Sex and gender

Sex and gender

John Archer

Barbara Lloyd

CAMBRIDGE
UNIVERSITY PRESS

Published by the Press Syndicate of the University of Cambridge
The Pitt Building, Trumpington Street, Cambridge CB2 1RP
40 West 20th Street, New York, NY 10011-4211, USA
10 Stamford Road, Oakleigh, Victoria 3166, Australia

First published in 1982 by Penguin Books Ltd., Harmondsworth,
Middlesex, England; revised, North American edition first published
in 1985 by Cambridge University Press
Reprinted 1987, 1988, 1989, 1992

Printed in the United States of America

Library of Congress Cataloging in Publication Data
Archer, John.
Sex and gender.
"First published in 1982 by Penguin Books Ltd.,
Harmondsworth, Middlesex, England" – T.p. verso.
bibliography: p.
Includes indexes.
1. Sex differences (Psychology) 2. Sex differences.
3. Sex role. I. Lloyd, Barbara B. (Barbara Bloom),
1933–   . II. Title. [DNLM: 1. Identification
(Psychology) 2. Sex Characteristics. BF692.2 A671s]
BF692.2A72   1985   155.3'3   84-20038

ISBN 0-521-26497-9 hardback
ISBN 0-521-31921-8 paperback

Contents

v

Preface

One impact of the women's movement of the 1960s was a reawakening of concern about the psychology of women and about sex differences in psychological research. The first wave of interest among psychologists, in the late 1960s and early 1970s, was often characterized by attention to biological explanations. At this time the influence of the women's movement was also being felt in anthropology and sociology. It was only later in the 1970s that social psychologists became interested in comparing the behavior of men and women.

The impact of social scientists and the contrast between their approach and that of more traditional psychologists of the early 1970s are reflected in the change of both explanations and terminology. The study of differences between men and women has moved from biological explanations to a consideration of the importance of broader social processes. The term *sex differences* was originally used in a vague sense by psychologists to indicate both socially derived distinctions between men and women and their biological differences. Recently this usage has been called into question, and increasingly the term *gender* is being used when referring to socially derived distinctions, leaving the term *sex* for biological differences. Our title and usage reflect this change.

In entitling our book *Sex and Gender*, we are extending its concerns beyond those of earlier, more strictly psychological accounts of "sex differences," although we do not ignore the topics found in them. This change in emphasis means that the issues involved in describing, measuring, and explaining sex (or gender) differences have become complex. We begin by considering these issues in the first two chapters. In Chapter 1 we look at some commonsense beliefs about the nature of men and women and consider the way in which these have influenced psychological accounts. We then consider the nature of research strategies used to study sex and gender and establish our usage of the two terms. In Chapter 2 we present three different approaches to the study of gender differences. We begin by drawing demographic portraits of men and women, since these produce views that, on the surface, appear to be objective. We then consider how psychological testing provides a description of the abilities of men and women. We conclude with studies of stereotyping, which brings us back to commonsense beliefs. In the remaining chapters we consider a range of topics that are of central importance in the discussion of sex and gender differences: physical attributes, sexuality, aggression and power, mental health, the family, intelligence and achievement, the development of gender differences, and social change.

We are indebted to Julia Vellacott, who first suggested that we write a book about sex differences. This project has led us back to old problems and into new fields and has ultimately helped us to consider the boundaries of the area known as the psychology of sex differences. Along the way, many people have given generously of their time and expertise. In particular, we thank Neil Berry, Lynda Birke, Glynis Breakwell, Ernest Brown, Mervin Glasser, Ken Gledhill, Carol Jacklin, John Lazarus, Mike Scaife, Bill Scott, Mary Sissons, and Helen Weinreich-Haste. Special thanks are due to Peter Lloyd.

Note to the American edition

When Cambridge University Press decided to publish an American edition of *Sex and Gender*, we set about "correcting" our spellings of words such as *behaviour* and *programme*. As we began this minor revision, we discovered many studies that had been published since our manuscript went to press. We have now added new and overlooked material where relevant. Although this is not a totally revised version of our 1982 book, we believe that we have clarified, enlarged, and judged a number of issues more adequately for our transatlantic readers.

John Archer, Preston, England
Barbara Lloyd, Sussex, England

1

Commonsense views and psychological research

Everyone has ideas about the nature of men and women and knows in a commonsense way what they are like. If that were the whole story, we, and the biological and social scientists whose research we report, would be wasting our time. But it is not. Commonsense views are only a part of the story; but they are an important place to begin, because they have had a major influence on the scientific study of sex and gender.

Commonsense views about differences between men and women were more widely accepted before the challenges of the modern feminist movement modified public consciousness. Since awareness of the prejudice inherent in commonsense notions has tempered contemporary images, we shall look at the popular culture of an earlier decade to find a typical example. It comes from "A Hymn to Him" in *My Fair Lady*, the musical version of Shaw's *Pygmalion*. The song may not appeal to you aesthetically; but whatever your reaction, bear with us, since it provides a clear example.

Henry Higgins is puzzled. After achieving a social triumph at a ball, Eliza Doolittle disappears. Higgins laments:

Women are irrational, that's all there is to that!
Their heads are full of cotton, hay and rags!
They're nothing but exasperating, irritating, vacillating, calculating,
    agitating, maddening and infuriating hags!
Why can't a woman be more like a man?
Men are so honest, so thoroughly square;
Eternally noble, historically fair;
Who, when you win, will always give your back a pat!
Why can't a woman be like that?

And so it goes on through several more verses. Rather than consider all of these, let us use the eight lines above to extract some general principles.

The first principle is that men and women differ fundamentally. Most comparisons take the form of a dogged pursuit of their differences, and our common humanity is either deliberately ignored or so tacitly assumed as to have much the same effect.

The second principle is that men are superior and women their inferiors. Henry Higgins is sure of this. He leaves us in no doubt that women are not a patch on men; in these lines he contrasts women's emotionality with man's steadfastness. In other verses he comments negatively on women's intelligence, conformity, vanity, and sensitivity to slights. You may wish to say that this is just a song – one man's view of the opposite sex. Nevertheless, with the exception of writing from the women's movement, it is difficult to find comparisons that err in the opposite direction by presenting women in an overwhelmingly positive light. This is hardly surprising, since commonsense views reflect the respective places of men and women in society, and in most cases men exert more power and have higher status in public life than women.

Rather than provide further examples of commonsense views from plays, films, and novels (Ellman, 1968), we shall use these two principles – that men and women differ fundamentally and that the differences involve female deficiencies – to analyze further everyday notions about physical, intellectual, and emotional differences between men and women. We shall then go on to consider the roles of the two sexes in society, commonsense explanations of them, and possibilities for change.

The commonsense emphasis on categorical (i.e., nonoverlapping) differences appears to be grounded in recognition of anatomical and functional differences in reproduction. These differences bolster the assumption that other physical, intellectual, and emotional differences have the same nonoverlapping distributions. If we return to the lines from *My Fair Lady*, we can see that men and women are regarded as totally different in their actions and mental makeup. Women are described as emotional and illogical ("irrational" is Henry Higgins's word), whereas men, by implication, are described as stoic and sensible.

Although it is no longer believed that men are intellectually superior to women, it is still widely held that the two sexes think differently and have a natural bent for different intellectual activities. The preponderance of boys and men studying pure science, mathematics, engineering, and architecture and the concentration of girls and women in biology, the arts, and language studies support this view. Not only are natural sciences and engineering seen as the special domains of men, but they are viewed as more complex and difficult. Boys and girls are believed to have different skills, and those of males are viewed as superior. Old ideas do not die easily.

Is it merely coincidence that the two sexes are regarded as fundamentally different both in physical form and in mental characteristics, or are mental and physical differences linked in some way? One widely held assumption is that bodily characteristics influence mental ones, but commonsense theories offer no explanation of the nature of this influence. In Victorian times even scientists regarded women as intellectually inferior, and reasons for this were sought in terms of the biological knowledge of the day (Burnstyn, 1971; Shields, 1975; Gould, 1978; Sayers, 1982). At present, the hormonal changes associated with the menstrual cycle, pregnancy, childbirth, and menopause are often implicated in women's alleged emotional lability, and the assumed lack of major hormonal change with the reputed stability of men.

The search for correlations between physical attributes and mental traits is one everyday way of explaining sex differences. Another is to consider the functions of men and women in biological and social spheres. In this way it is assumed that since only women bear and suckle infants, they must also be responsible for child care. But not all role assignments are based on categorical sex differences. It is also argued that because women are, on average, smaller and less muscular, this precludes them from a variety of strenuous and demanding occupations such as bricklaying or coalmining. This argument may be disguised as an attempt to protect women from strenuous and dangerous physical pursuits.

Until fairly recently there was little need to seek an explanation either for the coincidence of particular physical and mental traits in men and women or for the consequences of physical traits as seen in sex-specific roles. The traditional explanation according to both Jewish and Christian religious belief was that God had created woman to be the helpmate of man, but not his equal. It was the "natural order of things." As our society has grown more secular, biological ideas such as those of evolution and genetic inheritance have come to replace the deity in sustaining the natural order. But this is not unique to our society. In Tchambuli culture, where sex roles appear to be the reverse of those in our own society, their own explanation for the division is also found in biological forces (Mead, 1950).

At present there is a competing and fairly widespread view that sees the social environment as the source of differences between the sexes. Even physical differences, it is suggested, reflect the encouragement of boys and men to take part in sports and body-building activities and the restriction of girls and women to less demanding physical pursuits (Lowe, 1982). The process whereby social values are differentially inculcated is colloquially described as "conditioning." The term does not denote the technical procedures first outlined by Pavlov but is used in everyday speech to describe how people are influenced by society.

According to the conditioning view, sex differences in temperament and ability are not seen in terms of female inadequacy and weakness but as the result of societal (male) pressures that have resulted in female subservience and underachievement.

Acceptance of this type of explanation has produced a reaction from those who seek to defend traditional values. For many people interested in the social issues of our time, biological research and theory are seen as a way of explaining why contemporary society has created social problems through neglecting or disregarding human nature. Books of this genre that have caught the popular imagination include *On Aggression* (Lorenz, 1966), *The Naked Ape* (Morris, 1967), and *The Territorial Imperative* (Ardrey, 1967). In these works, man's aggression, his particular view of women as sex objects, and the legacy of his prehistory as a hunter are portrayed as inevitable.

These popular accounts of differences do not exist in a vacuum but are closely connected with perceptions of the desirability of change. For those who believe that the roles of men and women reflect their evolutionary origins, the natural place for women is in the home, looking after children. Emotional traits such as patience, tenderness, and sensitivity are seen as fitting them for their role as homemakers and mothers. It follows that drastic changes would be both undesirable and doomed to failure.

From the conditioning perspective, however, existing differences and even those traits that suit women to the care of children would be seen as susceptible to change. Unlike the popular biological account, this explanation, focusing on an upbringing that from an early age thrusts dolls in girls' arms and encourages competitiveness in boys, sees any changes as yet another pattern to be produced by conditioning.

In everyday thinking these two views and outlooks for change are associated with conservative and egalitarian ideologies. The conservative ideology sees present-day roles as part of the natural order and change as disastrous. As the popular romance novelist Barbara Cartland puts it, "All this striving and clawing into a man's world will eventually end in tears." The implication is that either women will not succeed or, if they do succeed, change will only bring unhappiness in its wake.

The egalitarian view stresses the inequality in present-day

differences between men and women and seeks to set this right through social change. The belief that differences reflect conditioning supports the possibility of change. Sex discrimination can thus be modified through legislation and education.

Although the egalitarian position based on belief in the possibility of change is typically that of feminists, there are a minority who see the problem of male power residing in biology. Men are regarded as more aggressive by nature and always likely to take it out on anyone weaker.

By and large, feminist writers question commonsense notions about men and women. They challenge both the emphasis on differences and the belief that those traits ascribed to men are more desirable. Descriptions of differences are seen as myths that are used to justify the subjugation of women, and men and women are seen as being more similar than popular beliefs would indicate.

Commonsense influences on psychological research

Commonsense views have had a major influence on psychological research. They have led to an emphasis on differences, and they have guided the discovery, characterization, and explanation of these differences.

A parallel with the commonsense view that presents men and women as fundamentally different can be seen in psychological research. Psychologists often look for differences between men as a group and women as a group without taking into account the wide range of variation among individuals of the same sex. Their main criterion for deciding that a difference between two groups is significant is *not* the magnitude of the difference alone but whether it would be expected to occur very often by chance. Significance is a measure of reliability, not of magnitude. It enables differences that are small in absolute magnitude but statistically significant to appear important when the variation within groups is low or the samples are large. The widespread use of significance-testing in psychology has led to the use of the term *sex difference* to refer to a range of significant differences that vary greatly in absolute magnitude.

The publication policies of psychology journals contribute to the emphasis on differences and the neglect of similarities. Such journals accept more readily reports in which statistically significant differences have been recorded, and so it is difficult to publish results in which no significant differences have been found. As a result there is no way to estimate the underreporting of findings of no difference (Maccoby and Jacklin, 1974; Lloyd, 1976).

Although we have shown how psychological research strategies support the pursuit of differences, there have been some signs of change. Tresemer (1975) has drawn attention to the need for estimates of the degree of overlap in the performances of men and women, and attention to the magnitude of sex differences has been recommended by Sherman (1978) and Jacklin (1979). A distinction could thus be made between different magnitudes of difference. It may be useful to think of these as lying on a continuum or scale. At one end are those characteristics on which every member of one sex is different from every member of the other (e.g., the genitals), and at the other are characteristics men and women share to an equal degree (e.g., intelligence). In between would be measures on which the sexes partially overlap. Although most psychological measures are of this sort, by referring to them as sex differences it is implied that they show little overlap.

Tresemer (1975, 1977) suggested that some estimate of the size of the difference in means or degree of overlap of the distributions would be a more useful way to compare men and women than significance tests. He identified three measures of overlap. Our discussions (Lloyd and Archer, 1981) of overlap also draw upon the earlier work of Levy (1967) and that of Oakes (1978).

Intellectual performance provides an example of the use of such measures. On average, men attain higher scores on tests of spatial ability (see Chapters 2 and 8). Although the magnitude of the sex difference often goes unreported, where the

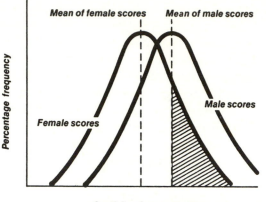

Figure 1.1. Percentage distribution of male and female spatial performance scores. The shaded area represents the 25 percent of female
scores that exceed the mean male scores.

information is available it is usual for about 25 percent of
women's scores to be above the mean value of men's (Lambert,
1978). Tresemer has described this as a medium to large difference, given the relative magnitude of effects usually found in
studies of sex differences. But as Figure 1.1 shows, there is a
considerable overlap of men's and women's scores.

Jacklin (1979) has also outlined ways to assess the magnitude
of sex differences and has analyzed a number of studies that
showed differences in measures of independence and intellectual efficiency. She concluded that these sex differences, although *statistically* significant, were "trivially small." Although
few of the studies we report are amenable to these modes of
precise analysis, we do try to keep in mind the magnitude of
the differences we are reporting and the degree to which men
and women are similar. For example, in Chapter 3 we consider
not only the typical course of physical development for men
and women but also the range that can occur within each sex
as a result of variations in normal and abnormal development.

The second commonsense principle – that women are inferior to men – has also been reflected in psychological studies. Fortunately, the influence of this belief has waned, and it is primarily when we look back over research of earlier decades that we detect its strong influence. Parlee (1975) has shown that in their 1968 review of sex differences in mental and behavioral traits, Garai and Scheinfeld used a term implying superiority to describe 46 percent of comparisons in which males scored higher, yet characterized comparisons in which females scored higher by such a term only 27 percent of the time. By this choice of language, men appear superior even though females scored higher in forty-one comparisons and males in only thirty-five. Attempts to prove women's general intellectual inferiority have given way to research on specific intellectual abilities, achievement motivation, and emotionality.

Although psychologists no longer set out to show that women are inferior, the influence of commonsense views is apparent in the choice of what to look at and in the borrowing of words from everyday speech to describe it. This occurs in at least two ways: Psychologists actively seek to measure differences described in ordinary language – that men are more aggressive or women more fearful – and they use everyday terms to describe differences reported in psychological research. These differences may have been encountered fortuitously, actively sought in theory-guided investigations, or derived from surveys of published findings.

Accidental findings of sex differences arise because psychologists regularly test both male and female subjects. In analyzing their data, they may happen to find a difference in the performance of the two sexes. Since journals encourage the publication of significant differences, these are reported and an explanation, or at least a label, is sought to describe them.

On the other hand, in theory-guided research, measures apparently unrelated to commonsense notions may be labeled in a way that transforms them into characteristics that appear to support the commonsense view. The work of Herman Witkin

(1967) on cognitive style (see Chapter 8) is an example of this. Witkin developed tests to measure the extent to which people perceive a particular visual stimulus as part of its surroundings or as an independent entity. (One test he used was the Embedded Figures Test–EFT; another was the Rod and Frame Test–RFT.) In many studies it was found that men are more often able to separate the stimulus from its background than are women (Maccoby and Jacklin, 1974). Witkin has argued that these perceptual differences represent wider differences in people's approaches to their environment–their cognitive style (Witkin et al., 1962).

A person who tends to separate the stimulus from its background is called *field-independent*, whereas someone who tends to perceive the stimulus as part of its environment is called *field-dependent*. This choice of terms implies an active, independent type of person and a passive, dependent person. Men typically show field-independent responses and women field-dependent responses on the EFT and RFT. This is important in view of Witkin's claim that the measures reflect a difference in the way men and women perceive the world (McGuinness, 1976). Had Witkin used different descriptive labels, such as "context sensitive," the social implications of the research would have been different. As it is, his labels support the commonsense view of women as inferior to men.

The influence of commonsense terms can also be seen in reviews of the literature. Since the research evidence on sex differences is large and fragmented, there is much reliance on such summaries, which organize and collate large numbers of varied findings. Of the many examples, we have chosen only two. Garai and Scheinfeld (1968) described a miscellaneous collection of measures on which women performed better than men and then labeled them "clerical abilities," implying that women naturally possess characteristics that suit them for one of the major female occupations in our society. Similarly, Gray (1971a) described as "fearfulness" a heterogeneous category of measures on which women showed higher scores. This not only confirmed the commonsense view of women's greater emotionality but also identified it with a label that is not highly valued. It is understandable that reviewers of sex-difference research need to generalize and to label their findings. Nonetheless, it is apparent that the identification and naming of these differences are influenced by commonsense views of the nature of the sexes.

Psychological explanations also provide parallels with commonsense accounts: These explanations are often sought in terms of either specific biological processes or social influences. They are linked to wider social issues in a manner very similar to the corresponding commonsense views.

Current biological explanations include evolutionary arguments, which have been offered in support of conventional divisions of labor and power relations between the sexes. A typical claim is that men possess evolutionary adaptations that enable them to dominate political life (Tiger, 1970; but see Hrdy, 1981, for a refutation of this view). Other biological explanations involve effects of sex hormones on the brains of men and women. These also reflect the increasing volume and sophistication of research on hormones and behavior in animals. Such theories have been cited by some opponents of femininism (e.g., Stassinopoulos, 1972; Goldberg, 1973) to buttress the view that the social roles of men and women have a biological basis, but they have received limited support in psychology.

The main alternative psychological explanation is that sex differences in temperament and abilities are the result of the different learning experiences of boys and girls (Mischel, 1966; see also Chapter 9). This view parallels the commonsense conditioning explanation, and it has been cited in support of an egalitarian view of sex roles.

Commonsense explanations imply that since biological processes are natural, they cannot or should not be changed. On the other hand, since experiential effects are seen as having no basis in biology, they are regarded as malleable. Although this

widely held commonsense view also influences psychological
accounts, it is incorrect. A person's personality or behavior
may be quite resistant to change and yet be the result of influences in his or her early or later environment. Conversely,
someone may inherit a predisposition toward a certain type of
behavior but, owing to the modifying effects of a particular
environment, may not develop this behavior. Commonsense
reasoning seems to have influenced the interpretation of biological research so that it has been used misleadingly to support particular ideological positions.

Research strategies

In this section we consider the various research strategies that
have been adopted by psychologists studying sex and gender.
One prestigious and influential approach is that of reductionism (Rose and Rose, 1974; Waddington, 1977). The various social and natural sciences are arranged in a series of decreasing
complexity from the social sciences to psychology, physiology,
chemistry, and physics; and events in a more complex science
are explained in terms of a more fundamental science. Reductionism has provided effective solutions to problems in the
biological sciences by offering biochemical and physical explanations of biological systems. Impressed by these successes,
many psychologists have sought biological and biochemical explanations for psychological phenomena. An added appeal of
this approach is the apparent reality of biochemical and biological processes when compared to abstract psychological phenomena (Lloyd, 1976).

   Many biological explanations of sex differences in psychological processing have employed reductionist arguments. The
main alternatives are explanations concentrating on analysis of
environmental influences acquired through learning. (See the
preceding section.)

   Both these viewpoints are limited: One considers only a person's biological properties, the other only the social environ-

ment. A more comprehensive account is provided when a person's individual characteristics are seen in the context of that person's interactions with the environment. We now consider three approaches that endeavor to understand sex differences by looking at the individual as actively seeking to make sense of the world. These approaches are described as "cognitive" because they stress the primary role of thought processes.

Kohlberg (1966) analyzed boys' and girls' ideas about sex roles from a cognitive perspective. He argued that these ideas are of a different nature at different ages and that they undergo a series of transformations that mark the boundaries of discrete stages in the development of understanding about sex roles. Kohlberg's theory, which is considered in more detail in Chapter 9, is concerned with changes in mental constructions through development. Other cognitive approaches examine the structures adults use to understand their social world. We consider two of these, first that of ethnomethodology and second the social–cognitive approach.

Ethnomethodologists are concerned with the ways in which a person constructs his or her view of the social world. Their starting point is the assumption that what we see as objectively "out there" is a result of our own construction (and that this is true whether we are ordinary people or scientists; see the beginning of Chapter 2). One person's construction may differ from another's, but each is true for each of them.

The ethnomethodological approach was applied to sex and gender by Kessler and McKenna (1978). In doing so, they made important points that challenged some commonsense notions about men and women. One assumption that is taken for granted both in everyday life and in most research on sex differences is that there are two biologically given classes, male and female. In fact, when we meet someone, we do not determine that person's sex in the same way that a biologist would sex an animal or a person – for example, by genital inspection or by examination of chromosome composition (Chapter 3). Instead, we mentally construct the person's gender from a wide range of cues, such as dress, way of moving, length of hair, beard growth, and breast development. Usually this process occurs quickly and unconsciously; but it has important consequences, since it forms the basis for selecting very different forms of social interaction in the future. Kessler and McKenna analyzed the process of gender construction and considered instances where it is not obvious and where people have to search for the relevant cues, as in the case of transsexuals.

In recognizing the *social* construction of the distinction between men and women, ethnomethodologists refer to the two categories as *genders*, reserving the term *sex* for distinctions made on the basis of biological criteria. The reader may feel that the *way* distinctions are made between men and women – whether by social or biological attribution – is of little practical consequence, since the resulting categorization would usually be the same. Nevertheless, it is of practical importance when we consider such marginal cases as that of the woman athlete who "fails" a chromosome test or of the transsexual who sees herself as a woman despite her masculine physical features. These cases show that sex does not define gender and that if a person adopts important aspects of the cross-gender role, he or she will be seen as being of that gender.

Ethnomethodologists urge a shift in research away from studying the *consequences* of having attributed gender to an examination of the attribution process itself. Little research of this type has been carried out, and most of that described in our book is on the consequences of attribution. Nevertheless, we regard the ethnomethodological approach as important because it concerns itself with the interaction of people with their environment and with the mental representations that are constructed in these social encounters. In doing so, it rejects the reduction of social events to biology or to simple environmental units.

The social–cognitive approach is another major departure from reductionist accounts of sex and gender. Like ethnomethodology, it focuses on the social context (hence "social") and people's attempts to understand this (hence "cognitive"). Our view of the social–cognitive approach derives from the writings of Kay Deaux (1977), Julie Sherman (1978), Sandra Bem (1981), and others. To explain the social–cognitive approach, it is useful to contrast it with the traditional view of psychological testing, which we present more fully in the next chapter.

In much psychological research on sex differences, measurements taken from specific tests or observational procedures are used to make generalizations about wider psychological attributes on which men and women are said to differ, such as aggression, emotionality, or mathematical ability. Differences in the average scores of men and women on a particular test that involves mathematical reasoning, for example, may be described as a gender difference in "mathematical ability." It is seen as a stable attribute or trait of individuals. This view, like reductionism, is based on transposing the scientific method from the natural sciences to psychology. In this case, it is precise measurement of the characteristics of individuals that is sought. Attempts to apply such rigorous measurement of abstract psychological characteristics, in a manner analogous to measuring physical features, encounter a number of difficulties, which the social–cognitive approach highlights. This broader view of psychological testing places both the psychologist and the person taking the test in a wider social context. Each of the participants has commonsense views about the nature of men and women and about the social setting of the test – in particular about whether the test favors masculine or feminine skills. In this approach, the emphasis shifts from trying to define and measure general traits to examining how men and women react to the experimenter and how they perceive the test conditions and requirements. These are seen as transactions that will be strongly influenced by the person's own commonsense views about the social attributes of men and women. These views exert influence on test performance and affect the measurement process.

Different transactions occur depending on the sex of the experimenter and of the person being tested. One intriguing example of the possible influence of the experimenter's sex on test performance was given by Sherman (1978), who suggested that tests involving male experimenters in darkened rooms may make female subjects uneasy because "such situations have been known to elicit unwanted sexual advances."

Men and women may have different ideas about how they should behave in a social setting. Deaux (1976a, 1976b) suggested that men generally endeavor to be assertive and women to be affiliative in any social situation and that being a subject in a psychological experiment or test is no exception. These different ideas about appropriate masculine or feminine behavior can be another source of influence in psychological measurements.

Certain tests may be viewed as masculine or feminine. Interest in them and motivation to succeed will differ for men and women. Sherman (1978) argued that this factor has been neglected in psychological research on sex differences. She cited research that shows that male superiority in one particular "spatial ability" test was not found if the same test was identified as measuring a more feminine skill. Previous experience, practice, and familiarity with test material will also differ for men and women, and this is again related to whether a test is associated with masculine or feminine abilities. Most reviews of sex differences have neglected the issue of unequal practice.

In contrast to the ethnomethodological view, the social-cognitive approach is still concerned with studying the consequences of attributing gender to a person rather than with the attribution process. Despite this important distinction, the two views have many features in common. Both accord a central place to the social meaning and social significance of sex differences. At present there is relatively little research aimed at evaluating the effects of commonsense notions about gender on the differences between men and women measured by psychological tests. What evidence there is suggests that ideas about gender roles directly and indirectly affect reports of psychological sex differences (Sherman, 1978). We believe that this line of inquiry will prove to be more productive than an emphasis on differences in psychological traits or the predominantly reductionist explanations usually offered to account for them.

Sex or gender?

We now return to the issue of terminology that was raised in connection with the ethnomethodological approach. Kessler and McKenna (1978) referred to men and women as two genders, since the usual way the two are distinguished is on the basis of social criteria. The term *sex* is restricted to cases where the distinction is made on the basis of biological criteria. Domestic animals, newborn infants, and Olympic athletes are divided into two sexes; but when we are introduced to a stranger, a *gender* is attributed to us on the basis of a variety of bodily and behavioral cues. Since this is the way men and women are usually distinguished, both in everyday life and in psychological research, it follows that most of the differences between men and women we describe in this book are based on social criteria. We refer to these differences throughout the remainder of the book as *gender differences*. Only when we are considering biologically based distinctions, particularly in Chapter 3, do we refer to them as *sex differences*. In practical terms, the distinction may appear trivial; but it becomes important to specify whether we are referring to sex or to gender in cases of abnormal sexual differentiation (Chapter 3) and when we consider societies in which there are more than two genders, such as the Omani, described in Chapter 4.

A distinction between the terms *sex* and *gender* is becoming widespread in psychology, but our use differs from that of Unger (1979), who suggested that *sex* relates to the label "male" or "female" that identifies the individual, whereas *gender* refers to the characteristic traits and appropriate behavior for members of each sexual category. We have adopted an ethnomethodological position that implies that the very identification of an individual as male or female depends on a complex attribution process. We have chosen to employ the strict criterion of attribution rather than the commonly employed strategy of using *sex differences* to refer to biological features and *gender differences* for social attributes. We believe that the distinction is often difficult to make in practice and that it implies that differences between men and women are *either* biologically produced *or* socially determined. We have already indicated the limitations of this view, which derives from commonsense notions and which seeks a reductionist explanation. Adopting a distinction based on attribution alerts us to problems. When attribution is derived from social criteria, whatever differences are subsequently found between men and women are called gender differences. In fact, biological differences would be expected to contribute to gender differences, but they would be mediated through an interaction with the environment according to a person's mental concepts – or commonsense ideas about men and women.

2

Men and women: three views from the social sciences

In Chapter 1 we explored the influence of commonsense ideas on psychological studies of men and women. Here we begin by considering commonsense ideas about the nature of scientific investigation; we then trace the influence of these ideas on the evaluation and credibility of three different ways of studying men and women.

In popular imagination a full picture of the scientist would include the dedicated Dr. Jekyll toiling in the laboratory to improve the lot of the human race, as well as the demoniacal Mr. Hyde. We are concerned not with the darker side but with the popular idealization of science that sees it as a straightforward, reliable, public procedure involving discovery by the ingenious scientist of "facts" residing in the outside world. The distinguished biologist C. H. Waddington (1977) caricatured this view of science as the "Conventional Wisdom of the Dominant Group" – a clumsy phrase to which he attached the evocative mnemonic "COWDUNG."

But is science as objective as naive opinion assumes? Waddington, as his acronym suggests, thought it is not. He emphasized that scientific knowledge is obtained by the scientist's making observations, a process he described as an active interchange between the observer and the objects of his study. The process is similar to that used every day in making sense of the world. According to Waddington, the distinction between scientific and nonscientific knowledge is only one of degree. In a scientific investigation the observations are made in a controlled and organized fashion (as experiments or surveys) in order to minimize the effects of observer bias and to ensure that the measurements could be replicated by other scientists. Observations that form the basis of everyday generalizations are less systematic, and little effort is made to control sources of bias. It is difficult to know whether other observers would come to similar conclusions under these conditions.

Adopting Waddington's view, we realize that scientists may try to limit the effects of observer bias but that scientific studies cannot be completely objective. Scientists inevitably see the world through the filter of their own culture and their particular experiences of it. Our society's notions about the nature of men and women function inevitably as a lens through which scientific findings are distorted.

The mechanics of particular kinds of investigation make some appear more objective and more credible than others. In this chapter we contrast three different ways of seeking and presenting knowledge about men and women. We begin by examining demographic accounts, which at first glance appear to rely only on simple counting and to be objective. Next we consider the results of psychometric testing, the application of standard tests and procedures to provide descriptions of the skills and abilities of men and women. Finally, we report the explicit study of commonsense notions in the social psychological investigation of stereotypes.

The demographic approach: Mr. and Ms. Average

The demographic "facts" about men and women are statistical averages taken from various government reports. For Britain we have used the *Annual Abstract of Statistics* (1983), the *General Household Survey* (1979), and *Social Trends* (1977, 1979, and 1984). We present these British statistics not only because we are more familiar with them, but also because they are published in a more accessible format. Comparable statistics for the population of the United States are usually broken down into racial and regional categories that make the gross male–female comparisons less striking.

Common sense holds that these official statistics provide truly objective evidence. This was a view also held by early sociologists. Durkheim compared fluctuations in the number of suicides with the movement of mercury in a thermometer. He believed that these fluctuations could be used to study social forces just as the rise and fall of mercury could provide valid information about a host of scientific processes. Contemporary critics point out that whereas the calibrated scale of the thermometer provides a more reliable measure than unaided sensory experience, official statistics do not have a straightforward relation to social phenomena. In order to compile the numbers of people committing suicide, it is necessary to determine in each instance whether a person took his own life while of sound mind. Attitudes toward suicide affect such judgments, and suicide statistics are compiled only after such judgments of ambiguous events have been made. Critics have argued that the meaning of the statistics remains ambiguous unless the judgmental processes are understood (Douglas, 1967).

We have already argued that total objectivity in terms of the detachment of the observer from the object of study is impossible, so it is hardly surprising to learn that official statistics are neither totally objective nor theoretically neutral. But there are different degrees of subjective involvement and observer participation. The census and social surveys are designed to minimize the influence of the people administering the questionnaire, and in surveys the choice of individuals to be included in the sample is carefully scrutinized. Such investigations aim to limit the role of the observer to an almost mechanical one of collecting and tabulating figures. Similarly, when the figures are published there are usually few comments, and the statistics are often presented as raw material for others to use and interpret.

Despite precautions in the administration and tabulation of census and survey results, decisions must be made at the beginning of an investigation about the categories to be included and the particular questions to be posed. An obvious bias in the statistics we present is the categorization of adult men and women in the work force. Men appear as a single entry in British Department of Employment figures, but women are broken down into two categories, married and unmarried. Other choices that make the picture presented by the statistics less than totally objective will become apparent as they are examined. These include problems of judgment in the classification of crime and in the decision to publish when unemployment is a factor.

The simplest question we can ask of census statistics is "How many men and women are there?" At first the answer appears straightforward. More boys than girls are conceived and born during any given period, but at every age male mortality is greater than that of females. Given the experience of our own society, it is surprising to learn that in parts of Asia women die earlier than men (El-Badry, 1969). We will look first at figures for Britain and then at comparable statistics for Ceylon, India, and Pakistan.

In the thirty- to forty-four-year-old age group, the numbers of men and women are approximately equal in Britain – 5.4 million and 5.3 million, respectively (*Social Trends*, no. 14, 1984). We find that there are 1,030 men for every 1,000 women when we consider people up to the age of forty-five, but after sixty, the ratio reflects the younger ages at which men die. Among people over the age of sixty in Britain, there are only 697 men for every 1,000 women.

Statistics confirm impressions that there are many lonely old women. The figures in Table 2.1 can be described as follows. Among people in their sixties women outnumber men slightly, but by the age of seventy-five there are four women for every three men. Among those living to eighty-four, women outnumber men almost two to one, while women predominate more than four to one among those surviving to eighty-five and beyond. Technically, the proportion of men to women is

Table 2.1. *Elderly people by age and sex (in millions)*

Age	Female	Male
60–64	1.6	1.4
65–74	2.8	2.2
75–84	1.7	0.9
85+	0.5	0.1

Source: Based on table 1.2 in *Social Trends.* no. 14 (1984).

known as the *sex ratio.* As age increases there is a decreasing sex ratio: that is, increasingly women outnumber men. Another way to look at these figures is to note that in England and Wales the current life expectancy at birth is 70.4 years for males and 76.5 for females (*Annual Abstract of Statistics,* 1983).

Census statistics from Ceylon, India, and Pakistan provide a challenge to the view that on average women can expect to live longer than men and that over the age of sixty there will be more women surviving that men (El-Badry, 1969). It depends on which part of the world one lives in; and in Ceylon, India, and Pakistan, containing one-fifth of the world's population, a female has a lower life expectancy than a male. Ceylon had the smallest difference in male and female expectancies – 61.9 and 61.4 years, respectively – according to the figures for 1960–2. The gap was larger in India, 41.9 years for men and 40.6 for women in 1951–60; for the period 1962–4 in Pakistan males had a life expectancy of 49.6 years compared to a female average of 46.9 years.

These figures are so strikingly different from those to which Westerners are accustomed that it is interesting to consider the explanations that have been offered to account for them (El-Badry, 1969). One is the greater mortality of females, particularly in the years of childbearing but also in infancy and childhood. A second but minor factor is a general tendency to undercount females. These explanations stand in sharp contrast to those put forth in Western society, where the greater incidence of coronary heart disease among men has been implicated in the consistently higher male death rate. Those very traits that we shall later consider as part of the masculine stereotype – aggressiveness and competitiveness – have been shown to increase the risk of coronary heart disease (Waldon, 1976). Many lessons can be learned from this brief excursion into comparative demography; one is that where you look will influence what you find. A second concerns the role of social values in determining life experiences.

The late Marcia Guttentag (Guttentag and Secord, 1983) attempted to link these demographic facts and social behavior by investigating changes in the sex ratio. Her work confirms the British statistics cited earlier and shows that in the United States there is a large population of women over age forty-five for whom there is no male partner. It is also suggested that when there is such a low sex ratio – many more women than men – divorce and illegitimacy rates are high, remarriage is higher for men, female-headed single-parent families become more common, and women feel less powerful and valued. These conditions can also be observed in the British statistics that follow.

What do British statistics say about the families in which male and female children grow up, about their education, careers, and other life prospects? Let us start with the most common type of households, one-family households, which comprise 72 percent of the total. By definition, these include at least one adult and one offspring. According to 1984 figures, 89 percent of all one-family households in England and Wales included an adult female and an adult male, and 11 percent are single-parent households (*Social Trends*, no. 14, 1984, table 2.4). It probably comes as little surprise to learn that the overwhelming majority of single parents are women (only one-ninth are men) (*Social Trends*, no. 14, 1984, table 2.9).

Who are the heads of these single-parent households? The largest group of women living alone with children are divorced (41 percent). Almost equal proportions (21 and 22 percent)

Table 2.2. *Socioeconomic standing of household heads (percentages)*

	Female unmarried	Female married	Male single- and two-parent
Professional	–	–	5
Employers and managers	2	–	14
Intermediate and junior non-managerial	13	26	14
Skilled manual	3	–	32
Semiskilled and personal service	8	8	11
Unskilled	4	3	3
Economically inactive	63	57	20
Never worked	7	6	–

Source: Based on table 2.5 in *Social Trends,* no. 9 (1979).

have never married or are separated from their husbands; 16 percent are widows (*Social Trends,* no. 14, 1984, table 2.9). Since men remarry more often than women after divorce, there are more divorced women: Of the 1,521,000 divorced people remaining unmarried in England and Wales in 1982 only 641,000 are men. This difference, along with the likelihood of children's staying with their mothers, partly accounts for the greater number of single female heads of households.

What do heads of households do for a living? We compare the socioeconomic backgrounds or broad occupational categories of male and female heads of households in Table 2.2. In making this comparison demographers generally regard men as the head of a household whether they are living with an adult female or as a single parent. Table 2.2 shows that children growing up in male-headed homes are better off economically; male heads of households are from professional, managerial, and skilled manual groups much more often than female heads are. Female heads of households are more likely to be unskilled, economically inactive, or never to have worked (there are no men recorded in the last category). These figures reflect the higher occupational status of men and underscore

Table 2.3. *Girls and boys attain-
ing A, B or C grades in O-level
examinations (percentages)*

	Girls	Boys
English	44	33
Mathematics	26	31
Physics	8	21
Chemistry	9	15

Source: Based upon chart 3.5 in *Social
Trends*, no. 14 (1984).

the obvious financial advantage to children of growing up in a
male-headed household.

It was not possible to update this table or Tables 2.5, 2.6, and
2.7, as figures were not published in the same format after
1979. The manner in which statistics are cross-tabulated intro-
duces yet another source of bias.

We shall return to gender differences in occupations after
first looking at education. The educational statistics tell two
different stories. Those based on attainment at the time people
leave secondary school show few substantial differences between males and females. The 1984 edition of *Social Trends*
reported fairly similiar proportions of girls and boys leaving
school with the same levels of qualifications, but differences
occur in the academic subjects studied for examination. We
have tabulated these results by subject. Table 2.3 shows the
percentage of each gender achieving a mark of A, B, or C in the
O-level examinations, which are taken at about sixteen years of
age. We discuss differences in verbal and mathematical achievement later in this chapter and in Chapter 8.

The destinations of school leavers, presented in Table 2.4,
show more marked differences. In a 1972 survey of "highly
qualified" British people – defined as individuals with at least
one degree – men outnumbered women three to one. Table 2.4,

Table 2.4. *Destinations of school leavers, 1981–82 (percentages)*

	Degree courses			Teacher training	Other full-time education	Employment
	University	Polytechnic	Other			
Females	4.9	1.5	0.4	0.7	25.2	67.2
Males	6.9	2.0	0.3	0.2	14.4	76.3

Source: Based on table 3.9 in *Social Trends,* no. 14 (1984).

Table 2.5. *Sixteen-year-olds entering different classes of employ-ment, Great Britain, 1974 (percentages)*

	Females	Males
Apprenticeships	6	43
Professional	1	2
Clerical	40	7
Other work with over 12 months training	6	10
Work with 8 weeks to 12 months training	12	7
Other	34	32

Source: Based on table 5.26 in *Social Trends,* no. 8 (1977).

published twelve years later, shows that women are gaining ground, although they are still outnumbered on degree courses. Entry into all types of postsecondary education are presented, and here women outnumber men. Types of further education that women enter in great numbers and men rarely are secretarial training and nursing. The initial judgment about what is a high qualification changes the conclusions we can draw from the figures.

A further issue is the occupational destination of the hun-dreds of thousands of school leavers who do not go on to full-time education. We must rely on 1977 figures, as statistics are no longer provided in this form. Here, Table 2.5 shows that gender differences are even greater than those appearing in further education. Only a small proportion of girls enter ap-

Table 2.6. *Major activity for economically inactive*

	Female	Male
At school or college	3	10
Permanently unable to work	5	14
Retired	21	70
Keeping house	69	1
Other	2	6

Source: Based on table 5.23 in *General Household Survey* (1979).

prenticeships, and a similarly small proportion of boys take up clerical employment.

Once in employment, the prospects for a young man or woman are again quite different. Both in manual and non-manual full-time employment men on average earn more than women. According to 1982 figures, the average full-time male worker earned £150.50 per week, whereas women averaged £99.00 per week. That men may work more hours than women and hence earn considerable overtime pay can account for part of this difference. Among manual workers the percentage of overall pay earned through overtime was 13 percent for men and 4 percent for women. If we examine hourly pay rates, we obtain a starker comparison: Among manual and nonmanual workers, women's earnings were only 73.9 percent of men's.

Before leaving the realm of statistical averages, let us look at people who are not working and at those who are involved in crime. Table 2.6 shows that of those who are not working, most men are retired and most women are keeping house.

Another set of figures that tend to confirm common expectations are replies to a question asking why people in Great Britain left their jobs in 1978. Among unemployed people over sixteen years of age who had previously worked, almost half the men reported being fired or made redundant (Table 2.7). The most common reason given for unemployment by women

Table 2.7. *Reasons for unemployment offered by previously employed (percentages)*

	Female	Male
Made redundant or fired	26	48
Dissatisfied with last job	28	20
Ill health	10	18
Last job temporary	7	4
Retired	–	3
Domestic reasons, pregnancy, and others	30	8

Source: Based on table 5.22 in *General Household Survey* (1979)

Table 2.8. *Persons found guilty of or cautioned for indictable offenses, 1982 (thousands)*

	Female	Male
Murder, manslaughter, infanticide	0.1	0.4
Violence against persons	5.5	52.3
Sexual offenses	0.1	9.2
Burglary	3.4	84.4
Robbery	0.2	4.3
Theft and handling stolen goods	78.6	245.9
Fraud	5.7	20.6
Criminal damage	1.0	12.4
Other (including vehicular offences)	4.3	56.8
Total:	98.9	486.2

Source: Based on table 12.9 in *Social Trends*, no. 14 (1984).

was domestic commitments, including pregnancy, but job dissatisfaction and loss followed closely behind.

The final set of figures that we present shows gender differences in indictable offenses (Table 2.8). For all categories men are convicted of more offenses than women. Almost 80 percent of indictable offenses committed by women fall into the cate-

gory of theft and handling stolen goods, yet this category accounts for only 54 percent of the offenses committed by men.
Violence against persons is almost ten times as common an
offense among men as among women, and criminal damage is
even more common for male than for female offenders. Many
of the differences that appear as neat statistics will be considered at greater length in later chapters.

Although we have used official statistics to provide a concise,
quantitative comparison of men and women, it is important to
remember the complex and often ambiguous judgmental processes that lie behind this precise presentation. In the chapters
that follow we sometimes take these findings at face value and
seek to account for them, but at other times we challenge their
veracity. For example, in Chapter 3 we consider explanations
for the shorter life span of men, and in Chapter 5 we question
the accuracy of reporting of violent crimes committed by
women. Even though the evidence presented in the preceding
pages comes from official reports and appears to be objective, it
too must be subjected to critical evaluation.

The psychometric approach: what psychologists measure

The picture of men and women that emerges from the psychometric assessment of individual differences is neither complete
nor completely objective. Standarized tests were developed to
meet practical needs. One of the pioneers in the field, Alfred
Binet, set out to find a way to identify those French children
who would not benefit from a normal state education. Once
identified, special provisions could be offered to cope with
their learning inadequacies. Research psychologists, too, have
devised tests, but these do not aim at predicting success in
practical situations – instead they are usually designed to assess
the validity of different psychological theories.

Psychometricians assume that individuals differ in a variety
of characteristics, that these differences can be defined and
measured objectively, and that the scores obtained are related

to other aspects of the individual's behavior. Each of these assumptions entails judgments in test construction. Characteristics are sought in which individuals do indeed differ, but at the same time they must be psychologically meaningful dimensions. Our understanding of human behavior would be advanced little by counting hairs on people's heads, but differences in the rate at which people tap a key might provide clues about motor skills or even persistence. Judgments about what is worth measuring involve the definition of concepts and the interrelations of different types of behavior. Even the construction of objective tests involves psychological theorizing.

Standardized tests are constructed to assess individual differences; hence they employ repeated measures on the same individual in order to derive stable values that can be used in comparing and ranking individuals. Aggregation over series of subtests on intelligence tests provides these reliable and stable estimates (Rushton et al., 1983). Theoretically motivated research on sensory processes and learning has not focused on individual differences and generally relies on single measures of important variables. It is hardly surprising to discover that many gender differences on standardized tests have been reported but that there is little consistent evidence for differences between men and women from studies of perception and learning where a single measure may be used to estimate the value of a variable.

The conclusion that we find what we are looking for is further strengthened by noting that some intelligence tests, such as the Stanford–Binet Scale, were deliberately devised so that overall scores would show no consistent differences between males and females. This was achieved by carefully balancing those subscales on which one gender performed better with other subscales on which the other gender excelled. Despite difficulties in test construction, the introduction of standardized tests enabled more objective selection than previous reliance on interviews, teachers' judgments, and other informal selection methods. Given these caveats, the obvious question

"How intelligent are men and women?" turns out to be complex and difficult to answer.

The commonsense concern with natural differences versus conditioning leads to two different sorts of questions. One can be posed as "How much native wit do men and women possess?" while the other can be stated as "How much has each gender learned?" Psychologists have moved away from this formulation ever since it became clear that natural endowment, learning, and even experience with being tested all affect performance (Vernon, 1955).

The psychometric emphasis on individual differences makes it difficult to compare men and women even when we realize that test performance is multiply determined. The vast body of reports on individual differences contains comparisons across age, social class, culture, order of birth, and race. Differences between men and women might cut across any of these or co-vary with them. Even more limiting is the unevenness of available results. Reports are heavily biased toward certain age groups, primarily the captive audiences of students at all levels. These highly selected samples show higher than average ability and are most often made up of white, middle-class individuals (Maccoby and Jacklin, 1974; Hyde, 1981).

Interpretive difficulties do not end with the collection of original data. The classic summary of Maccoby and Jacklin from which we begin was criticized soon after publication both for making more of the evidence than one reviewer believed was justified (Fairweather, 1976) and for overlooking evidence that another psychologist believed indicated further important differences between men and women (Block, 1976a, 1976b). Since their summary, which dealt primarily with research carried out between 1966 and 1973, further evidence has accumulated and been reviewed (Harris, 1978; Sherman, 1978; Wittig and Petersen, 1979).

We begin by considering the picture that Maccoby and Jacklin constructed on the basis of their understanding of the results of many standard intelligence tests. In looking first at measures of general intellectual abilities, we cannot be too surprised that few clear differences were reported. We saw earlier that intelligence tests were originally constructed to provide similar overall scores for males and females.

Constructing a summary table of results comparing the scores of males and females on intelligence tests is one way to present a picture of psychometric gender differences. Maccoby and Jacklin (1974, table 3.1) compiled such a table with forty-six entries. We do not reproduce it here, as there are few surprises. Although a variety of tests were used, no clear gender differences emerged. Only three studies reported results from testing people over the age of twenty-one. Two of these showed no significant differences, although a third reported that the intelligence quotients (IQs) of men improved more than those of women when tested at intervals over a thirty-eight-year period (Kangas and Bradway, 1971). As the study was concerned more with change than with absolute levels of IQ, its results, based on the performance of only forty-eight people, gave but a limited picture of gender differences in general intelligence.

It is worthwhile pausing to consider the two tests from which these results were derived. The Stanford–Binet (S-B) Scale and the Wechsler Adult Intelligence Scale (WAIS) are, like most intelligence tests, made up of a variety of items. The S-B is scored only to yield a composite IQ, whereas the WAIS yields separate verbal and performance IQs. Consistent gender differences have been reported on particular subscales but not on composite IQs.

The measure of verbal IQ on the WAIS is based on scores in answering twenty-nine general-information questions, understanding fourteen comprehension items (for example, proverbs), defining forty words, solving fourteen arithmetic problems, and remembering strings of digits. The performance IQ is based upon the ability to say which part is missing in twenty-one incomplete pictures, to translate a digit-symbol code, to reproduce a variety of designs using red- and white-sided blocks, to arrange pictures in a series so that they tell a coherent story, and to assemble objects.

Even a brief examination of the subtests that contribute to the two WAIS IQ scores indicates the variety of abilities required to produce high scores. In order to solve arithmetic problems, both computational skills and verbal understanding of the questions are necessary. Such is the variety of tasks that it is difficult to describe all the abilities these tests are measuring. It is likely that males are good at some things and females at others, but composite scores that are based on the combination of many subtasks mask these gender-related differences.

Factor analysis is a complex statistical technique that psychometricians have used to analyze the different abilities their tests measure. Specifically, they examine the relationships between a large variety of tests or even among test items. Factors are identified from the matrices yielded by these measures of relationship. A factor described as spatial ability has consistently revealed differences between men and women showing a clear male advantage.

Again it is useful to look specifically at the kinds of tests used to measure spatial ability. One extensive review of gender differences in spatial ability organized empirical results under six headings: recall and selection of shapes, mental rotation and identification, geometric and mathematical skill, chess, sense of direction, and auditory perception, including spatial elements in music (Harris, 1978). This presentation included mathematical skill under the heading "spatial ability." Maccoby and Jacklin reported it separately as one of three well-documented gender differences in intellectual ability. They found a male superiority in mathematical ability, which they described as beginning in early adolescence. Although Maccoby and Jacklin listed spatial and mathematical abilities separately, they recognized that mathematical performance may reflect spatial skill. The relative importance of spatial and verbal processing in problem solving may account for the failure to find clear gender differences in tests of mathematical ability.

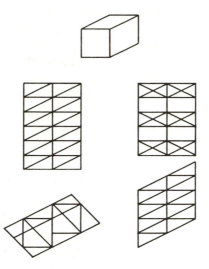

Figure 2.1. An example of the Witkin Embedded Figure Test. The subject is first shown one of the complex figures in the lower two rows, followed by the simple figure above. The simple figure is then hidden and the subject must find it embedded in the complex pattern. The time taken to do this is scored.

Examining tests that consistently show a male advantage in spatial ability, we find that the clearest evidence comes from tasks that involve making mental transformations in three-dimensional space (Fairweather, 1976). Typically, a person is shown two slightly different line drawings of patterns representing piled blocks and is then asked whether rotating one pile would make it appear exactly like the other. From early adolescence, males excel.

The recall and detection of shapes, particularly as measured by the Embedded Figures Test (EFT), also provides consistent evidence of a male advantage. The magnitude of the difference is such that 25 percent of female scores are above the mean for male scores (Hyde, 1981). In this test, individuals are briefly shown a simple geometric figure and, after it has been removed, required to find the figure in a complex drawing (see

Figure 2.1). Before adolescence boys and girls tend to perform in a similar fashion, and the few significant differences that have been reported are inconsistent, some showing that boys excel and others that girls perform better (Maccoby and Jacklin, 1974). Many studies have reported a male advantage during adolescence, which has been shown to continue into middle age and to be present in a variety of cultures (Harris, 1978). Performance on the EFT has been interpreted as indicative of an individual's more general ability to "disembed," or separate, figure and ground. The more general ability has been called field independence or an analytic cognitive style (Witkin et al., 1962). The description of women as less analytic, or field-dependent, because of lower scores on tests such as the EFT has been challenged by a number of psychologists (Sherman, 1967; Harris, 1978). One argument against the view that the male advantage in the EFT rests primarily on a disembedding skill is that disembedding is a complex process comprised of a number of constituent skills. Visual coding and visual memory are believed to contribute to successful performance, as well as spatial ability.

Studies of geometric and mathematical skills were also included in Harris's (1978) review of spatial ability research. He claimed that male superiority was evident only in branches of mathematics where spatial ability is important, such as geometry. In other branches of mathematics that rely more heavily on verbal understanding, the evidence for gender differences is less consistent (Maccoby and Jacklin, 1974; Harris, 1978).

In his survey of spatial ability Harris also considered tasks such as chess playing, musical composition, and a variety of tests that assess an individual's sense of direction. The evidence for a gender difference varies from study to study, and again this may reflect the relative contribution of spatial skills and other abilities to total performance.

Before we leave the area of systematic testing, it is necessary to consider verbal ability. It is a commonsense belief that women have the edge here, but the psychometric data are less clear.

Maccoby and Jacklin (1974) and earlier reviewers reported a slight female advantage, which Hyde (1981) and Tresemer (1975) both estimated to be much smaller than the spatial difference. But the evidence is contentious, and Fairweather (1976) even claimed that the data show a slight male advantage.

Let us consider the developmental evidence regarding verbal ability. Maccoby and Jacklin failed to find a *clear* female advantage in early childhood. But studies undertaken with children from disadvantaged families show that there is an initial female superiority although by three years of age boys achieve equal verbal competence.

Even more puzzling are studies carried out with English schoolchildren (Brimer, 1969). When more than eight thousand children between the ages of five and eleven years were tested on vocabulary items, boys showed an advantage from six to eight years, but there were no other significant differences. Results from the United States are more consistent with commonsense notions, as a female superiority was reported when children age five to eight were tested with verbal items from the Stanford–Binet Scale.

Although Maccoby and Jacklin suggest that a female advantage emerges in adolescence, the results on which they base their conclusions are not consistent. The few studies of adults are contradictory, some reporting a male superiority and others a female advantage, particularly in verbal reasoning and vocabulary (Bayley and Oden, 1955; Blum et al., 1972). The evidence for a female superiority in verbal abilities is certainly not as convincing as that which has been marshaled to show a male advantage in spatial skills.

Until quite recently the picture that emerged from an examination of the results of careful tests of intellectual functioning was one of limited differences between men and women. Stereotypes could not be readily fueled by such evidence, but meta-analytic research, the review and synthesis of sets of results, may modify our conclusions. Rushton et al. (1983) argue that psychologists need to aggregate their measures in order to derive more reliable estimates and more accurate descriptions. In demonstrating the usefulness of this approach they cite Block's (1976b) critique of Maccoby and Jacklin. Block (1976b), who also asserted that single measures can be unreliable, had combined variables and then examined the pattern of male and female superiority. In the domain we have been considering, intellectual functioning, the method of Rushton et al. yields seven dimensions. These include the already familiar verbal, spatial, and quantitative abilities but add "set breaking responses to insight problems," which shows a striking male advantage: "anagrams – breaking up words into new words," which yields a moderate female advantage: and two dimensions along which there are no clear differences – "descriptive, analytic sorting style" and "auditorially oriented responses." Although this meta-analysis does not substantially challenge earlier conclusions, it emphasizes the relationship between the procedures psychologists use and the results they report.

The social psychological study of stereotypes: commonsense beliefs

Turning to the social psychological study of stereotypes we gain a new perspective. Psychologists who study stereotypes employ precise quantitative methods in order to describe socially shared beliefs. The process they investigate, the assignment of traits according to group membership, is one of everyday life. We noted in Chapter 1 that the commonsense approach to gender differences is based on this attribution of abilities and characteristics according to gender.

In early social psychological research on stereotypes people were given long lists of adjectives and asked to choose those that applied to particular racial and ethnic groups (Katz and Braly, 1933). Similar techniques have been used to study gender stereotypes (Williams and Bennett, 1975). It is assumed that these methods reflect the stereotyping process itself – that people make sense of their social world by categorizing other individuals according to easily observable characteristics that signal age, gender, or race and by then attributing other adjectives or traits on the basis of group membership (Secord and Backman, 1964). The relationship between group membership and other traits is difficult to explain and may appear arbitrary. A black might disclaim being superstitious (Katz and Braly, 1933) just as a woman would take issue with being seen as frivolous (Williams and Bennett, 1975), although in the popular imagination both these descriptions appear apt. A study of gender stereotyping in thirty nations that reported considerable cross-cultural uniformity in the assignment of traits by gender suggests that the process is not completely arbitrary (Williams and Best, 1982).

A more precise relationship between the process of categorization and the contents or traits invoked in forming stereotypes has recently been proposed; it focuses on intergroup relations rather than on the characteristics of isolated groups (Doise, 1978). Beliefs about the nature of particular groups are held to reflect the relations that exist between these groups. If the conflict between men and women for education and jobs were to increase, we might expect that the traits assigned according to gender would provide sharper contrasts between men and women. In this chapter we take a more static approach; we use the work of social psychologists to provide an objective appraisal of commonsense notions of gender.

The most extensive research on gender stereotypes has been undertaken at universities in the United States. We start by comparing three American studies and consider the view of men and women that emerges from them. We then look briefly at a study of English university students.

We begin with a straightforward study, that of Williams and Bennett (1975). They asked university students to indicate which adjectives from a list of 300 were typically associated with either men or women. The students were able to categorize over 90 percent, or 272, of the adjectives as belonging to either women or men. There was considerable agreement about this

Table 2.9. *Adjectives associated with women, with evaluative classification*

Affected	−	Feminine	o	Prudish	−
Affectionate	+	Fickle	−	Rattlebrained	−
Appreciative	+	Flirtatious	o	Sensitive	o
Attractive	+	Frivolous	−	Sentimental	o
Charming	+	Fussy	−	Soft-hearted	o
Complaining	−	Gentle	+	Sophisticated	o
Dependent	o	High-strung	o	Submissive	o
Dreamy	o	Meek	o	Talkative	o
Emotional	o	Mild	o	Weak	−
Excitable	o	Nagging	−	Whiny	−

Source: Based on Williams and Bennett (1975) and Gough and Heilbrun (1965).

assignment among female and male students. Tables 2.9 and 2.10 show those adjectives that were agreed upon by 75 percent of all students (females and males combined). This criterion estab-lished 30 adjectives describing women and 33 describing men. They are presented with an evaluative classification of each adjec-tive – positive (+), negative (−), or neutral (o) – that had been developed in an earlier study (Gough and Heilbrun, 1965).

Williams and Bennett's results are similar to gender-stereotype findings published by Komarovsky in 1950 and re-ported repeatedly since then (by, e.g., Rosenkrantz et al., 1968, and Ellis and Bentler, 1973). Investigators often find that greater value is ascribed to male attributes, and these tables support a similar conclusion. Fifteen adjectives in each list have either positive or negative connotations. Of the adjectives asso-ciated with women, 5 are positively valued whereas 10 are negatively valued. The values attached to the masculine stereo-type are the mirror image, 5 negative and 10 positive.

Judgments of typical feminine and typical masculine traits provide a very familiar picture – and so they should, since com-monsense beliefs are used to make judgments about typical women and men. But there are also a few surprises. Adjectives

Table 2.10. *Adjectives associated with men, with evaluative classification*

Adventurous	+	Disorderly	−	Realistic	+
Aggressive	o	Dominant	o	Robust	o
Ambitious	+	Enterprising	+	Self-confident	o
Assertive	o	Forceful	o	Severe	o
Autocratic	o	Handsome	o	Stable	+
Boastful	−	Independent	+	Steady	o
Coarse	−	Jolly	o	Stern	o
Confident	+	Logical	+	Strong	o
Courageous	+	Loud	−	Tough	o
Cruel	o	Masculine	o	Unemotional	o
Daring	−	Rational	+	Unexcitable	o

Source: Based on Williams and Bennett (1975).

such as *Coarse, Disorderly, Jolly,* and *Severe* are not usually found among the attributes of the masculine stereotype. On the feminine list, *Appreciative, Complaining,* and *Sophisticated* are unexpected. Williams and Bennett asked students to choose from an extensive list of adjectives and gave them instructions suggesting that each adjective could be attributed either to a typical woman or a typical man. These procedures may have contributed to the unexpected findings.

The two studies we consider next – those of Sandra Bem who developed the Bem Sex Role Inventory, and of Janet Spence, who devised the Personal Attributes Questionnaire – differ from the simple-choice approach we have just examined. They differed, too, from earlier studies in which masculinity and femininity were viewed as two ends of a single continuum, a position reviewed and criticized by Constantinople (1973). Separate dimensions of masculinity and femininity were used. Bem asked students to rate the desirability of traits along these dimensions, and Spence asked students to describe the ideal and the typical male or female.

Initially Bem (1974) asked four groups of university students to rate the desirability of 400 traits in order to find 20 adjectives

Table 2.11. *Traits from the Bem Sex Role Inventory classified by dimension*

Feminine	Masculine	Socially desirable or undesirable
Affectionate	Acts as a leader	Adaptable
Cheerful	Aggressive	Conceited
Childlike	Ambitious	Conscientious
Compassionate	Analytical	Conventional
Does not use harsh language	Assertive	Friendly
Eager to soothe hurt feelings	Athletic	Happy
Feminine	Competitive	Helpful
Flatterable	Defends own beliefs	Inefficient
Gentle	Dominant	Jealous
Gullible	Forceful	Likable
Loves children	Independent	Moody
Loyal	Individualistic	Reliable
Sensitive to others' needs	Leadership abilities	Secretive
Shy	Makes decisions easily	Sincere
Soft-spoken	Masculine	Solemn
Sympathetic	Self-reliant	Tactful
Tender	Self-sufficient	Theatrical
Understanding	Strong personality	Truthful
Warm	Willing to take a stand	Unpredictable
Yielding	Willing to take risks	Unsystematic

Source: Based on Bem (1974).

characteristic of women and 20 characteristic of men. Table 2.11 presents the adjectives she found to be feminine and masculine. Some adjectives were not specifically applied to women or men, although they were rated as generally more or less desirable. Twenty of these undifferentiated but clearly desirable or undesirable adjectives were included in the inventory in order to determine an individual's tendency to exaggerate in a positive or negative direction. Bem (1979) has defended this choice vigorously in the face of subsequent attack (Locksley and Colten, 1979; Pedhazur and Tetenbaum, 1979). We consider the controversy in Chapter 10. Here we are interested in the particular content of the gender stereotypes that these methods yielded.

Spence and her co-workers developed their Personal Attributes Questionnaire (Spence et al., 1975) from an earlier test of "sex role" stereotyping (Rosenkrantz et al., 1968). They asked university students and other groups of people to select items that described either a typical woman and man or an ideal woman and man. Judgments of a typical woman and man were more extreme and resembled other reports of stereotypes. People made less polarized judgments in describing their ideal woman and man. This suggests that there is a potential for change. Although people recognize that current gender roles are polarized and report this in their typicality judgments, their ideal ratings are less polarized. At some future time people may see the roles of women and men as less polarized.

Fifty-four dimensions along which ratings of typical women and men showed clear and statistically significant differences were used to make up their final questionnaire. The less extreme ratings of ideal woman and ideal man were used to identify those items specific to one gender. The 13 dimensions along which the ideal woman and ideal man differed comprised their sex-specific items. The other 41 dimensions did not yield any significant differences in descriptions of the ideal, but on 18 of them both woman and man were rated at the feminine end of the continuum – these items were labeled "female-valued" items. On the remaining 23 dimensions both the ideal woman and the ideal man were placed on the masculine end of the continuum; these were labeled "male-valued" items. The Personal Attributes Questionnaire is presented in Table 2.12 with the female-valued, male-valued, and sex-specific items grouped together.

In comparing these three studies, we begin by looking at the sex-specific items from the Personal Attributes Questionnaire (Table 2.12), since these showed masculine–feminine polarization even of ideal ratings. In the future we would still expect to find these differences between women and men. None of the 7 female entries from the 13 sex-specific items appears either in the list of adjectives associated with women according to Williams and Bennett or in Bem's list of feminine traits. The sex-

Table 2.12. *Personal Attributes Questionnaire items*

18 Female-valued items

Aware of others' feelings	Enjoys music and arts	Likes children
Considerate	Expresses tender feelings	Neat
Creative	Gentle	Strong conscience
Devotes self to others	Grateful	Tactful
Does not hide emotions	Helpful to others	Understanding
Emotional	Kind	Warm to others

23 Male-valued items

Active	Good at sports	Not timid
Acts as leader	Independent	Outgoing
Adventurous	Intellectual	Outspoken
Ambitious	Interested in sex	Self-confident
Competitive	Knows ways of world	Skilled in business
Does not give up easily	Makes decisions easily	Stands up under pressure
Feels superior	Not easily influenced	Takes a stand
Forward	Not excitable in minor crisis	

13 Sex-specific items

Female		*Male*
Cries easily	Religious	Aggressive
Excitable in major crisis		Dominant
Feelings hurt		Likes maths and science
Home-oriented		Loud
Needs approval		Mechanical aptitude
Need for security		Sees self running the show

Source: Based on Spence et al. (1975).

specific male items in conjunction with the other two lists yield a clear masculine stereotype. Even in an ideal world the male role is more consistently specified. *Aggressive* and *Dominant* are found on all three scales. *Loud* appears here and also in Williams and Bennett's list (Table 2.10).

Comparisons with the 18 female-valued and 23 male-valued items show additional overlaps with the other two studies. Once more these are greater for the masculine stereotype. *Ambitious* and *Independent* appear on all three lists, while *Acts as leader, Athletic, Competitive,* and *Makes decisions* are also included in Bem's masculine dimension. Altogether, 6 of Bem's masculine traits appear among the 23 male-valued items in Table 2.12. An additional 2 male-valued items – *Not excitable* and *Self-confident* – are found in the Williams and Bennett list. Eight of the 23 male-valued items are to be found in previous lists.

Two of Spence's female-valued items occur in precisely the same form on Bem's feminine dimension. These are *Gentle* and *Understanding. Expresses tender feelings* and *Likes children,* as well as *Warm to others,* are similar to descriptions in Bem's feminine category. This lenient comparison produces a 5-item overlap with Bem's list. As there are only 18 female-valued items in the Personal Attributes Questionnaire, the proportion of overlap calculated in this manner is slightly larger for female items (28 percent) than that for the male-valued items (24 percent). *Gentle* appears in the Williams and Bennett list, but only *Emotional* adds a new item of overlap and brings the total across the three measures to 6: The male stereotype appears slightly clearer.

A distinction suggested by the sociologists Parsons and Bales (1955) in relation to the family provides a division that can be used to characterize these descriptions. They summarize the traits ascribed to women as being indicative of emotion and label them as constituting an expressive dimension, while they see the traits that describe men as being concerned with action or an instrumental dimension. This view of the family echoes commonsense judgments and stereotypes of masculinity and femininity and is not without its critics.

We can now ask how the composite pictures of women and

men yielded by these three measures compare with results from an English study. The traits listed on two or more scales to describe women are *Affectionate, Emotional, Feminine, Gentle, Likes children, Tender, Understanding,* and *Warm.* The list of traits associated with men includes *Acts as leader, Aggressive, Ambitious, Assertive, Competitive, Dominant, Forceful, Good at sports, Independent, Loud, Makes decisions easily, Masculine, Not excitable,* and *Self-confident.*

How do these views compare with those of students in England? A heterogeneous group of people attending Open University summer schools were asked to rate their own gender and the other gender along 21 dimensions (Burns, 1977). In addition, they were asked to rate their own gender as they imagined a member of the opposite gender would rate it. This study, which asked students to give three different viewpoints, is complex, and we report only a part of it. The perception of each gender as seen through their own eyes and their view of the other gender group are similar to those found by the procedures used in the American studies. The widest discrepancies were found between a gender's view of itself and its beliefs about the opposite gender's view of it, but we will not pursue these as there is no counterpart in the three American studies.

Women perceived women as showing *Affection, Expressing anger verbally, Somewhat creative,* and *Taking things personally.* Men saw women as *Showing affection* and *Taking things personally* – and here agree with women's judgments about women. But men also saw women as *Crying easily, Somewhat kind,* and *Warm.* Superficially it appears that English women and men were less in agreement than Americans, but it should be noted that in Williams and Bennett's study judgments of own and other gender were combined without indicating discrepancies: Students were only asked to indicate whether an adjective was associated with a woman or a man, whereas the English students were required to locate women and men at points on each of 21 dimensions. This may in part explain the differences between the attributes the English students used in describing women and the American list – *Affectionate, Emotional, Gentle, Feminine, Likes children, Tender, Understanding,* and *Warm. Taking things personally* and *Cries easily* may be aspects of *Emotionality*, but *Somewhat creative* and *Expressing anger verbally* are new dimensions of a feminine stereotype arising from the English findings. *Creative* appears as a female-valued trait, though not as a sex-specific attribute, in Table 2.12.

Each of the approaches we have considered provides information about the nature of men and women. Can we say that one approach is more scientific or objective, indeed more credible than the others? Even our cursory examination of these three methods of investigation, (demographic, psychometric, social psychological) suggests that in each there is an aim to reduce bias and provide replicable results, but that none is without problems. The answer to our question must surely be no – we cannot say that one of these descriptions portrays men and women more faithfully than the others.

In demographic and psychometric research the definition of concepts is a source of ambiguity that can lead to reliance on intuitive commonsense notions. Although social psychologists use our everyday terms in studying stereotypes, their results vary according to the questions they ask. Terms selected to describe typical men and women in gender roles as these are currently enacted in society differ from those traits chosen when people are asked to describe gender roles of men and women in the future – how they would ideally see them.

Although the need for such attention to detail may at times appear fiddling if not positively boring, it is a necessary part of every scientific investigation. It is one characteristic that distinguishes scientific investigation from naive understanding. We believe it is essential in any scientific discourse on the nature of gender. Nonetheless, that discourse remains sensitive to the influences of commonsense. In the absence of clearly specified theories, ambiguities in defining our variables and in describing our results lead us to fall back on our intuitive, commonsense understanding of men and women.

3

Physical sex differences: evolution, development, and cultural significance

In the first two chapters we introduced some issues that are important for understanding the scientific study of sex and gender and showed how differences between men and women had been studied from three diverse points of view within the social sciences. We turn now to more detailed examination of specific topics. We begin in this chapter by looking at physical differences. First we consider the evolutionary origin of sex and of the bodily forms of the two sexes; we then outline the physical development of boys and girls; and finally we consider briefly the elaboration and cultural use of physical sex differences – their contribution to gender.

Evolution: Where did sex begin?

As recently as a hundred years ago, many people were apparently satisfied with the Adam-and-Eve answer to the question of the origin of the two sexes. But the general acceptance of Darwin's theory of evolution, which constitutes a cornerstone of modern biology, has eroded the credibility of religious sources.

Although there has been some return to religious fundamentalism in recent years in the United States, at present there is no credible scientific alternative to evolutionary biology as an answer to questions about the origins of sex. Although science may be able to compete with religion in terms of credibility, it cannot do so in the certainty of the answers it offers. Much about the evolution of sex and sex differences has yet to be

48

explained. The current theories of evolutionary biologists do, however, provide an intriguing and rather different way of looking at this familiar subject.

What is sex?

Before we can ask about the origins of sex and of the bodily forms of the two sexes, we must ask a further question: In biological terms, what does sex entail? The answer may seem clear enough in human terms. But even this is not so. In our discussion of the ethnomethodological approach in Chapter 1, we noted that human beings tend to identify a person as a man or a woman by constructing the person's gender from a variety of cues, including physical attributes such as physique, beard growth, and breast development. But from the wider perspective of the evolutionary biologist, who is familiar with a whole range of animal species, these physical differences between men and women – which help us to assign gender – are not sufficiently widespread in the animal kingdom to be useful in answering the general question "What is sex?"

Even the feature that many men and women regard as *the* essential difference between them – possession of a penis or a vagina – is not one that can be used for defining sex over a wide range of animal species, even if we were to confine our discussion to those animals in which fertilization takes place internally. In birds, for example, the male does not have a penis. In fact, mammals are the only animal group in which the male does possess a true penis, although a comparable male appendage ("intromittent organ") that is inserted into the female body is present in many other forms of animal life where there is internal fertilization. There are, for example, paired bony projections called claspers in male cartilaginous fish such as sharks and dogfish.

The existence of a chromosomal difference between men and women is fairly widely known, particularly as this distinction is the one used for defining the sexes for the purposes of professional sporting competitions. Competitors in women's Olympic athletic events have to undergo a sex test, which is an assessment of their sex chromosomes. Every human being (and indeed every multicellular animal) starts life as a single fertilized egg cell. In the nucleus of the human egg cell, there are forty-six chromosomes, forty-four (twenty-two pairs) called autosomes and two sex chromosomes. The latter are both relatively long and identical in females (designated XX), but in the male one of them is an incomplete structure carrying little genetic material (the Y chromosome), thus leaving many genes on the longer X chromosome unpaired.

All cells in a woman's body except the egg cells contain two X chromosomes, and all the cells in a man's body except the sperm cells contain one X and one Y chromosome. In the germ cells, the egg and sperm cells, only half the chromosomes are present, so that female cells all contain one X chromosome, and male cells contain either an X or Y chromosome. These pair up to form either XX or XY in the fertilized egg, in roughly equal proportions. Usually there are slightly more males than females at conception in most mammals, but this difference declines with age owing to relatively greater male mortality at all ages.

Although the Y chromosome has practically no functional genes, the X chromosome has a number, including those responsible for fifty-seven unwelcome conditions such as color blindness and hemophilia. Most of these harmful genes are *recessive*, meaning that if they are paired with another of a different type, they will not be expressed. In the female, the possession of two X chromosomes usually results in these harmful genes being overridden; in the male, they are much more common, because the Y chromosome is ineffective in counteracting them, as it possesses practically no functional genes. Characteristics such as color blindness, which result from the expression of these recessive genes, are termed *sex-linked*.

A straightforward procedure is available to determine

whether a cell contains more than one X chromosome and thus to identify the genetic sex of a person. Cells from the mouth are prepared and stained. A distinctive spot of color called the Barr body indicates more than one X chromosome – a female. This test has been used to "sex" Olympic competitors.

But even chromosomally defined sex is not a general enough characteristic to answer the question "What is sex?" for all animals. The possession of two X chromosomes may be an adequate defining characteristic for the female sex in mammals, but this is not the case for fish, amphibians, and birds: In these animals the female has the shorter chromosome and the male two longer X chromosomes. In some animals, sex is determined not by chromosomal differences but by their environment. In the coral-reef fish *Anthias squamipinnis*, for example, the absence of a male in the immediate surroundings causes a female to undergo a sex change. But if a male can be seen (even in an adjacent fish tank), this reversal is inhibited by his presence (Shapiro, 1979).

Can we define sex in a general way, one that will satisfy the wider viewpoint of the evolutionary biologist? The answer is that we can. Fundamentally, sex is defined in terms of the gametes or germ cells an animal produces – whether these are sperms or eggs. If an animal produces a gamete that is large, contains food, and is immobile it is called an egg cell and would be defined as female. One that is small, contains no food resources, and is mobile is defined as a male.

Why did sex evolve?

Having provided a general definition of male and female in terms of the unequal size and mobility of their germ cells or gametes, we now consider why this arrangement developed – in other words, why sex evolved. To answer this we consider two more specific questions. One is why sexual reproduction evolved at all. The second is why the two types of gametes are located in different individuals (males and females) in some species whereas in others, such as snails and earthworms, they both occur in the same individual (hermaphrodites).

Why sexual reproduction evolved at all has puzzled evolutionary biologists. There are several consequences of sexual reproduction that might put a sexual animal at a disadvantage compared with an asexual one. Asexual reproduction involves the budding or cloning of a genetic "carbon copy" from the parent individual, whereas in sexual reproduction only half of each parent's genetic material is passed on to each offspring. Therefore, twice as much time and energy has to be expended in order to pass on the same amount of genetic information in a sexual process. There is also the risk that a sexual parent might mix his or her genetic material with that of a genetically disadvantageous individual, thus producing poorer offspring than by an asexual process. The act of mating itself involves a number of "costs," such as the expenditure of time and energy in courtship and copulation and increased risks from predation, overeager mates, and infectious diseases (Daly, 1978).

Since sexual reproduction involves these disadvantages, why did it evolve at all? The reason seems to be that mixing the genetic material from two individuals – which occurs during sexual reproduction – results in far greater individual variation in the resulting offspring, and this variation is highly advantageous if a species is to adapt to a changing environment (Maynard Smith, 1971). Since asexual reproduction only results in the formation of individuals who are genetically identical to their parents, it cannot produce sufficient variation for the organism to adapt to changing conditions. Although sex is both risky and costly, it has provided a way in which organisms have continually been able to produce sufficient variety in their offspring to increase the chances of their survival in changing environments.

According to this explanation, the usefulness of sexual reproduction is confined to certain fairly restricted circumstances, occurring when an organism produces a large number of offspring that are likely to inhabit rather different environments from those of their parents. Although this may provide an explanation for the origin of sexual reproduction, it is clear that not all sexually reproducing animals exist under such circumstances today. Birds and mammals, for example, produce relatively few offspring, and sexual reproduction may actually be maladaptive in these circumstances; but these animals, having lost the preadaptations necessary for reverting to asexuality, continue to reproduce sexually (Williams, 1975).

A second question about the evolution of sex is why two different-sized gametes (eggs and sperm) have arisen. If the important aspect of sexual reproduction lies in the fusing of genetic material, why are two different-sized germ cells necessary? In many one-celled organisms, sexual reproduction does take place through the fusion of two identically sized gametes. But in most multicellular organisms gametes of unequal size – male and female – are produced.

Parker and his colleagues (1972) discussed the possible evolution of different-sized gametes from same-sized gametes. They suggested that there are two opposing selection pressures acting on gamete size in many-celled organisms: The first is that individuals can increase their number of fertilizations by producing many small gametes rather than few large ones; the second is that the provision of a large food store in the fertilized egg cell (*zygote*) increases its chances of surviving to maturity. (In a one-celled organism a large food reserve is unnecessary, since it does not have to develop into a much larger organism.) Parker and his colleagues used a computer simulation to demonstrate that the only stable evolutionary response to the two selection pressures is the production of two different gamete sizes, each of which is a response to one, but not both, of the selection pressures.

It is suggested that small-sized gametes (*spermatozoa*) originated as a response to selection for high productivity; but these gametes lack adequate food reserves and hence they can only produce viable offspring if they fuse with larger, food-carrying gametes (*ova* or *egg cells*). The smaller gametes would quickly

develop adaptations that would enable them to be more successful in fusing with the larger gametes than these would be
in fusing with one another. Once this happened, the larger
gametes would begin to lose their initial motility and there
would be selection for increased motility among the smaller
gametes, resulting in the characteristically active spermatozoa
(Parker et al., 1972).

The third question concerning the evolution of sex is why
different-sized gametes are produced by different individuals,
males and females. Since we ourselves belong to a species in
which there are two sexes, we tend to regard separate sexes as
the natural order of things. Although this arrangement does
occur throughout the animal kingdom, and in a number of
plants, many organisms are hermaphrodites, that is, each individual is capable of producing both types of gamete. In most
hermaphroditic species, cross-fertilization occurs, thus providing the mixing of genetic material that seems to account for the
evolutionary success of sexual reproduction. Why, then, are
not all animals cross-fertilizing hermaphrodites? There appears
to be no clear answer to this question. There is, however, one
fairly obvious advantage of two sexes over hermaphrodites: In
the latter, each individual must maintain two sets of gonads
and reproductive ducts, both of which are complex and expen-
sive in terms of energy expenditure (Williams, 1975). Identifying the particular circumstances under which hermaphrodites
would be at an advantage over two separate sexes is a particularly difficult problem, and a convincing theoretical explanation
for the occurrence of hermaphroditism has yet to be offered
(see Ghiselin, 1974; Williams, 1975).

Evolution of sex differences in animals

Sexual dimorphism is the term used to refer to differences in
anatomy, physiology, and behavior between males and females of the same species. It is a phenomenon that is widespread throughout the animal kingdom, and of course occurs

in the human species. If there is only one fundamental difference between males and females – that of gamete size – why
have such a wide variety of other differences evolved? Why,
for example, do the sexes of many vertebrates differ in size and
other physical characteristics? Why are many male birds more
brightly colored than their female counterparts? Why do cocks
crow but not hens? And why do men but not women develop
beards, and women but not men develop prominent breasts?

The usual evolutionary explanation for sexual dimorphism is
derived from Charles Darwin's speculations on the subject in
The Descent of Man and Selection in Relation to Sex, first published
in 1871. Darwin suggested that there are two selection pressures determining which individuals produce the most offspring: competition between males for females and selection by
females of certain male characteristics in preference to others.
The first pressure, male competition, has been used to explain
the origin of the complex antler development of the male deer.
Large antlers are assumed to be the result of large-antlered
ancestors' successful competition with other stags for access to
fertile females. The second type of selection pressure, female
choice, has been used to explain the origin of the elaborate tail
of the peacock. This time it is assumed that females choose
males with the most elaborately developed tails. Darwin called
these forms of selection "sexual selection." It is important to
realize that he only addressed himself to the question of how
male characteristics evolved and that such a male-centered
view of sexual selection has persisted until the present day.

One of the most influential modern views of sexual selection
is that of Robert Trivers (1972). Although published a century
after Darwin's work, it is still concerned mainly with male competition and female choice (again neglecting selection of female
characteristics). Trivers suggested that these types of sexual
selection can be viewed as consequences of the different-sized
gametes in the two sexes. He suggested that since the female
provides all the food reserves for the fertilized egg, the male's
contribution to the offspring represents much less in expendi-

ture of time and energy than that of the female. Trivers argued that the number of offspring a female can produce is limited by her ability to produce egg cells, since a relatively large amount of energy is necessary to produce the food reserves in these cells; on the other hand, no such limit operates in the case of the male. A male's reproductive success will not be limited by gamete production but by his ability to fertilize the egg cells of females, that is, by his access to fertile females. Trivers infers from this that the ways in which the two sexes can maximize their reproductive success will be different – males by mating with as many females as possible, and females, which require only one successful mating to fertilize their eggs, by choosing the male with the best genetic endowment or one that will make the best parent (if parental care is involved). The result is competition among males for access to females with unfertilized eggs and selection by females of genetically fit males, the two forms of sexual selection originally envisaged by Darwin.

If Darwin's view of sexual selection and Trivers's argument sound notoriously like a familiar view of human conduct – of males trying to sow as many wild oats as possible and of females remaining coy and choosy – this is not surprising. Such a view of human conduct – some would say "human nature" – has clearly influenced both views of animal nature, and they provide a further example of scientific thinking reflecting commonsense notions prevalent in the wider society.

Irrespective of the source of Trivers's inspiration, are his assumptions about the relative contributions of the male and female in gamete production correct? They are not necessarily so, for the following reason: Female animals produce a certain number of egg cells (many or few, depending on the species), each with its store of food. But the male sheds a far greater number of sperm cells, together with their accompanying fluid. Only if one compares the energy expended in producing *one* egg cell with that expended in producing *one* sperm cell is Trivers's assumption obviously correct. But since males produce far more sperm cells than females produce egg cells, males may make up in numbers what they omit in terms of food resources. The relative contribution of male and female to the total amount of gamete production is not a simple matter of assumption (as Trivers suggested). It would require empirical measurement and is likely to vary from one animal species to another.

This objection to Trivers's assumption is not a crucial one for his whole theory, since he used his point about the relative contribution of the sexes to the fertilized egg as a basis for considering a much wider range of possible differences in the contribution of males and females to reproductive processes. Using a term borrowed from economics, Trivers regarded each parent as "investing" in its offspring: the greater the investment the greater the chance that the offspring will survive to perpetuate themselves (and hence their parents' genes). Trivers defined *parental investment* as any contribution by a parent that increases an offspring's chances of surviving and reproducing itself while also reducing the parents' ability to produce future offspring. Some examples of parental investment are the energy expended in gamete production and activities such as feeding and protecting the young. The total range of possible activities that this description covers is very difficult to combine and quantify in a single value, and this difficulty limits the usefulness of Trivers's subsequent speculations. We can say, however, that features such as giving birth to live young, production of enclosed eggs, and lactation all represent high degrees of parental investment.

Trivers suggested that the (supposedly) smaller contribution of males to gamete production will, if there are no other factors involved, result in males competing for access to females. But he also extended this argument by suggesting that the sex that makes the lower parental investment will compete for access to the sex that makes the greater parental investment. This more general point does not depend on his initial assumption about gamete production being correct, since *parental investment* is a wider concept. This concept provides a reason for either sex competing for access to the other or showing mate choice. Trivers argued, however, that the usual case will still be that of male competition and female choice, basing his argument partly on the usual investment imbalance at fertilization forming the basis for a subsequent imbalance in parental investment. Whatever the logic of this assumption – and it can be convincingly disputed (e.g., Dawkins and Carlisle, 1976) – many animal sex differences do seem to fit Trivers's predictions. For example, Trivers's theory predicts that male competition, and hence sexual dimorphism, will be most marked in animals where there is practically no male parental investment, that is, no paternal care or protection. In such cases, the difference in reproductive success between individual males will also be greatest, and so will the mortality difference between the sexes. There are many examples that fit these predictions: In the elephant seal, for example, the males are considerably larger than the females, male competition is pronounced, and a successful male can hold a "harem" of about forty females, whereas an unsuccessful one obtains no females (Le Boeuf, 1974).

Trivers's theory also predicts that when the male's investment approaches that of the female, competition between males will be lessened, as will sexual dimorphism in size, aggressiveness, and mortality. This occurs in all birds that form relatively permanent pairs (i.e., are monogamous), which is the majority of species. As predicted, they show relatively small sex differences.

Trivers's theory also predicts that in cases where male parental investment is the higher, females will possess typically "male" characteristics such as bright plumage, larger size, and aggressiveness. This occurs in some wading birds, where the male is the sex that incubates the eggs and shows parental behavior, whereas the female mates with several males (i.e., she is polyandrous).

Thus, parental investment and sexual dimorphism do appear to be related in the way Trivers suggested. This does not necessarily mean that sexual dimorphism has always evolved as a consequence of prior differences in parental investment, since *parental investment* refers to an assortment of activities that may have arisen either relatively early or late in evolutionary history. One would expect, therefore, that there will be cases where sexual dimorphism has arisen prior to or independent of sex differences in parental investment and that Trivers's theory can only provide a partial explanation for sex differences in animals.

There are indeed cases of sexual dimorphism that Trivers's theory cannot explain. For example, in many mammalian species the female is slightly larger than the male, and it has been suggested that this is more common than is generally supposed (Ralls, 1976, 1978). Trivers's theory would predict that where the female is the larger sex, there should be greater parental investment by the male than the female (as in polyandrous wading birds: Jenni, 1974). However, in mammals where the female is larger, the male does not make any appreciable contribution to parental care – nor is the larger size of the female accompanied by typically "male" characteristics, as it is in female polyandrous birds. Ralls also cited examples from other groups of animals: The female guppy is larger than the male, but the male is still the more aggressive and brightly colored sex. These two features can be explained in terms of parental investment, but we should still have to offer another type of explanation for the larger female size.

What, then, is the explanation for large females? Ralls (1976, 1978) offered several possibilities, but there is really very little evidence on the subject. The first possibility is the "big mother" hypothesis: Simply put, big mothers make better mothers – "better" in this context referring to their ability to leave more surviving offspring. It is known that larger size is associated with greater reproductive success in women and in domestic ewes, but both these examples come from species in which the male is larger than the female. Ralls suggested that under certain conditions (e.g., where there was the possibility of prolonged food shortage) the benefits of large size would become more pronounced and might result in the female becoming larger than the male.

A second possibility is that males and females may reduce competition between the sexes by feeding from different food sources. This has been suggested to account for some sex differences found in birds (Selander, 1972). Ralls suggested that the same process might in some cases produce large females, but at present this remains purely hypothetical.

A third possibility, again lacking concrete examples for its support, is that certain resources, such as food or nesting sites, may be more crucial to females and hence lead to competition between females, resulting in large size in the same way that this is produced by competition in the male.

Whatever the explanation, it is clear that Trivers's theory cannot explain Ralls's large females. Ralls's suggestions are not particularly convincing as explanations for large female size, but they do represent a departure from the tradition of explaining sexual dimorphism solely in terms of male competition and female choice. Changes resulting from selection pressures on the female for efficient mothering, female competition, and specialized adaptations in the two sexes for different types of food foraging tend to take the focus of attention away from the male.

Hrdy (1981) has extended consideration of selection pressures acting on the female in a comprehensive review of the behavior of nonhuman primates. She views female competition as an essential basis for primate social organization. Hrdy argues that because female competition is less overt than that of the male, it has been ignored in early accounts of the behavior of female primates. Females compete for food resources and for the opportunity to breed and to raise offspring without being harassed by other individuals. Such harassment may have serious consequences for reproductive success, including inhibition of reproduction through social stress and infanticide by males or in some cases by other females. Hrdy goes on to argue that there are many aspects of primate–and human–evolution that can be explained by considering competition among females.

Evolution of human sex differences

We can never be certain about the evolutionary origin of human sexual dimorphism. There is no shortage of opinions on the subject, simply because it is so difficult to demonstrate that any particular one is incorrect (see, e.g., Freedman, 1964; Morris, 1967; Tiger, 1970; Hutt, 1972a; Goldberg, 1973; Morgan, 1972). What we shall attempt to do here is to relate some of these views to the general theories discussed in the previous section.

First, there are the possibilities raised by Darwin's discussion of sexual selection and by Trivers's theory. Darwin (1871) suggested that the larger average size, strength, and muscular development of men and the greater male aggressiveness (Chapter 5) could all have originated as a result of male competition. Trivers (1972) suggested that higher male mortality (Madigan, 1957) may also have originated in this way. (But see also the section on demography in Chapter 2). Tanner (1970) attributed men's beards to a similar origin, in terms of their intimidating appearance. Darwin (1871) suggested that these masculine features (including beards) originated partly through female choice.

An alternative explanation for the greater average size, strength, and musculature of men is that these features are adaptations for cooperative hunting of big game. This "hunting hypothesis" has been used to explain a range of masculine psychological characteristics such as the existence of all-male groups (Tiger, 1970), male dominance (Tiger, 1970), and throwing accuracy and spatial ability (Kolakowski and Malina, 1974). In the "hunting hypothesis," only selection pressures on the male are considered (see Slocum, 1975; Leakey and Lewin, 1979). Many views of human evolution are of this type, and cooperative hunting is often cited as the driving force in making us the intelligent creatures we are today (e.g., Washburn and Lancaster, 1968; Alcock, 1975). Commenting on this view, Hrdy (1981, p. 5) writes: "Curiously, few anthropologists have asked why intelligence never became sexlinked or why–if intelligence evolved among males to help them hunt–Nature should have squandered it on a sex that never hunted."

Male hunting is only one side of the coin: In most present-day hunter-gatherer societies, the women do not sit around at home while the men hunt the meat; there is a division of labor in food finding–men hunting animals and women gathering plant food–and women usually contribute more to the diet than do the men (Martin and Voorhies, 1975; Leakey and Lewin, 1979). Thus if men show adaptations for a hunting existence, women should also show adaptations for plant gathering. The division of labor into hunting and gathering might have arisen as a way of reducing competition between the sexes for food finding: In the previous section we mentioned Selander's explanation of this adaptation in birds.

As we have seen, there are several theories to account for the evolution of male features, but there has been less speculation about the female, and what has been offered usually emphasizes the male (Hrdy, 1981, is a notable exception). Women are generally regarded as showing a number of features that make them unusual compared to other female primates. For example, female sexual interest is less clearly related to the stage of the human menstrual cycle, and there are no external visual signals of sexual receptivity in women as there are in other female primates. In addition, the mammary glands develop into their adult form at puberty rather than during the first pregnancy, and body hair has been lost to an even greater extent than in the human male.

The standard explanation for prolonged female sexual interest, popularized by Morris (1967), is that it promotes long-term relationships between the sexes, and therefore provides a favorable environment for child rearing (see also Napier, 1971; Crook, 1972; Lovejoy, 1981). In our closest living relative, the chimpanzee, there is practically no association between members of a mated pair other than for copulation (Lawick-Goodall, 1971). Although human sexual acts can be as transient as this, there is usually some form of prolonged association between human sexual partners. Sexual interest and activity throughout the female cycle are viewed as contributing to prolonging the length of time mated pairs remained together. Nevertheless, other psychological characteristics, such as the capacity for exclusive emotional attachments and sexual jealousy, would also be required for any more permanent associations to have arisen. Whatever adaptations the human species possess in this respect, these certainly operate inefficiently, compared for example with those that produce true monogamy in birds. The term *pair bonding*, derived from research on birds, has been used to refer to human partners, but it is perhaps a misnomer since in humans the so-called bonds are often heavily dependent on cultural sanctions.

Recently, some authorities on the fossil evidence for human evolution have agreed with Morris in emphasizing human "pair bonding" (Lovejoy, 1981; see also Johanson and Edey, 1981). On the other hand, Hrdy (1981) is critical of this view in the light of comparative studies of the behavior of nonhuman primates. It is well known that truly monogamous species show little difference in body size or form between the sexes (see Trivers's theory in the previous section). Polygynous mating systems (i.e., those with one male and several females) are associated with differences in size and form between the sexes, and human sexual dimorphism lies within the range normally associated with polygyny (Short, 1980; Hrdy, 1981). Hrdy also argues that truly monogamous species do not show high levels of sexual activity across the female cycle. On the other hand, females of some polygynous primates are sexually active when they are not ovulating. These observations show that we are not dealing with a uniquely human feature, nor with one that is characteristic of monogamy, thus raising considerable doubts about the "pair bonding" explanation.

Hrdy's own explanation is that it has been evolutionarily advantageous for females of several basically polygynous group-living species to conceal their time of ovulation so that no single male could be certain of paternity. In many primate species where paternity is predictable (through the female continuously associating with one male), other males will, if given the opportunity, attack infants, and considerable mortality results. Disguising paternity, by concealing the time of ovulation and becoming more promiscuous, would be an effective female evolutionary strategy for ensuring that males who lacked these infanticidal tendencies evolved. It would also enable females to induce males to behave paternally toward infants, since paternal care is characteristically shown by primate males to infants that may be related to them. Hrdy argues, therefore, that many features of human female sexuality are adaptations for increased female promiscuity evolved within an originally mildly polygynous mating system rather than as adaptations for increased monogamy.

The usual explanation for other female characteristics such as breast development at puberty, lack of body hair, and a rounded figure is that these sexually attractive features have arisen through male choice. This was first suggested by Darwin (1871) and extended and popularized by Morris (1967), who viewed the human female as consisting largely of a collection of adaptations for sexually arousing the male – or, as he puts it, for "making sex sexier." This explanation was further publicized – with appropriate illustrations – by a British tabloid newspaper because it fitted neatly with our society's definition of women as "sex objects," a feature the British popular press exploits to sell newspapers. Morris argued that both these features and prolonged sexual interest (i.e., lack of clear signs of estrus) have evolved to promote "pair bonding."

However, in view of Hrdy's convincing argument against the pair-bonding idea, this seems unlikely. In Hrdy's view, Morris would be correct in speculating that these features had evolved "to make sex sexier," but not to serve male interests. In fact the opposite is suggested – that these features, together with the unreliable female orgasm, have evolved to promote sexual activity with several male partners, a feature that works against the interests of males! Throughout human history, Hrdy argues, the majority of the world's cultures have tried to counteract female promiscuous sexuality and to reassert male control over paternity.

Hrdy does not specifically discuss how women's breasts might have evolved. They represent a unique feature in the primate world in that they develop before they are required for lactation, they are conspicuous, and they contain a large amount of fatty tissue. These features cannot be easily explained in terms of their adaptive value in milk production (although they could be adaptations for supporting the milk-producing and milk-dispensing tissue of the breast). The obvious erotic significance of the female breast in our culture and in many other cultures (Short, 1980) makes Morris's theory that they are primarily for sexual attraction appear convincing in the absence of an alternative.

Such an explanation overlooks the importance of adaptations for ensuring survival, efficient reproduction, and good infant care in less affluent and well-fed times than our own (reflecting what Hrdy, in another context, calls "an American supermarket mentality"). Female breasts may have originally occurred as part of a general increase in fatty deposits in the female, so as to enable her to survive periods of food shortage. The female has to provide food for herself and for her infant when she is pregnant or lactating. This will entail a much greater food requirement than for the male, who only has to feed himself. It is also important for the female to produce a constant supply of milk in spite of hard times, and the fatty tissue in the breast would help to achieve this.

Other features of the human female are more obviously adaptations for reproduction – for example, the wider pelvis to accommodate the infant's head, which has increased in size during the course of evolution, during childbirth.

Some aspects of human sexual dimorphism have clear reproductive functions common to all mammals. The mammalian penis, for example, arose as an adaptation for efficient internal fertilization, and similar organs have developed as a result of parallel evolution in several other animal groups. Internal fertilization is a prerequisite for another characteristic of mammalian reproduction – that the young develop inside the mother and are born alive rather than enclosed in an egg. This is called *viviparity*, and it has resulted in specializations of the female reproductive organs to house the fetus (the uterus), to allow nutrient and waste product exchange between the embryo and the mother (the placenta), and to transport the full-term fetus to the outside world (the vagina).

Milk production appears to be of more ancient origin than viviparity, since it occurs in primitive egg-laying mammals such as the spiny anteater (Sharman, 1976). In fact, the mammary glands may have decreased in importance during the course of mammalian evolution, yielding part of their function of feeding the developing young to the placenta.

To sum up, there are several hypotheses that might account for the evolutionary origins of human sexual dimorphism: male competition, female choice, hunting-and-gathering specializations, female competition, and adaptations directly or indirectly related to reproductive success in the female.

The development of physical sex differences

In humans there are not only the obvious physical sex differences in reproductive organs, secondary sexual characteristics, and physique, but also some less obvious differences in physiological processes (Glucksmann, 1974). In this section, we consider how these differences arise in normal development, describe certain abnormalities, and discuss the normal variations in the developmental process that can lead to within-sex differences. The issue of within-sex variation reflects our concern with the extent to which sex differences show overlapping distributions, which we discussed in Chapter 1.

We first describe the three "sex hormones" that feature prominently in accounts of sexual development. The main hormone produced by the testes is testosterone; this, together with hormones of the same general type but produced in other parts of the body, are called *androgens*. The main hormones produced by the ovaries are estrogen and progesterone; the hormones of the same general type are referred to as *estrogens* and *progestogens*, respectively. Both types of "female" hormones show cyclical changes in their output from the ovary: This produces the estrous cycle (in most mammals) and the menstrual cycle (in primates). Both involve periodic release of an egg and changes in behavior toward males. The menstrual cycle is distinguished by monthly vaginal bleeding, caused by the shedding of the uterine wall.

These so-called male and female hormones are not confined to their respective sexes. The ovaries and testes each produce all three hormones, and the adrenal glands, situated above the kidneys, secrete androgens in both sexes. The ovaries and the adrenal glands of women produce androgens that affect hair growth under the arms and in the pubic region (Glucksmann, 1974); the testes produce a small quantity of estrogens, but at present there are no known physiological effects.

The developmental process

Prenatal development. There is no difference in male and female development during the first six weeks after conception. At this time the embryonic sex organs (*gonads*) are identical in the two sexes. The Y chromosome of the male is crucial for ensuring that the embryonic gonad will develop into a testis, and this occurs by enlargement of the inner part of the embryonic gonad at about six weeks of age. In the female, no gonadal development occurs at this time: Instead, at about twelve

Sex and gender

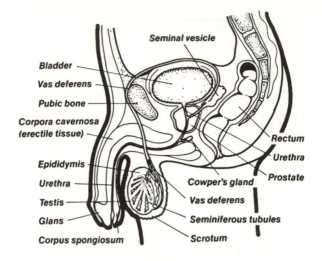

Figure 3.1. The male sexual and reproductive organs: side view. From Hyde (1979).

weeks the outer part of the embryonic gonad develops into an ovary, and this development is completed during the sixth or seventh month of pregnancy. At that time the ovaries will contain all the three hundred to four hundred egg cells that will be released during the woman's future life, as well as an additional hundred thousand that will not be used (Money and Ehrhardt, 1972).

During early development we all possess the rudimentary internal ducts for our own and for the opposite sex. At about three months after conception those for our own sex enlarge, whereas those for the opposite sex degenerate. This process depends, in the male, on the secretion of two hormones from the testis: The first, testosterone, causes enlargement in the male (Wolffian) ducts, which develop into the vasa deferentia, epididymis, and seminal vesicles (see Figure 3.1); the second, an unidentified substance (possibly a peptide usually called factor X or Mullerian-inhibiting substance), causes the female (Mullerian) ducts to degenerate (Simpson, 1976; Goy and Mc-

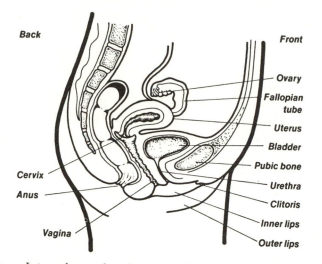

Figure 3.2. Internal sexual and reproductive organs of the female: side view. From Hyde (1979).

Ewan, 1980). The testis functions early in development, and testosterone synthesis has been reported in the human fetal testis at eight to ten weeks after conception, only two to four weeks after testis development has begun (Reinisch, 1976). In the female, absence of these two hormones results in degeneration of the Wolffian ducts and development of the Mullerian ducts to form the oviducts, uterus, and vagina (see Figure 3.2).

The final step in sexual differentiation is the development of the external genitals. Both male and female organs develop from a single undifferentiated structure: The presence of an androgen, dihydrotestosterone, during the third and fourth months of pregnancy causes the formation of a penis and scrotal sac, whereas the female clitoris and labia develop if this androgen is absent (Money and Ehrhardt, 1972; Imperato-McGinley et al., 1974; Goy and McEwan, 1980).

The crucial importance of the presence or absence of testicular androgens for normal sexual differentiation in mammals was first realized in 1947, following publication of animal experiments performed by Alfred Jost. He demonstrated that castration of the male rabbit fetus early in life resulted in the development of female reproductive structures (Jost, 1972). Research that followed showed that sexual development was similar in human beings and in other mammals.

The adrenal glands of male and female fetuses secrete small amounts of androgens, as do the adult glands. Since masculine development is dependent on the presence of androgens in the fetus, these adrenal androgens could be expected to produce some degree of masculinization in female fetuses. Research on rats and on rhesus monkeys has suggested that the hormone progesterone protects the female fetus from the possible masculinizing effects of fetal androgens, since progesterone is produced in much greater quantities by female than by male fetuses (Resko, 1975; Shapiro et al., 1976). At present, it is not known whether these findings can be generalized to other mammals, including humans.

In rats and mice, androgens from the fetal (or immediately postnatal) testes affect the developing brain of the male in a way that influences both the physiology and the behavior of the adult animal (Goy and McEwan, 1980). The behavioral influences range from the facilitation of masculine sexual behavior to nonsexual activities such as fighting, exploring, and playing (Archer, 1975; Olioff and Stewart, 1978; Goy and McEwan, 1980; Blizard, 1983). Several writers have suggested that testosterone may affect human brain development – and hence behavior – in a similar manner (e.g., Hutt, 1972a; Goldberg, 1973), but experimental studies on monkeys indicate that only some of the findings from rats and mice extend to primates, the taxonomic order to which human beings belong (Resko, 1975; Herbert, 1976; Gray and Drewett, 1977). Speculations from human clinical studies that prenatal androgen treatment can also "masculinize" the play activities of girls (Money and Ehrhardt, 1972) are controversial, since the studies were flawed methodologically (Quadagno et al., 1977). These issues are discussed further in Chapter 9, where developmental influences on gender differences are considered.

Another controversial theory about human behavior, also derived from studies of rodents, is that of Dörner (1976), who suggested that low levels of testosterone during fetal development predispose human males to become homosexual. Dörner based his theory on research using male rats. These studies found that testosterone normally affects areas of the young rats's brain that later influenced adult sexual behavior, resulting in the reduction of female patterns and the enhancement of male sexual behavior in adulthood (Gray and Drewett, 1977). Low levels of androgens result in a reversal of these effects. Dörner claimed that a similar process generally occurs in human males, so that insufficient testosterone during development would result in what is effectively "behavioral feminization," which he equates with homosexuality. But there is a logical flaw in this argument. The effects produced by androgens in rats influence the animal's preferred role in the sexual act – whether it mounts or solicits mounting. Human homosexuality is defined by the choice of sexual partner, and not the preference for an active or passive role in intercourse. If correct, Dörner's theory would also predict that exposure of human females to testosterone during fetal life would result in their showing lesbian preferences when they are sexually mature. Studies of women exposed to fetal androgens indicate that this is not the case (Money and Ehrhardt, 1972).

Despite these objections, Dörner's theory has continued to attract interest, as evidenced by subsequent work by his research group on human subjects. In order to explain this work, some background information about the rodent research is necessary.

If a male rat is deprived of androgens at a crucial stage early in life, it will show the typically female cyclic pattern of sex hormone secretion when it is an adult (Goy and McEwan, 1980). It is this process that underlies the estrous cycle of the female, and it is controlled by a structure in the brain called the hypothalamus. This is where androgen acts during the development of the male – abolishing the cyclic pattern of hormone release. One feature of the cyclic pattern is that the pituitary gland will show increased secretion of luteinizing hormone (LH) in response to increases in estrogen levels. This process normally includes ovulation, the release of egg cells. Male rats castrated early in life will, like normal female rats, show a rise in LH levels in response to estrogen administration (Goy and McEwan, 1980).

Dorner (1976) found that when homosexual men were each given an estrogen injection, a rise in LH output typically occurred between seventy-two and ninety-six hours later. But such an increase was not found in heterosexual and bisexual men (Goy and McEwan, 1980). Dörner argued that the male homosexuals' LH response is a sign of a female pattern of hormone release and that this must have originated from low levels of androgens at a crucial stage in their fetal life (i.e., that they are comparable to rats castrated early in life). However, other evidence from rhesus monkeys and humans all indicates that early androgen treatment – or lack of it – is not the crucial factor affecting the pattern of hormone secretion in these species (Resko, 1975; Herbert, 1976; Gray and Drewett, 1977). In other words, monkeys and people are not like rats in this respect.

Dörner's theory provides several features characteristic of the reductionist approach described in Chapter 1 (see the section "Research strategies"). First he makes unsubstantiated generalizations from studies of "lower" animals to human behavior and physiology; secondly, he assumes that because physiological and psychological events are associated with one another, the first must cause the second – yet there is ample evidence that psychological states influence physiology (Ellis, 1982; Sommer, 1982). In seeking a hormonal "cause" of homosexuality, Dörner defined a social and psychological phenomenon in terms of an abnormality of individual development, and in doing so supported the view that it is an illness for which a physical cure should be sought and administered. We consider psychological aspects of the development of sexual partners and some alternative views of homosexuality in the next chapter. For the moment, we conclude by noting the lack of firm support from research on human beings for Dörner's theory – and for other hormonally based theories of homosexuality (Birke, 1982).

Infancy and childhood. Although testosterone is crucial for early sexual development, its level declines just before birth (Knorr et al., 1974). Until comparatively recently it was thought that it remains negligible throughout childhood; but it has been reported that male infants show higher concentrations of testosterone at birth than females (Maccoby et al., 1979). Studies have also shown a rise in testosterone during the first six months following birth (Tanner, 1978), although the significance of this is unknown at present. One possibility is that in the human infant the period of sexual differentiation of brain structures occurs after birth. Relative to other primate infants, human babies are developmentally immature (Gould, 1980). In other mammals that give birth to immature young (e.g., the rat and the ferret), the period of sexual differentiation of the brain occurs after birth (Goy and McEwan, 1980). If this were also the case for human infants, research reviewed in the previous section on possible *prenatal* influences would have focused on the wrong period of development.

The most notable sex difference during infancy and childhood is that girls grow faster and reach puberty before boys do. They also stop growing earlier. Individual developmental age can be assessed accurately by measuring bone and tooth development and comparing these measures against a set of standards (Tanner, 1970). Before birth girls are shown to be more advanced than boys, and at birth they are on average four weeks ahead. This difference is maintained until about sixteen to eighteen years of age, and is reflected in other measures, such as those indicating motor coordination (Tanner,

1970). Girls also reach puberty before boys: The first outward sign of puberty, increased growth rate, occurs about two years earlier in girls.

The cause of these differences is unknown, but there is evidence that the timing of puberty is affected by prenatal testosterone; thus girls and female rhesus monkeys who had been exposed to testosterone during fetal development show delayed puberty (Resko, 1975; Money and Ehrhardt, 1972).

The other physical sex differences found during childhood are generally less pronounced versions of adult sex differences. Girls begin life slightly shorter than boys, and they remain shorter until about eleven years of age, when they overtake boys for about three years as a result of their earlier onset of puberty. Girls also weigh slightly less at birth and continue on average to be the lighter sex except for a few years around the age of puberty (Tanner, 1970).

Puberty and adulthood. Most of the well-known physical differences between men and women begin to appear at puberty, triggered by the action of the sex hormones – testosterone in the male and estrogen and progesterone in the female.

In boys, testosterone produces a number of changes similar to its effects in many other male mammals: The voice deepens, sweat gland activity is increased, body hair distribution changes, and muscular development is increased, particularly in the neck, chest, and shoulders (Glucksmann, 1974). Testosterone also has a number of less well-known physiological effects; for instance, it promotes growth in the skeletal system and increases the size of the heart and lungs, the capacity of the blood to carry oxygen, and the body's ability to neutralize the waste products of muscular exertion. The last three are, however, considerably influenced by the level of physical training and activity (Lowe, 1982).

In girls, the rise of estrogen levels leads to breast development, fat redistribution, and the beginning of the menstrual cycle. The growth of female pubic and axilla (underarm) hair is produced not by estrogen but by adrenal androgens (Tanner, 1970). Estrogen and progesterone show cyclic fluctuations during the menstrual cycle, estrogen levels rising during the earlier, follicular phase and progesterone during the later, luteal phase (progesterone is produced by the corpus luteum, which develops in the ovary after ovulation). Far greater hormonal changes occur during pregnancy, when the levels of these hormones, particularly progesterone, are greatly increased. Thus in the female, puberty marks the beginning of a series of hormonal changes that have complex regulatory effects on reproductive life, whereas in the male the hormonal changes are of a simpler nature, affecting mainly the production of secondary sexual characteristics.

The bodily changes that begin at puberty are largely maintained during adult life. In men, testosterone levels show a gradual decline throughout the middle or later years. In women, reproductive life ends much more abruptly sometime between the ages of forty-five and fifty-five, when estrogen levels decline dramatically, called the menopause. A variety of bodily reactions may also be experienced, including dryness of the vagina and urethra, circulatory disturbances or "hot flashes," and symptoms of general discomfort such as insomnia, headaches, and possibly depression (Evans, 1979). These are the transient reactions that occur while the hormone levels are declining. In addition, there are longer-term changes associated with normal aging but exaggerated by some aspect of the postmenopausal hormonal state. These include loss of skin elasticity and greater bone brittleness (Sherman, 1971; Evans, 1979; Birke and Best, 1980).

One sex difference supposedly widespread in mammals is a greater average life span in females than in males (Trivers, 1972; Glucksmann, 1974). This occurs in the human species; but as we have shown in Chapter 2, it is subject to reversal in parts of present-day Asia. Several possible explanations have been put forward for greater male mortality: Trivers (1972), for example, suggested that testosterone has a number of indirect effects that combine to lower the life expectancy of males, and he cites some (admittedly limited) evidence that castrated male rats and human eunuchs live longer than their normal male counterparts.

Waldron (1976) reviews evidence to show that the higher male mortality in the United States occurs because more men die from conditions that are a consequence of activities related to the male role and stereotype – for example, smoking, drinking, using guns, and working in hazardous occupations. Whatever the precise causes of the sex difference in mortality, one important consequence in our society and in many others is that during the later years of adult life women increasingly come to outnumber men of their own age group; another is that women will be more likely than men to have to face the distress and strain of bereavement during the later part of their life. Again, we cannot divorce bodily differences from their social consequences and meaning.

Variations in development

Having described the typical pattern of development, we now consider variations in development that produce an overlapping distribution of physical characteristics in men and women. The reproductive organs generally show no overlap between members of the two sexes. The secondary sexual characteristics, which develop at puberty, are more variable: A woman may be flat-chested or she may develop large breasts, and a man may or may not develop hairs on his chest. The two sexes show a degree of overlap on these characteristics, some fat men showing feminine-looking breast development and some women having relatively abundant body hair. There is even more overlap in general features such as physique, height, and rate of development, that vary widely within each sex.

Variations in development may produce these different degrees of overlap between the sexes. Since the reproductive organs' characteristics generally show no overlap with one another, it can be inferred that normal sexual differentiation is a fairly rigid process, not prone to producing wide variations. There are, however, a small number of people whose reproductive organs show characteristics of both sexes, although this results from fairly drastic modifications in the developmental processes. We consider some of these cases of abnormal development below.

Since there are fairly wide variations within each sex in secondary sexual characteristics and in the processes controlling growth and maturation, we can infer that for these features normal development is more flexible. Such variations can be produced by a larger number of smaller and more gradual changes than those producing abnormal sexual differentiation.

Abnormal sexual differentiation. Abnormalities in sexual development provide a valuable source of information about factors necessary for normal development, supplementing the information gained by experimental studies of animals. Regrettably, such knowledge is gained as a result of human suffering, but it has also proved useful in treating some of the disorders. Abnormal sexual differentiation, perhaps more than most other disorders, will have complex psychological repercussions. Gender is among the first distinctions that children make in classifying others in their social world, and it is crucially important for the developing self-concept. Parents also interact with their infants and children on the basis of this distinction. Any ambiguity in a person's physical sex at birth upsets these social processes and will have serious psychological consequences.

The work of John Money and his colleagues on the various clinical conditions involving abnormal sexual development has had considerable impact. Their approach takes into account the social and psychological implications of the disorder when choosing a course of treatment (Money and Ehrhardt, 1972), but is nevertheless controversial (Raymond, 1979; Fried, 1982).

Abnormal sexual differentiation can result from additional or

missing sex chromosomes, from a specific gene affecting a crucial aspect of sexual differentiation, or through abnormal hormonal conditions. Soon after the first successful attempts to
stain and view the human sex chromosomes in 1956, a number
of possible abnormalities were reported. Some of these corre-
sponded to previously known clinical conditions. For example,
women who were previously characterized in terms of Turner's
syndrome – first described in 1938 – were found to possess only
one X chromosome in each cell, designated XO. Their internal
and external reproductive organs appear typically female as a
result of the absence of the Y chromosome. There are, however, a number of other abnormalities that result from the
single-chromosome composition, such as short stature and rudimentary and inactive sex organs (Mittwoch, 1973).

Men previously described as showing Klinefelter's syndrome
were found to possess an additional X chromosome or chromosomes. The XXY constitution is the most common abnormality,
although up to three extra X chromosomes or additional Y
chromosomes have been recorded. The Y chromosome ensures
male development, although the additional X chromosome results in small, inactive testes and in many cases in breast development (Simpson, 1976). A rarer condition occurs in people
who possess a normal complement of sex chromosomes and
yet develop bodily characteristics of the opposite sex. This is
caused by a gene that affects sexual differentiation. The most
dramatic examples appear to be men, but the individuals actually have two X chromosomes. Although they occur rarely,
such cases are of considerable interest in helping to discover
the way in which normal sexual differentiation is brought
about. According to our account of sexual differentiation in the
previous section, such an occurrence should be impossible,
since the presence of the Y chromosome triggers the development of the testes and male differentiation. XX men, although
having small testes and signs of androgen deficiency, are
otherwise very similar to XY men in appearance. The most
likely explanation for their condition is that part of the Y

chromosome, which includes a gene that controls male development, has moved to another chromosome (Simpson, 1976). Such a gene – which causes testicular development in the absence of a Y chromosome – has been found in mice, and Ohno (1976) suggested that this is the result of a small piece of the Y chromosome moving to one of the other chromosomes (an autosome). A similar explanation may account for human XX males.

Although there are cases in which male differentiation occurs in the presence of XX chromosomes, the reverse case of complete female differentiation in the presence of XY chromosomes is not known in the human species. XY females occur commonly, however, in the wood lemming, and, unlike human chromosomal anomalies, they are fertile. XY female wood lemmings probably possess a gene on the X chromosome that suppresses the male-determining effects of the Y chromosome, and they appear to represent a mechanism, unique in mammals, for producing surplus females (Fredga et al., 1976). The germ cells of XY females all contain X chromosomes, so that for the purpose of reproducing they are identical to XX females. All the offspring produced by a mating between a male and an XY female are female, since all the XY offspring will contain the Y-suppressing gene.

The testicular-feminizing syndrome is a clinical condition that causes feminization in the human genetic male, but it does not supress the effects of the Y chromosome, as occurs in the remarkable case of the wood lemming. Instead, the Y chromosome proceeds to differentiate the testis normally and it produces testosterone, but this has no effect on any of its usual target organs (Mittwoch, 1973; Simpson, 1976). Since most male differentiation results from testosterone action or from the action of the testosterone metabolite dihydrotestosterone, no male differentiation can occur, and the resulting individuals develop into women. Their development differs from that of normal females: In particular, testes are present, although they remain inside the body and produce no sperm.

There is also no uterus, since its development has been suppressed by the Mullerian-inhibiting substance secreted by the fetal testis (Mittwoch, 1973). Externally, the only difference from the typical female body lies in the absence of pubic and axilla hair growth, since these are normally controlled by the action of androgens.

The description in the previous paragraph is of the "complete" testicular-feminizing syndrome. It is now known that various incomplete forms are possible – for example, with male internal ducts but female external genitals (Goy and McEwan, 1980). One remarkable case of partial feminization was described by Imperato-McGinley et al. (1974) among families in an isolated town in the Dominican Republic. These individuals are genetically male (XY), but with an enzyme deficiency that prevents testosterone being converted into dihydrotestosterone. As a consequence they show feminization only in those features whose development is controlled by dihydrotestosterone, that is, their external genitals. They therefore appear to be girls at birth, but since male genital, muscle, and voice development at puberty are testosterone-dependent, they give the appearance of changing into boys at puberty. In particular, the testes descend into the formerly labia-like scrotum, and the previously clitoral phallus grows into an organ four to six centimeters in length that is capable of erection (Imperato-McGinley et al., 1976). The individuals are known locally as *guevedoces*, meaning "penis at twelve."

Controversy has been generated by the author's claim that since the *guevedoces* were reared as girls, and *apparently* had no difficulty adopting a male role after puberty, their gender identity and sexual orientation must have been hormonally induced. This claim runs counter to the widely accepted view of gender identity and to most of the other clinical evidence (see Money, 1976, for an initially hostile response). We shall return to these issues in Chapter 9, on the development of gender differences.

Just as lack of androgenic action feminizes genetic males, so the presence of androgenic action during development can masculinize a genetic female. The androgenital syndrome (AGS) is a genetically transmitted condition involving a deficiency of various enzymes necessary for the synthesis of adrenal hormones, and it indirectly leads to the accumulation of large quantities of androgenic substances during fetal development. These produce masculinization of females, the extent of which can be partial or extensive; thus genital appearance at birth may be typically female with a small degree of clitoral enlargement, or it may appear to be completely male.

In the late 1950s, similar masculinizing effects were reported in the female babies born to mothers who had been treated with synthetic progestogens administered to help prevent possible miscarriages (Simpson, 1976). These substances evidently had an additional androgenic effect that had not been anticipated.

Occasionally a human being develops into a true hermaphrodite, with ambiguous external genitals and both testes and ovaries. Genetically, a hermaphrodite may be XX or XY or have cells of both types, but the developmental origin of the condition is unknown (Simpson, 1976).

These various abnormalities illustrate the complex and precarious nature of the developmental process and show that the apparent inevitability of the division into physically distinct sexes is one we take for granted all too often.

Variations in normal development. Individual differences in secondary sexual characteristics are well recognized and have been remarked upon since Old Testament times: Thus Jacob said to his mother Rebekah, "Behold, Esau my brother is a hairy man, and I am a smooth man" (Genesis 27:11). The modern counterparts of Esau and Jacob can readily be observed wherever the male body is on view.

Some women may show a relatively marked degree of hair growth, particularly on their legs, arms, and face, whereas others have relatively little body hair. But it is more difficult to observe differences in body hair growth in women than in men (at least in Western societies), since there are social pressures for them to remove all traces of body hair except their pubic hair. Young women may be made anxious about very normal growths by commercial interests marketing hair-removing products and by women's magazines portraying idealized versions of feminine beauty. Normal variations in development are labeled unfeminine according to culturally defined norms, which seek to deny or minimize the natural results of the developmental process.

Secondary sexual characteristics develop as a result of the action of testosterone or estrogen at puberty. There are several possible sources of variability in these characteristics: differences in the sensitivity of the body to hormones, different levels of sex hormones in individuals of the same sex, and non-hormonal influences.

Considering the first of these, it is known that individual differences in the sexual behavior of male rats – which is controlled by testosterone – depend not on differences in testosterone levels but on differing sensitivities to the hormone (Gray and Drewett, 1977). The extreme case of total lack of sensitivity to testosterone – in all parts of the body and at all ages – occurs in the human testicular-feminizing syndrome, discussed in the previous section, where the body develops as a female. More subtle variations in sensitivity to androgens could account for some individual differences in body hair growth in both men and women.

Secondly, the levels of the sex hormones themselves may vary in different people, during both prenatal development and adulthood. Resko (1975) reported a wide range of individual differences in the levels of testosterone found during fetal development in male rhesus monkeys, and he suggested that these differences might produce different degrees of "masculinization" of the developing brain (but see earlier for a discussion of this in relation to Dörner's theory of homosexuality). Ellis (1982) has reported a 5–10 percent overlap between androgen levels in male and female fetuses.

A wide range of variation has been found in the testosterone levels of adult men, both between individuals and within one individual at different times (for example, Doering et al., 1974). Body hair growth is known to be directly related to testosterone levels in young men (Tanner, 1970), so that differences in testosterone secretion are presumably an important cause of the variation in body hair growth between different men.

Individual differences in sex hormone levels may also result from processes that are less closely related to the individual's genetic makeup: The environment and consequences of behavior can exert important influences on hormone secretion. For example, emotional stress causes marked reductions in the levels of both male and female hormones in human beings and other mammals (Archer, 1979), and in several species of mammal the male responds to the presence of a sexually receptive female with a rise in testosterone secretion (e.g., Purvis and Haynes, 1974; Katongole et al., 1971). Measurements carried out on a human male subject also showed that testosterone levels increased during and immediately after intercourse (Fox et al., 1972). Indeed, an anonymous male zoological fieldworker who was about to leave a remote island even claimed that his beard growth was enhanced by the anticipation of future sexual activity ("Effects of Sexual Activity . . . ," 1970).

Ellis (1982) suggests that a wide range of situations, such as defeat, social isolation, and inescapable punishment, which he characterizes as PIF (prolonged and/or intensely frustrating experiences), all cause androgen levels to fall. In contrast, PIE experiences (prolonged and/or intensely exhilarating experiences), such as a successful response to a challenge, repeated sexual encounters (and their anticipation), and successful competition with another individual, all cause androgen levels to increase.

All these variations in sex hormone levels may affect the development and maintenance of secondary sexual characteristics. Other bodily processes, of a more general nature, may also influence such characteristics: For example, breast development in both men and women is affected by their total amount of body fat.

Sex hormones affect physiological processes involved in skeletal growth, muscle development, and fat deposition, providing a major contribution to the greater average height and muscular development of men and to the more rounded physique of women. However, features such as height and physique show a wide variation within each sex and overlap between the sexes, as many other influences are also operating.

We have shown some of the reasons why the sexes overlap in terms of physical characteristics, different degrees of overlap being apparent in different cases. We have also given one example of an attempt to minimize this degree of overlap – the removal of body hair by women.

The social meaning of physical sex differences

So far, we have discussed physical sex differences in terms of their evolutionary origins and individual development. But as we have also indicated, physical sex differences have a significance and meaning in human social life in addition to their interest for the biologist. Social traditions tend to use biological features as instruments of culture (Sahlins, 1977). Gender – the social distinction – involves the elaboration and evaluation of physical sex differences.

Physical sex differences have important social functions quite unrelated to their original biological function. For example, at birth the human genitals provide the crucial signal for deciding which of two very different life experiences the child will be exposed to, as a boy or girl (see Chapter 9). The importance of this initial signal is perhaps only realized when one considers the anxiety and distress of parents of a baby born with ambiguous genitals. Money and Ehrhardt (1972) reported that "parents whose minds are in doubt about their baby's authentic sex tend to monitor the child's behavior with supervigilance, *looking vainly for signs to resolve their doubt*" (p. 153, our italics).

Until they find such a sign, the parents will not be sure whether to reward traditionally masculine or feminine behavior, something that is taken for granted with a normal baby.

The physical characteristics that come to distinguish the sexes at puberty are less important for discriminating between the two genders, since many distinctions have been established from birth onward. But they do provide social signals that indicate the completion of male and female physical development. The responses to such signals vary in different cultures. For instance, menarche, the onset of menstruation, may in one culture be used to signify in a positive way the onset of womanhood, whereas in another it may be regarded as private and shameful and be used to transmit more negative ideas (e.g., Sherman, 1971; Birke and Best, 1980).

In modern Western society most girls know what to expect at menarche, although earlier studies in the United States showed that many girls were unprepared for menstruation, especially in working-class samples (Sherman, 1971). Although menarche is essentially private in our society, it is often taken to indicate that a girl has outgrown the tomboyish activities of childhood and should begin to act like a woman. In the novel *Kinflicks* by Lisa Alther (1977) the heroine is still a keen football player at the age of thirteen, and her first menstrual period takes her by surprise: "So unprepared was I for this deluge that I assumed that I had dislodged some vital organ during football practice the previous afternoon." After embarrassed reassurance that what had happened was indeed normal, her mother adds, "No more football. You're a young woman now" (p. 40).

The outward signs of puberty appear more gradually in boys. To define a single point as indicating the attainment of manhood requires much more arbitrary or culturally variable signals. In many societies it is often based on undergoing an initiation ceremony at a particular age rather than on physical development.

A further social use of physical sex differences is to provide a rationale for justifying the different roles of men and women.

For example, the greater average size and strength of men is commonly used to justify the restriction of many physically demanding and dangerous occupations and sports activities to men. Thus men predominate in active roles in the military, police, and fire-fighting services, undertake heavy work in the construction industry, handle heavy trucks and farm tractors. Sports activities, especially those requiring speed, strength, and stamina, have traditionally been the domain of men. Do physical differences between the sexes necessitate the exclusion of women from these activities, or do the physical differences merely provide a convenient justification for our social customs?

On average, men possess a number of physical advantages that potentially enable them to perform better than women in sports in which speed, strength, or stamina is important. Men generally are larger, stronger, and more muscular than women; they can also carry higher concentrations of oxygen in their blood and are better equipped to deal with the waste products of physical exertion. These are only average differences, however, and, with the exception of height, are all characteristics that can be improved considerably by appropriate training (Lowe, 1982). The argument that, because men are *on average* better equipped physically for energetic sports, such sports should be totally reserved for men ignores both the variable overlapping distribution of physical abilities in men and women and the potential for improvement as a result of training.

The discouragement or exclusion of women from taking part in traditional sports, at least as serious competitors, would seem to derive mainly from cultural rather than physical considerations (Dyer, 1977; Lowe, 1982), with the latter being used to justify their exclusion. In the earlier part of the century, women were regarded as being unsuited for strenuous athletic events. The first women's races were introduced into the athletic program of the Olympic Games in 1928 (Keating, 1978), but middle- and long-distance races were regarded as too exhausting for women. It is only comparatively recently that middle-distance races have been included in major international athletics competitions and world records at these distances recognized for women. The serious participation by women in long-distance events, culminating in the marathon (twenty-six-plus miles), is an even more recent development. The percentage difference in world records for middle- and long-distance races between men and women has narrowed over the past thirty years (Dyer, 1977).

Various reasons were given for discouraging or preventing women from participating in sports, and sex differences in physical abilities constitute only one of these. At one time appeals were made to what seemed to be the natural order. In a badminton magazine of seventy years ago, women were advised to "leave the rough outdoor pastimes to those for whom they are naturally intended – men" (Keating, 1978). The same sentiments may still be voiced, but they are now taken less seriously and have been supplanted by the more culturally based, though equally powerful, belief that sports achievements are incompatible with culturally defined femininity. Thus it is regarded as "undignified" for women to wrestle or box or run in long exhausting races. The cultural pressures that discourage women from engaging in sports will restrict their activity and training and thus serve to accentuate further the average sex differences in physical abilities.

In a rather different way, sex differences in reproductive function are used as the basis for wider differences in social roles. The most obvious of these differences is the child-care role of women, which is based on the mammalian method of reproduction, in which the female bears and suckles the offspring. We suggest that the mammalian method of reproduction has not so much dictated women's exclusive child-care role as provided the necessary conditions that have resulted in this role being adopted in most human cultures. As a result, women have generally been excluded from other activities, particularly those concerned with public power and status (Rosaldo and Lamphere, 1974; Rosenblatt and Cunningham, 1976).

Our last example of the cultural use of physical sex differences is sexual attractiveness. There are many ways in which a culture defines and minimizes or emphasizes sexually attractive bodily features. Our culture in particular emphasizes the physically attractive features of young women – in fact, they are used to market almost any type of wide-selling product. Clothes, padding, and cosmetics can be used to accentuate physical sex differences, and this is again a notable occurrence in modern Western society. The sex difference in body hair growth is accentuated by women removing hair from under their arms and from their legs, and differences in complexion are heightened by makeup. The rounded female figure may be accentuated by tight-fitting jeans in younger women and maintained by foundation garments in older women. Women's breasts are made higher and more prominent by a bra, and padded bras are available for making the breasts look larger.

Although the less adorned sex, men have by no means escaped such devices. Height is an important feature for sexual attractiveness in men, and small stature is often a cause of great anxiety. Shoes with built-up soles are marketed with this problem in mind. Emphasis on the attractiveness to women of a muscular physique has diminished in recent years, so that even the successors of the old Charles Atlas type of advertisements now emphasize health and fitness rather than the female admiration for bulging muscles. Men's jackets have traditionally contained padded shoulders, which are an attempt to simulate a more broad-shouldered, muscular appearance, an emphasis that is less apparent in more modern jackets.

With the advent of tight trousers and jeans, some men have even tried to accentuate the bulge produced by the male genitals. Elvis Presley is reputed to have had his own way of doing this, but there are now commercially made appliances available. Advertisers extol the attractions of "Fantastic padded pouches! Padded and moulded to add to your masculine outline under tight jeans. . . . no one will know your secret!" (advertisement in *Sunday Times* [London], January 15, 1978).

In conclusion, there are a number of different ways in which physical sex differences assume cultural as well as biological importance. In other words, they become used, modified, and often accentuated as part of our ideas about the real and ideal attributes of the two gender groups. We have concentrated on examples from contemporary Western society, but there are, of course, other examples available in other cultures.

4

Sexuality: psychobiology, psychoanalysis, and sociology

We began our detailed examination of sex and gender in Chapter 3 by asking how and why sex evolved. In this chapter we consider the human sexual experience from three different perspectives: those of psychobiology, psychoanalysis, and sociology.

We use the term *psychobiology* to denote the classic modern studies of Masters and Johnson and of Kinsey, which aim to provide antiseptic, empirical descriptions of adult sexual behavior. They seek answers to questions such as "What are the measurable physiological correlates of orgasm?" and "In what circumstances do people find sexual satisfaction?"

In examining the psychoanalytic approach, we move from the readily observable world of physiological function and conscious experience to explore the meaning of sexual experience in our remote inner world of the unconscious. Here we seek answers to different sorts of questions. We pursue the origins of adult sexual satisfaction in early childhood experiences and ask how the child's recognition of anatomical sex differences influences adult personality.

In the final section we consider the use of sexuality in defining social roles and the influence of social values on sexuality. To gain a perspective on our own society's definitions of the roles of men and women, we consider the Omani solution. In this closed and traditional Islamic society a third gender role, that of the male transsexual, is important in maintaining the highly contrasting roles of male and female. The Omani acceptance of transsexual behavior contrasts with our society's treatment of deviant practices.

The three approaches differ in their modes of study and in the data they seek to explain. The objective methods of Masters and Johnson provide precise physiological descriptions of sexuality, but they ignore the deeper levels of meaning pursued by psychoanalysis. Although the unconscious bears the marks of an ordinary understanding of anatomical sex differences, it interprets them in ways that are not available to common sense. Whatever its elaborations and complexities, the unconscious is influenced by culture. Discussion of the three Omani gender roles provides a contrast that forces us to reconsider our gender role system based only on male and female roles and to think about sexual alternatives beyond those of adult heterosexuality.

The physiological measurement of sexual behavior

The studies of Masters and Johnson attracted considerable publicity when they appeared in the 1960s, but public attitudes toward the study of human sexuality had already begun to change with publication of the Kinsey reports more than a decade earlier. Scholarly interest in sexuality existed before the twentieth century, but our inheritance of a Victorian morality made even the scientific study of human sexuality controversial and long delayed. Ancient Chinese physicians writing within the Taoist tradition carried out careful observations and offered advice that enabled both women and men to achieve great sexual satisfaction (Chang, 1977). The Talmud, one of the major repositories of the Jewish tradition, contains detailed instructions concerning not only sexual satisfaction but also contraception. Love and procreation, like food, were considered important aspects of life.

When it was initially reviewed by the comparative psychologist Frank Beach (1966), the work of Masters and Johnson was compared with the fundamental studies of the digestive system undertaken a century earlier. The delay in studying sexual functioning reflected repressive social attitudes and not a lack of scientific technology. Neither the physiology nor the behavioral aspects of human sexuality were considered suitable for open discussion or even for dispassionate, objective, scientific study.

Here we can only discuss highlights of Masters and Johnson's research. Interested readers can pursue further details in their two major works, *Human Sexual Response* (1966) and *Human Sexual Inadequacy* (1970), or in accounts that appear in textbooks on sexuality (e.g., Katchadourian and Lunde, 1980).

The human orgasm

The four-stage description of the sexual response that Masters and Johnson provide emphasizes similarities rather than differences between men and women and is based on their observations of ten thousand orgasms, or *sexual cycles* as Masters and Johnson label them. Of these, three-quarters were the sexual cycles of women, but this still leaves a sizable number (twenty-five hundred) of observations of men's orgasmic behavior. Their aim was to provide sound physiological information about sexuality and to dispel myths about women and men that had been maintained through ignorance. In addition to orgasms achieved through heterosexual intercourse in one of three positions, satisfaction by self-stimulation was studied. For example, they observed women's use of a plastic phallus and, in a few cases, stimulation of the breasts leading to orgasm. The artificial phallus contained photographic equipment that recorded, for the first time, the internal changes in women that accompany arousal and gratification.

Their four-stage description of orgasm applies both to women and to men (see Table 4.1). It is independent of the nature of the sexual activity, autoerotic or heterosexual, as well as the source of stimulation, tactile or psychological. The activities of the sex organs differ according to their anatomical structures, but the mechanisms of arousal are similar: vasocongestion and myotonia. The first is the filling of the pelvic region

Table 4.1. *Bodily changes during the sexual response*

Female	Male
Excitement phase	
Consistent nipple erection	30% nipple erection
25% sex tension flush	
Plateau phase	
75% sex tension flush	25% sex tension flush
Tension in hands and feet	Tension in hands and feet
Generalized muscle tension	Generalized muscle tension
Hyperventilation	Hyperventilation
Rapid heartbeat	Rapid heartbeat
(100→160 per minute)	(100→160 per minute)
Orgasmic phase	
Specific muscle contractions	Specific muscle contractions
Hyperventilation	Hyperventilation
Rapid heartbeat	Rapid heartbeat
(100→160 per minute)	(100→160 per minute)
Resolution phase	
30–40% sweating reaction	30–40% sweating reaction
Hyperventilation	Hyperventilation
Decreasing heartbeat	Decreasing heartbeat
(150→80 per minute)	(150→80 per minute)

Source: Based on Katchadourian and Lunde (1980).

with an increased supply of blood and other fluids, and the second is a general and widespread increase in muscle tension.

The excitement phase varies in the sources of stimulation that trigger it, its length, and whether tension will increase to reach the plateau phase or dissipate. The vagina rapidly produces a lubricant, the clitoris swells, the cervix and uterus move upward. One feminist writer and physician (Sherfey, 1973) compared the production of the vaginal fluid in the excitement phase to the rapid appearance of the penile erection. Viewed in this way, observable evidence of sexual arousal is available to both men and women.

In the plateau phase there are further changes in both sexes due to vasocongestion. The tip of the penis may increase in size and deepen in color, and the outer passageway of the vagina narrows. These changes are specific to the structure of each sex. Unlike the erect penis, the erect clitoris tends to disappear into its hood.

The contractions of the orgasmic phase initially occur with a frequency of one every 0.8 second in both sexes, although only males experience ejaculation. The rate slows down after five to twelve contractions in women but after only three to four in men. Once the orgasmic phase is reached, these responses become involuntary.

In the resolution phase following orgasm, congestion gradually disappears and muscles relax. While women in the resolution phase may react to further stimulation and experience additional orgasms, men experience a refractory period of at least some minutes during which another erection cannot be achieved whatever the nature of the stimulation. The multiple orgasms that Masters and Johnson observed appeared to be identical to earlier ones and were often described by women as feeling more intense.

Masters and Johnson's work drew attention to similarities in the physiological responses of the sexes. Now, more than a decade after their research first came to popular notice, we all recognize these similarities and may forget that Masters and Johnson provided an innovative perspective. Technical criticism about their description – for example, that it is difficult to separate the excitation and plateau stages – throws no doubt on their major conclusions that, functionally, men and women achieve sexual satisfaction in a similar manner even though anatomically they differ.

In addition, there are two other myths this research program sought to dispel. Masters and Johnson put forward the idea of a simple orgasmic mechanism in women. As we shall see in the next section, the Freudian view of mature female sexuality places considerable emphasis on the vagina as a source of satisfaction distinct from the clitoris. Masters and Johnson's evidence showed that the clitoris not only receives stimulation but is also crucial in transmitting feelings of arousal. The vagina, on the other hand, is relatively lacking in nerve endings and thus relatively insensitive.

The physiological source of sexual excitation in women is once again being questioned. In the 1970s it was suggested that in addition to the orgasm described by Masters and Johnson, which involved contraction of the orgasmic platform (the longest outer one-third of the vagina), there was a form of orgasm measurable in terms of uterine contractions. It was also suggested that most women experience a blending of the two types (Perry and Whipple, 1982).

Another Victorian myth Masters and Johnson sought to dispel was the notion that morally correct women "endured" sexual relations whereas only "fallen" women enjoyed them. In fact, in their early studies observing intercourse with prostitutes, they rarely witnessed female orgasm. Ordinary women having sexual relations with their regular partners provided the bulk of their evidence of orgasmic behavior.

Before considering women's and men's reports of their sexual experiences, let us examine some differences Masters and Johnson observed. Along many dimensions there is considerable overlap in the behavior of women and men, but men are generally more variable than women in achieving orgasm. Frequency of orgasm over a lifetime is an exception, and here women are more variable. If we think of this dimension as running from never at one end to a very great number at one time at the other end, we find women spread evenly along it. Many women, though perhaps not as many as was thought fifty years ago, have never experienced orgasm. At the other end there are a number of women who experience multiple orgasms, and their high rate cannot be matched even by very young men.

The men observed by Masters and Johnson achieved fewer orgasms at any one time and experienced more failures than women. Although three times as many female cycles were observed, only 118 failures to achieve orgasms were recorded for

women. In 2,500 male cycles there were 220 failures. Before rush-
ing to conclusions about the sexual natures of women and men,
we should note that all participants were volunteers capable of
achieving orgasm. Perhaps only women who were particularly
sure of their performance offered to participate in the study.

Sherfey (1973), who has drawn heavily on Masters and Johnson's work, argued that the female has an almost limitless capacity for sexual pleasure and would no doubt disagree with
our cautious interpretation. In her view, female sexuality is
physiologically constituted to outdistance the male and has
been held in check only by the rise of civilization and by male
oppression of women in the pursuit of private property and
individual ownership. Here we have a view of female sexuality
that is the complete opposite of a Victorian ideal. "Natural"
woman is seen as more highly motivated to achieve sexual
satisfaction than "natural" man.

Arguing from a sociobiological standpoint, Symons (1979)
questioned Sherfey's description of a limitless and continually
pleasure-seeking female sexuality. Indeed, he asserted the converse and suggested that sexuality is immaterial to female evolutionary history. Recently, Hrdy (1981) challenged Symons's
conclusions by conducting a careful examination of primate
and fossil evidence. Although the last word has yet to be written, Hrdy provides wise counsel. She states, "When a paucity
of information is combined with poignant interest, controversy
is the inevitable result. So it is scarcely surprising that the few
authors writing in any detail about the evolution of women's
sexuality have come to radically different verdicts" (p. 163).

Sources of sexual satisfaction

The classic studies of Kinsey, which describe the cultural patterning of the sexual response, appear to contradict Sherfey's
view: Men are reported to achieve far more orgasms. The Kinsey
studies provide a new dimension. We have so far concentrated

primarily on the mechanisms or physiology of the sexual response. Kinsey and his colleagues examined the array of arousing events and behaviors that lead to orgasm and the conscious factors that affect the experience of sexual satisfaction.

Their first book *Sexual Behavior in the Human Male* (1948), was based on interviews with 5,300 American men, mostly white. A similar report based on interviews with 5,940 American women was published in 1953. The description of male orgasms as "sexual outlets" has a quaint ring today, but Kinsey's findings belong to the contemporary scene more than to Victorian notions of sexual behavior, which they explicitly challenged. Although the Kinsey reports describe men as sexually more active than women, they present no major challenge to the conclusions drawn by Masters and Johnson. Indeed, the Kinsey data on multiple orgasms in women, which were initially received with scepticism, were buttressed by the later studies.

The array of activities that lead to orgasm were divided by Kinsey into six major categories, roughly equivalent for women and men. These are masturbation, nocturnal sex dreams (or emission for men), heterosexual petting, heterosexual intercourse, homosexual relations, and intercourse with other species. Although slightly more women than men were interviewed, it was men who reported more orgasms. Nonetheless, Kinsey maintained, as did Masters and Johnson later, that physiologically the orgasmic potential and response of the sexes were similar. Let us look at a few aspects of the behavior of men and women before comparing them.

We begin with the first book, which reported the sexual behavior of men. Kinsey found very clear effects of age and class on the sexual behavior of men. An older commonsense view recognized that men experienced fewer orgasms as they got older, but it was generally assumed that men reached their peak of orgasmic frequency somewhere in their twenties and only began to experience a decline in their forties. A very different picture emerged in terms of the number of sexual outlets per week recorded by Kinsey. On average, men were shown to reach a peak in adolescence, and a decline from this early peak was reported by the late twenties. Kinsey showed that sexual behavior often continued into the seventies and eighties.

Kinsey used education as a major indicator of social class. Although he sometimes employed a tripartite system, separating those who had attended primary school only, secondary school, and finally college or university, he often grouped together those of primary and secondary education and compared them with people who had had higher education. Kinsey found that lower-level men reported the majority of their outlets in genital intercourse – premarital, marital, or extramarital, with prostitutes, or in homosexual relations. His upper-level sample reported far more masturbation, petting to orgasm, or nocturnal emissions. The upper-level men grew less faithful the longer they were married, whereas lower-level men showed the opposite pattern, growing more faithful with age.

No doubt one of the most widely discussed findings of the report on male sexual behavior was the statistic showing that 37 percent of men had at one time or another engaged in homosexual behavior. The form in which this result was reported reflects Kinsey's views on the nature of homosexuality. He believed that it was incorrect to describe an individual as either homosexual or not in an all-or-nothing fashion. Instead, he devised a seven-point scale that ran from 0 to 6. Individuals who reported never having achieved sexual satisfaction with persons of their own sex scored 0, and those of exclusively homosexual experience scored 6. A great many individuals were to be found at points in between. His definition of homosexuality is problematic. We return to it in our discussion of the social definition of gender and its relation to sexuality.

In his report on women, Kinsey noted less clear-cut evidence for the effects of class and age. The only activity affected by class was extramarital intercourse, which echoed for women the class-determined patterns of infidelity first described for men. A greater incidence of homosexual relations was reported by upper-level than by lower-level women. The effects of age were different and more gradual. Women slowly built up to a peak of orgasmic frequency, which generally occurred in their late twenties and early thirties. It was maintained until their fifties, and only then did it show a gradual decline.

Religion, which had had a negligible effect on men's sexual behavior, emerged as the most important factor influencing satisfaction for women. Women who described themselves as religious achieved fewer orgasms in any circumstances; in particular, they were less likely to achieve orgasm in heterosexual intercourse. Historical factors, such as date of birth and cultural attitudes influencing socialization, also affected female sexuality. Women born after 1900 reported more orgasms in all contexts. We could say that women were breaking free of the constraints of Victorian values.

Since much of Kinsey's second volume is concerned with comparisons of women and men, we can only sample the differences between the sexes reported by Kinsey. There are fascinating behavioral differences, such as the female peak of outlets through nocturnal dreams in their forties compared to the male peak in the late teens and the more pronounced decline in masturbation as a source of satisfaction after marriage for men than for women. But one of the most interesting contrasts is Kinsey's own formulation of the differing natures of female and male sexuality. He saw female sexuality as being based on physical stimulation, while he ascribed the frequency and regularity of male gratification to men's susceptibility to psychological stimulation. Though he was careful to avoid an explanation in physiological terms, Kinsey believed that men were more easily conditioned and thus became susceptible to a variety of psychological stimuli. This view of the differential effects of learning, which presumably accounted for the sharp class differences in male behavior, overlooked the equally plausible hypothesis that women too were conditionable but that they had been conditioned not to respond with sexual arousal in the same situations that men found stimulating.

Reporting physiological arousal

A study of university students provides a partial test of the Kinsey hypothesis. These students would be described as sophisticated in terms of the older Kinsey data in that almost 80 percent of them had had intercourse and 84 percent of the women reported experiencing orgasm. Heiman (1975) used recently developed devices that record vaginal and penile pulse and blood pressure to measure the students' physiological arousal while they were listening to four different kinds of stories.

One group heard romantic stories and another erotic tales. In addition to a control group, who heard neither erotic nor romantic stories, a fourth group listened to a mixture of the two. Each student participated in two sessions. With few exceptions, only students listening to erotic or mixed erotic and romantic stories showed evidence of arousal. Women found the stories in which women were the initiators and the main focus the most arousing. Men showed a similar but less marked preference for this type of story. The next most arousing story for both sexes featured a male initiator and focused on the female. In physiological terms – that is, pulse rate and blood pressure – it appeared that there was little difference in women's and men's physiological arousal reactions.

Heiman also examined a related question: the conscious recognition of their physiological arousal by the two sexes. The students were asked to report any general arousal, specific genital arousal such as erection or lubrication, or more diffuse genital arousal. These self-reports were then compared with the physiological measures. By and large, women were not as accurate as men in reporting their own arousal. It is interesting to note that there were more errors made by those women who experienced arousal to nonerotic stimuli – that is, romantic stories or control stories. It would seem that sophisticated women may experience and recognize physiological arousal in exciting circumstances, but they are less willing, perhaps even unable, to report arousal when the context of the stimulus fails to provide socially acceptable support for their sexual feelings. These results suggest that Kinsey's findings may reflect differences in women's and men's reports of their sexual arousal rather than in their physiological responses to particular types of stimuli.

A recent study (Steinman et al., 1981) has reported similarities and differences in men's and women's arousal using both physiological and subjective measures. University students were shown various erotic and neutral films; both men and women exhibited greater physiological arousal when erotic material was viewed. Both found films of male homosexual encounters the least physiologically arousing and group heterosexual behavior the most physiologically stimulating. But men found both female homosexual and heterosexual films highly arousing, whereas high levels were recorded only for heterosexual films among the women. Although the physiological measures were treated as equivalent for men and women in much of this analysis, differences in magnitude of response were reported along with differences in the pattern of responses.

Four subjective measures were used: a continuous, mechanically recorded measure of psychological arousal, a verbal rating of arousal and a written assessment of pleasantness after each stimulus presentation, and finally, an overall assessment of arousal during the postexperimental debriefing session. These were found to produce roughly equivalent results and to correlate with the physiological measure. The pattern of interrelation between subjective and physiological measures differed for men and women, and a relationship between pleasantness and subjective arousal was reported only for men. The intricate patterns of arousal reported in this study are governed by rules of social acceptability, but the precise grammar of this domain remains to be described.

Current reports of sexual experience

The Kinsey reports reflect the social attitudes of the 1940s in their use of the term *sexual outlets* to describe orgasms. *The Hite Report* (1976) and *The Hite Report on Male Sexuality* (1981) are also products of their time. The first book, based on the questionnaire responses provided by three thousand American women volunteers, contains vivid verbatim accounts of women's masturbation, their feelings at orgasm, and their evaluation of various aspects of their sexuality. The second book makes clear Hite's redefinition of the term *sexuality*. Heterosexual genital intercourse is considered only one specific source of sexual pleasure and satisfaction. This focus on heterosexual genitality has been identified as a masculine bias in research on sexual behavior by a number of feminist writers (e.g., Rossi, 1973; Tiefer, 1978). In the context of this criticism it is particularly interesting that older men who took part in Hite's study reported a greater variety of ways to gain sexual satisfaction than did younger man and focused less on genital intercourse than did younger men.

A unifying theme of the first *Hite Report* is the author's assertation that the female potential for sexual satisfaction is equal to, if not actually greater than, that of the male. It is possible, of course, that women who hold such views are more likely to volunteer to complete questionnaires about sexuality. The work of Masters and Johnson and the speculations of Sherfey are quoted by Hite to support her claim of a great female potential for sexual pleasure.

We shall examine data provided by ten thousand British women who replied to a questionnaire that *Woman's Own*, a popular mass-circulation magazine, published in an attempt to assess the applicability of the American findings to the British scene. The two samples differ in many ways. The American sample included women from fourteen to seventy-eight years, but the majority of *Woman's Own* replies were from women under thirty, who reported frequencies of intercourse of two or three times a week. Another difference is that the women who sent their replies anonymously to *Woman's Own* appear to be more inhibited than Hite's American respondents. One example is the woman who ridiculed her own "liberation" by noting that she found it impossible to show her completed questionnaire to her husband. The British women voiced more dissatisfaction with their rates of intercourse. Just over half the women reported regularly experiencing orgasm in intercourse, and they admitted faking satisfaction to please their partners.

There are differences, too, in attitudes toward masturbation. American women may describe masturbation very explicitly, but the British sample is much more reticent. While 36 percent of the latter said they never masturbated and just over half that they did, the rest simply failed to answer. This semipublic study on a different population, sampled by very different techniques, still manages to convey a sense of active female sexuality, though it lacks the explicitness of the *Hite Report*. The editorial staff of *Woman's Own* are not as explicitly feminist as Shere Hite, and their readers may lack the explicitly ideological commitment of the American sample. There have been many studies of the conscious experience of sexuality, but we now turn instead to consider explanations of sexuality that speculate about its representation at an unconscious level.

Psychoanalytic explanations of sexuality

Psychoanalytic theory encompasses a variety of explanations of the patterning of sexuality and the dominance relationships between men and women. These accounts are virtually unique among psychological theories, as they reflect a deep concern with irrational aspects of human behavior. In considering psychoanalytic explanations of sexuality, we begin by moving back in time as well as changing the level of our attention. By 1905, when Freud first published the classic *Three Essays on the Theory of Sexuality,* he had developed a revolutionary view of the nature of human sexuality. His theory derived primarily from his clinical experience with psychologically distressed, mainly neurotic, patients and not from physiological measurements or reports of normal sexual behavior. To understand Freud's view of the inner world, it is necessary to begin by examining his approach to mental functioning and the unconscious. We then move on to examine the sources of adult genital sexuality in infant experiences.

The unconscious

It is essential to appreciate Freud's theory of mental functioning and the role of the unconscious in order to understand the *Essays* and the psychoanalytic view of sexuality. The academic psychology of Freud's day was a psychology of conscious experience, that which was accessible to trained, introspective reflection. Normal individuals were viewed as rational and their thought was believed to obey the rules of logic. Freud found his way to the unconscious through attempting to understand the symptoms, fantasies, and dreams of his patients.

Most of us recognize our conscious thought and would not quarrel with Freud's view of it as obeying the laws of logic, or *secondary process. Primary process,* or unconscious mental functioning, which obeys different rules, is not readily accessible or acceptable. A couple of concrete examples will help to bring the unconscious into focus. First, let us imagine a hypnotist telling a person he has put into a trance that when the person wakes up he will feel thirsty and ask for a cup of tea. Although the suggestion subsequently appears forgotten, conscious thought has been modified to the lingering suggestion. A more familiar example is the common experience when our own unconscious plays tricks on us – say, we wish to introduce someone we know to another friend but for the moment the name is gone, lost in our unconscious, or, more technically correct, in our preconscious.

In order to understand the meaning of symptoms and fantasies, Freud set about studying the mental functions of the unconscious, which he believed were determined neither by reality, time, order, nor morality, nor by the rules of logic. Initially, Freud regarded dreams as providing special access to these processes; later, the interpersonal relation established during therapy, the *transference,* was used to understand the unconscious meaning of thought and action.

This discussion begins with consideration of the unconscious because its crucial role in all mental functioning is often overlooked by those who attack the psychoanalytic interpretation of sexuality. As Juliet Mitchell (1974) notes, it is by applying only the rules of logic rather than those of the unconscious that many feminist critics distort the theory and find it wanting.

Unless we believe that the infant is born rational, with knowledge of the world, the unconscious and its functions must be seen as primary in the infant. Essentially, Freud viewed an infant as hedonistic, seeking satisfaction and withdrawing from "unpleasure" as these are experienced in his or her inner world. Primary processes lead the hungry infant to hallucinate the experience of feeding if the feed fails to arrive when the need is felt. But the hallucination does not satisfy the biological hunger, and so slowly, out of such failures to find pleasure or escape unpleasure, the infant begins to recognize the outer world or reality. In his structural theory, Freud (1923) described the agency that deals with reality as the *ego* and that arising from the instincts or drives as the *id.* Even after the reality principle and the ego are well established, they do not replace the pleasure principle and the id. Feelings and thoughts that were unacceptable to the world of reality, to the ego, do not disappear but are pushed into the unconscious, or repressed, and seek expression disguised by the processes of unconscious thought. The dynamic or conflicted quality of mental life reflects the tension between the ego and repressed feelings and thoughts. It is with this inner world of the unconscious and the id that Freud's explanation of sexuality begins.

Psychosexual development

Freud sought an understanding of adult sexuality in the earliest experiences of the infant. This does not imply that he believed interpersonal, object-oriented (that is, person-oriented), genital sexuality was present in infancy. Rather he considered that the mature heterosexual response, whose measurement we examined in the first section, had motivational origins in early sensual experiences. Although his view of infantile sexuality was unconventional and led to censure by his medical colleagues, Freud persisted in relying on his work with his patients, and his understanding of their emotional problems continued to guide his theorizing. From his female patients he heard tales of childhood seduction and rape by their fathers; although he initially believed their accounts to be true, he gradually came to view them as fantasies expressing repressed sexual wishes. In neurosis Freud observed the repression of infantile sexual wishes, but in the "perversions" – sado-masochistic practices, fetishism, and homosexuality – Freud believed that he could discern the direct expression of infantile sexuality. In order to understand these far-reaching conclusions to which Freud was led by his clinical experience we must examine the nature of this "polymorphously perverse" infantile sexuality and follow the developmental path that results in adult heterosexuality.

We begin by considering the classic Freudian theory of infantile sexuality and its development, noting in particular similarities and differences in the routes taken by women and men. The theory itself has a developmental history, and we consider some of the changes that have been introduced in the last seventy-five years as the result both of further clinical investigations and of researchers' observations of children.

Our account of Freud's use of the term *instinct* is as concise and incomplete as our statements about mental functioning and the structures of personality. Freud viewed instinct as a concept on the borderline between biology and psychology. Unlike external stimuli, which release reflexes, instincts have their source in the human body, and this makes withdrawal an impractical method for a person to use in dealing with them. The component sexual instincts have sources of excitation in the erogenous zones of the lips, mouth, and anus as well as in the genitals. Initially, they function independently, only becoming organized as adult libido in the course of development. The sexual instincts are the mental representations or symbols of these bodily excitations. The strength of the instinct is determined both by its bodily origins and by its role in the individual's psychological system. The aim of the instinct is satisfaction and, in Freud's system, the reduction of tension. A moment's reflection on the number of ways in which human beings gain sexual satisfaction tells us that sexual aims are achieved through a great variety of objects, both interpersonal and material. It was in infantile sexuality that Freud sought an explanation for this diversity of sexual aims and objects.

Freud viewed human sexuality as differing in important ways from that of other animals. Not only are we flexible in terms of aims and objects, but the female lacks the extreme periodicity of most other mammals. As we noted in Chapter 3, women are sexually receptive continuously throughout most of their adult lives. Freud (1940) drew attention to another difference that he held to be of major significance for psychological development – the latency period. He believed that our species experiences a unique sexual moratorium that even the most closely related primates lack – our closest animal relations, chimpanzees, reach sexual maturity at about five years of age. Normally, during this latency period, after the age of five or six, the urgency of sexual interests normally abates and the child's attention is deflected to other pursuits, such as learning the culture. The bodily changes that occur at puberty reawaken sexual interest, and in the course of this development sexuality reaches its adult genital form.

Freud's earliest descriptions of infantile sexuality reflected his preoccupation with the essentially bisexual nature of human beings. His study of embryology made him aware of the early parallel development of male and female internal organs. In the original formulation of the oral, anal, and phallic stages, Freud (1905) drew no distinctions between the development of girls and boys. The acts of feeding, defecating, and urinating, from which each of the component sexual instincts arise, were, he believed, undifferentiated by sex. In both girls and boys the aim of the oral instinct is sucking, and later biting, and the normal object is the breast. In the anal stage the aim is either expulsion or retention, and the appropriate object is the stool or feces. Even the phallic stage was seen as similar: Girls, Freud believed, have not yet discovered the vagina, and both girls and boys view the mother as phallic. The clitoris was held to function as a small penis and to be the source of erotic feelings. The aim of phallic fantasies for both boys and girls is penetration. He wrote: "So far as the autoerotic and masturbatory manifestations of sexuality are concerned, we might lay it down that the sexuality of little girls is of a wholly masculine character. . . . The leading erotogenic zone in female children is located at the clitoris, and is thus homologous to the masculine genital zone of the glans penis" (1905, pp. 219–20). The phallocentric character of Freud's view, evident in such passages as this one, became the focus of much feminist criticism of Freud (e.g., Stockard and Johnson, 1979).

At this point it is useful to return to the interpersonal relationships of the developing child; in focusing on the sexual instincts as they originate in the erogenous zones, we may overlook the social psychological aspects of development. Originally in the *Three Essays* Freud expressed his view that separate female and male sexuality develops only at puberty. Focus on the love relationships of the child leads to a reformulation of the account of psychological differentiation around the child's recognition of the anatomical differences between men and women. Freud believed that both boys and girls interpret the differences as a lack in the female. In this way the boy's love for his mother leads to fear of his father's jealousy and retaliation through castration. In the girl's disappointment at not having a penis, she abandons her mother who had made her this way and turns to her father, hoping to make up for her loss. The sexual instincts and love relationships within the family come together in penis envy, fear of castration, and the Oedipus complex.

Further work on the Oedipus complex appeared after the original publication of the *Three Essays* and after Freud's final reformulation of his theory of instinct (1920, 1923, 1924, 1925, 1931). The life instincts, or Eros, were seen in opposition to the destructive instincts, or Thanatos. This meant not only that each individual struggles with masculine and feminine trends in the Oedipal conflict, but that for each there is both a positive, erotic element and a negative, destructive factor. Before we consider this additional complexity, we need to examine Freud's views of masculinity and femininity in greater detail. Freud considered the terms *masculinity* and *femininity* difficult and confusing. He identified three different senses in which the terms were used. We have described one of these, the biological sense, in Chapter 3. In our discussion of stereotypes in Chapter 2, we examined social psychological attempts to quantify commonsense understanding of masculinity and femininity. The meaning of masculinity and femininity, crucial in psychoanalytic theory, refers to activity and passivity, but it is only with the development of adult sexuality that this distinction can be made and become meaningful for the individual.

We have already noted that in the phallic phase Freud saw both boys and girls as essentially masculine. The focus of their phallic sexuality is active and penetrating. For boys, the active aim in the Oedipus complex remains the active penetration of the mother, but passive penetration by the father is also a possibility. To further complicate the picture, there are passive aims directed toward the unrelinquished phallic mother, or fantasy mother, and active aims directed toward the father. But typically, male development continues the active aim of the phallic stage and is directed toward the female. The other possibilities are repressed and lost in the unconscious. They may return as symptoms or, when repression fails, as those adult practices that Freud labeled "perversions."

For the boy, threat of castration leads to the resolution of the Oedipal conflict and the establishment of the *superego,* or moral agency. Freud saw the beginnings of sexual differentiation for the girl in her recognition of her own and her mother's imagined loss of the penis. In his later writings Freud was precise in describing the consequences of the girl's discovery of the anatomical difference. In 1925 he wrote: "Thus the little girls' recognition of the anatomical distinction between the sexes forces her away from masculinity and masculine masturbation on to new lines which lead to the development of femininity" (p. 256). For the girl, the castration complex leads to feelings of inferiority and penis envy. It is in order to regain the lost penis that the little girl turns to her father and to fantasies of replacing her mother.

The Oedipus complex for the girl is a secondary development dependent on phallic sexuality, recognition of the anatomical differences between the sexes, castration anxiety, and penis envy; but it, too, gives rise to the superego, though in a weaker form. Given all these conditions, it may be difficult to appreciate that Freud in fact saw the Oedipus complex as simpler for the girl to resolve than for the boy (1924). Its resolution leaves the girl with a passive aim – to be penetrated – and at puberty a new source of sexual excitation, the vagina. We have already noted in the first section of this chapter that Masters and Johnson asserted that at a physiological level the clitoris and not the vagina is the main source of pleasure. Freud was describing the psychological experience and not just its bodily source. Nonetheless, Masters and Johnson's work has been used to attack psychoanalytic views of female sexuality. Recent studies of the musculature of the vagina suggests that there is in fact more than one physiological source of the female's experience of orgasm (Graber, 1982); plainly, the last salvo has yet to be fired in this controversy.

The paths leading to the resolution of the Oedipus complex are different for girls and boys, but the resolution is a major developmental landmark for all children. The incorporation of parental standards in the superego results in the development of internal constraints on action. The post-Oedipal child is believed to repress the component sexual instincts – oral, anal, and phallic – and is prepared at an unconscious level for sex-appropriate aims and object choices in adulthood. The earlier component instincts are now fused in a mature structure. Repression during latency frees sexual energy for other activities, and the sublimated energy can find fulfillment in intellectual and artistic pursuits. Indeed, a certain amount of such repression is considered essential for development in the early school years.

Freud's phallocentric theory of infantile sexuality was the target of criticism almost from its inception. Hostility arose not only from those who condemned the very idea of childhood sexuality but also from within the psychoanalytic group. Karen Horney (1924) challenged the notion of penis envy as an inevitable consequence of the girl's discovery of her genitals. Horney suggested that girls are jealous of boys' achievements in being able to urinate a greater distance, see their genitals, and more easily manipulate them. She was one of the earliest critics to consider the issues of control and power and the influence of the male position in society on the formulations offered by Freud and other male psychoanalysts. Melanie Klein's clinical work with very young children resulted in detailed descriptions of the first year of life and led to greater awareness of the mother's role in psychosexual development. From the work of Horney, Klein, and Ernest Jones a second, *gynocentric* position developed within psychoanalytic theory (Stockard and Johnson, 1979). Among theorists of an explicitly psychoanalytic orientation, both views, the phallocentric and the gynocentric, can still be found.

Juliet Mitchell (1974) defended Freud's phallocentric view by arguing that he sought to explain our unconscious understanding of sexuality as it developed in a particular milieu. The influence of culture is inevitable. Only if culture and society were to change would your unconscious change, too.

Freud (1931) himself was aware of many shortcomings in his account of infantile sexuality. In 1905 he acknowledged in the *Three Essays* that he knew more about the sexuality of boys than of girls. While he always retained the firm conviction that full female sexuality only develops from the castration complex, he urged his psychoanalytic colleagues to examine the pre-Oedipal period more closely. He recognized the special importance of the girl's relationship to her mother and the sources of her psychosexual identity in it.

Critics who basically accept the psychoanalytic view of psychosexual development have revised the theory as the result of careful observations of infants. Typical of this approach is the work of Galenson and Roiphe (1977). From their observation of seventy infants, half of them male and half female, they reported differences in genital play and the age, within the first year of life, that it occurs. They described infant female masturbation and suggested the existence of elements of fantasy from their observations of preoccupation and emotional love. This evidence, together with their clinical work with children, led them to suggest a differentiated sense of gender identity as early as eighteen months. They also noted awareness of anatomical sex differences in the second year. While accepting Freud's views about penis envy and the feminine castration complex, they saw these in relation to the two-year-olds' fear of loss of love objects and his or her anal concerns. According to Galenson and Roiphe, by two years of age girls and boys follow very different paths in the psychological development of their inner worlds.

The work of Galenson and Roiphe can be linked to another trend within psychoanalytic thinking, represented, for example, by Sayers (1982), who sees the gynocentric view of Horney, Klein, and Jones as rooted in a biological essentialism. Just as the phallocentric approach might be construed as deriving from male anatomy, so a distinctive female psyche is alleged to arise from the female infant's interaction with her body. This view is most clearly expressed in the writings of the French feminist psychoanalyst Luce Irigaray. She identifies a uniquely female desire, the representation of bodily excitations arising from female genitalia (1977).

Criticisms of Freud's theory are legion, but we have chosen in the remaining space to concentrate on an explication of psychoanalytic theory by the psychoanalyst Roy Schafer (1977), as this allows us to return to the evolution of sex. We present only one of the arguments Schafer raises in a paper examining problems in Freud's psychology of women. Schafer asserted that in a most curious way Freud turned on his own discovery of the psychological plasticity of human sexuality in terms of its aims and objects and eventually espoused the values of nineteenth- and early twentieth-century evolutionary biology. From these Freud posited procreation and heterosexual genital intercourse as the normal outcomes of development, but he sought an explanation for this in terms of the diverse currents of infantile sexuality. Thus he considered pleasure of an exclusively oral or anal nature immature and perverse, while nonprocreative (e.g., homosexual) intercourse he characterized as an inversion.

We share Schafer's view of the irony of the situation. We owe to Freud and the insights of his clinical investigations our own vision of human psychosexual development as a process relatively free from biological imperatives, yet Freud's deep personal commitment to the procreative values of Western society led him to consider the outcome of psychosexual development in terms of biological necessity. His theory suggests a biologically instinctual drive toward species propagation at the same time as it points to an explanation in terms of the psychological representations of diverse sensual experiences. The structure of Freud's argument encourages neglect of questions of cultural learning and social values and instead focuses attention upon the anatomy of sex differences and hypothesized imperatives of species survival. At the very time that Freud was able to account

psychologically for the allegedly natural revulsions and anxi-
eties that the perversions arouse, he himself was trapped by the
prevailing scientific and commonsense theories of his day. As
we have noted in Chapter 1 and elsewhere (Archer and Lloyd,
1975), the clarity and apparent certainty of biological explanations is powerful and very seductive.

The decision to examine criticism only from within the psychoanalytic movement reflects our recognition of the impact of
Freud's thinking on the understanding of sexuality in the
twentieth century. In order to give full attention to its complexity, we have ignored many other critics. Those who disagree
fundamentally with concepts such as the unconscious and infantile sexuality attack psychoanalytic theory, but they often
fail to illuminate the nature of this influential theory. Rather
than examine sociological critiques of psychoanalytic theories
of sexuality, we next consider the use of sexuality in defining
people's positions in society.

Social uses of sexuality

At the beginning of this chapter we approached the issue of
the similarities and differences in women's and men's sexual
experiences from the viewpoint of an outside observer or rational participant observer. Our examination of psychoanalytic
explanations introduced a new level of analysis and the inner
world of feelings and fantasies. We considered theories about
the effects of infantile experiences in shaping men's and
women's unconscious attitudes – the aims and objects of their
sexual pleasure. Here we will examine the impact of sexuality
on the definition of roles in society and the impact of social
values on sexuality.

The xanith *of Oman: a third gender role*

We begin by looking at a report of the *xanith* of Oman, an Arab
sultanate on the eastern side of the Arabian penisula (Wikan,

1977). Wikan suggested that the Omani gender system can best be understood by thinking of it not in terms of the two gender roles with which we are most familiar, those of male and female, but by viewing the *xanith* as a third gender. After examining Wikan's ethnographic material, we consider the issue of homosexuality and its relation not only to the definition of rules in society, but also to the worlds of unconscious sexuality and of normative sexual statistics. We begin by describing the behavior of the *xanith* from their own viewpoint and from that of Omani men and women, and only then do we consider their gender identity.

Wikan's analysis was aimed at elucidating sociological aspects of gender identity, and so she gave little attention to questions concerning the historical or psychological origins of the *xanith*. The *xanith* are biologically men. They sell themselves in passive homosexual relationships, but these transactions are not their main source of income. They work as skilled domestic servants and are in great demand, earning a good wage. Their dress is distinctive, cut like the long tunic worn by men but made of pastel-colored cloth. Although they retain men's names, they violate all the restrictions that *purdah*, the system of female seclusion, imposes on men. They may speak intimately with women in the street without bringing the women's reputations into question. They sit with the segregated women at a wedding and may see the bride's unveiled face. They may not sit or eat with men in public or play the musical instruments reserved for men. The *xanith*'s manners, perfumed bodies, and high-pitched voices appeared effeminate to Wikan. She described the *xanith* as transsexuals in the sense that their essential sexual identity is that of a woman rather than a man.

Transsexuals are no longer a great rarity in our own society. In her book *Conundrum*, Jan Morris (1974) described her own journey from boyhood, through the army, marriage, fatherhood, and a successful career in journalism to her long-sought identity as a woman. In her case and that of many less well-

known transsexuals, the path to achieving their desired identity is an arduous one involving hormone treatments, deliber-
ate study of the habits in dress, movement, and speech of the
desired gender, and finally surgery. In our own society the
change implies not only learning to behave in the gender-
appropriate manner, but in changing one's anatomy to the extent medical techniques will allow.

The Omani situation is illuminating because male transsexual
passage here is a more social phenomenon. There are three
quite different possibilities open to the *xanith*. Should they
wish to become men again, they need only marry and prove
themselves able to perform heterosexual intercourse with their
brides. Some *xanith* never choose this path and remain as
women until they grow old, when having given up prostitution and homosexual intercourse their anatomical sex again
places them – though perhaps only tenuously – in the category
of old men. In addition, Wikan reported that some *xanith* become women, then men, and then women again. This comparative ease of passage, based as it is on behavior rather than
anatomy, is one of the pieces of evidence Wikan provided in
arguing that Omani *xanith* represent a gender role – a third
one – intermediate between Omani male and female gender
roles. She argued that its function is to maintain the sharply
differentiated roles of men and women, which we shall examine more closely. If *xanith* is indeed a role, this may explain the
relative ease with which men pass from the male category into
xanith and back again to male. The fact that in old age, when
they are no longer sexually active, *xanith* are again classed with
men suggests that these transitions are of a different order
from those that transsexuals in our own society experience. In
our own society the passage must be complete and involves
something more than just role-appropriate behavior.

Before accepting Wikan's argument, let us consider the evidence she offered in asserting that the *xanith* represent a third
and intermediate gender role. In a sense this proposition is
difficult to entertain, so contrasting and exhaustive are our con-

cepts of male and female gender roles. Wikan (1978) defended her claim – that the *xanith* function as a third gender role – from attack by two anthropologists. In answering Brain's (1978) criticism that Wikan had overlooked other anthropological studies of homosexuality, she pointed to the need for precision in labeling behavior such as dressing like the opposite gender, entering into contracts (for instance, marriage) as if one were a member of the opposite gender, or engaging in sexual relations with members of one's own gender. The degree of institutionalization, too, is crucial for her analysis, and she points to the important difference between being able to recognize sexual deviants from their dress or walk and the socially recognized suspension of rules such as those that seclude women from any men except biological men socially categorized as *xanith*. In Omani society, sexuality is embedded in a precisely specified rule system that defines socially recognized roles.

Shepherd's (1978) criticisms arose in the context of her own fieldwork in Mombasa, a town on the east coast of Africa that has had centuries of contact with Oman. In Mombasa Shepherd found both male and female homosexuals, and this led her to question the completeness of Wikan's gender role analysis based on male prostitutes alone. In replying, Wikan stressed the importance of analyzing the situation both in terms of the behavior that can be observed by the anthropologist and in terms of its meaning for the actors. Wikan attacks Shepherd's assertion that Omani men act as *xanith* for economic reasons and that these then influence their status in the society. The money the *xanith* receive for sexual behavior is not their main source of income, and the *xanith* may even offer payment to other men when they become old and less attractive. These same data refute Shepherd's argument that homosexuals are treated as inferiors in the manner of married women who sell their sexual favors for economic security. Economic motives alone cannot provide an adequate explanation, for, as Wikan points out, no amount of money can guarantee that a *xanith* will pass the test of manhood on his wedding night.

At this point we might wish to return to the inner world of psychoanalysis in seeking an explanation of *xanith* behavior and character. The Omanis seem willing to accept that certain people's natures are different, and their social stance in these cases is one of noninvolvement; concern is confined to closest kin. A husband may feel shamed by his faithless wife, or parents may be saddened and grieved by their son's passive homosexual tendencies, but social concern is strictly limited. Again, our own society provides a sharp constrast. A question we can ask is the degree to which social recognition and the drawing of boundaries – for example, in designating people transvestites, transsexuals, or homosexuals – influences our own view of them and their own views of themselves. This issue has been raised by Foucault within a French intellectual tradition, and he has considered it in his history of sexuality (1979). Foucault saw Western society as aiming to classify everything, even things that, he believed, are essentially unclassifiable. He held that the aim of this classification is to allow differential status to be attached to categories of people.

The problem of classification and of the ease with which it can be imposed becomes a useful principle in reconsidering the gender-role system in Oman. Omani women wear their hair long, carrying it forward from a central parting, and are clothed in tight-waisted, brightly patterned tunics. Their heads are covered, as are those of men. But men wear loose-fitting white tunics and have short hair. The *xanith*'s hair is of medium length, and they never cover their heads; their solid-colored tunics are close-fitting, and they wear makeup. Wikan believes that these distinctions are essential and reflect *xanith* status not as biological women but as another category, as third gender. She argued that, given Omani patterns of dress, were *xanith* to assume the full women's costume their anatomic status as males would be ambiguous. Dress serves to define three distinct social categories.

The Omani gender-role system becomes understandable when we look at the roles of men and women and their attitudes toward sexuality. Oman was first opened to the Western world in 1971, so it is not surprising to discover that gender roles there are defined in terms of strictest Muslim custom. From the age of three, girls must be covered except for their hands, feet, and face. At puberty they don the facial mask that is removed only before women and closely related men – fathers, husbands, sons, and brothers. Fathers arrange their daughters' marriages, and once married a woman may not leave her home without her husband's consent. Yet Wikan warned us not to assume that women are unhappy or subjugated, for in response to this modesty and dignity women are treated by men with honor and respect.

Men are perceived to have a strong sex drive that is difficult to control and requires frequent release. Ideally, a man seeks satisfaction with his wife; if he is a migrant laborer or unmarried, problems arise. Strictly speaking, prostitution is illegal, but both male and female prostitutes are available. Besides costing five times as much as a man, going to a female prostitute involves a third party, the husband, while going to a *xanith* is a transaction between two independent people. Prostitution is condemned, but to understand its place in the gender role system Wikan contended that we must appreciate Omanis' commonsense psychology. Omanis entertain ideals about behavior but appreciate that the world is imperfect. Since the image of themselves that people seek to construct is one of good manners, of behaving tactfully, politely, morally, and amicably, they observe but do not sanction deviant behavior in any but the most intimate relationships. In addition, they view others in their full complexity and restrain from judging on the basis of a single act or an isolated set of acts. So widespread is this tolerance that Wikan found her own coolness toward a promiscuous woman being questioned in her circle of Omani friends. In this setting, male homosexuality is tolerated and serves to perpetuate the view of women as pure and honorable. So well defined is the *xanith* role that a man who seeks release with him in no sense risks his sexual identity, since the "man" always performs the act of penetration.

Beyond heterosexual gender roles

The Omani view of deviance also contrasts sharply with that of our own society. Although legal sanctions against sexual relations between men have been relaxed in the United States and England, the French laws are still repressive. Even where not viewed as criminal, homosexual pleasure is nevertheless often considered sick. It was only in 1973 that the American Psychiatric Association removed homosexuality from its list of diseases and, as discussed in Chapter 3, research still aims at "cure" (Dorner, 1976). Unlike the Omani attitude toward isolated acts of behavior, our society takes a different view of homosexual practices. For at least one hundred years we have categorized people who pursue homosexual pleasure as homosexuals, a distinct class of persons. In Omani society sexual behavior is embedded in a broader rule system. A *xanith* can expect to be treated like a man if he performs sexually with a woman. In our society the designation "homosexual" carries with it moral implications as well as rules of behavior.

The literature on homosexuality has been growing at a great rate ever since the emergence of the gay liberation movement in the 1970s. The thesis we present below, though not representative of this literature, is provocative in that it not only draws heavily on Freud's views on sexuality but is also concerned with the impact of society in molding sexual desire. The original anti-Oedipus argument attacking the procreative family was presented by Deleuze, a French philosopher, and Guattari, a Marxist psychoanalyst (Deleuze and Guattari, 1977). We draw heavily on Hocquenghem's (1978) analysis of their work.

To describe a particular kind of sexual desire as homosexual, Hocquenghem asserted, is to make an arbitrary division along the continuum of desire, a division that, he and many others (e.g., Foucault, 1979) have claimed, is imposed on sexuality by Western society to achieve its capitalist ends. Before we consider these claims, let us examine the assertion that the attempt to classify sexual desire as either heterosexual or homosexual is artificial.

We have just noted that in Oman efforts are made to avoid condemning an individual on the basis of isolated acts of behavior. In contrast, in our own society we seem very ready to make new classifications. The term *homosexual* evolved fewer than a hundred years ago as a means of denoting a category of people – those who participate in particular kinds of sexual acts (Weeks, 1978). The evidence reviewed in the first section showed that homosexual behavior occurs along a continuum; Kinsey's scale from 0 to 6 should make us cautious of simple all-or-nothing classification. But Hocquenghem argued that the aim of our society is not truth – rather, its categories are repressive. The identification of the sexually deviant legitimizes their repression and strengthens heterosexual, procreative sexuality. He argued further that any repressed deviant tendencies within those who identify themselves as heterosexual will lead them to persecute and condemn those openly identified as deviant.

This argument reflects Freud's concern with unconscious motives. Recognition of the polymorphously perverse nature of all human sexuality makes even those most interested in repression suspect. The language of the anti-Oedipus discourse is altered in the psychoanalytic discourse as presented in the reformulation of Freud offered by Lacan (1966). The reformulation is an attempt by Lacan to rid psychoanalysis of its biological language and to explore the unconscious in terms that he believed to be more appropriate, those of linguistics and of symbolism. In keeping with this project, instinct becomes desire, the penis gives way to the symbolic phallus, but the Oedipus complex remains at the core. For Lacan, as for Freud, the resolution of the Oedipus complex is the turning point in the child's development: It marks the child's recognition of authority and his or her loss of omnipotence, for the phallus symbolizes the patriarchal order. It is our society's patriarchal order that demands repression and renunciation of a polymorphous sexuality. No longer can the child obtain just what he or she desires; the authority of the father stands between the child and the child's desire for the mother. It is not the biological father but language and the symbolic order that gain ascendancy in the child's mental functioning, in the unconscious. The authority of the social order is centrally symbolized by the phallus.

We concluded the discussion of psychoanalytic explanations of sexuality with Schafer's criticisms of Freud's return to evolutionary biology in his efforts to understand adult genital sexuality – masculinity/femininity, activity/passivity. Lacan described a similar course of development, but in his account the unconscious bears the imprint of society through the social definition of masculinity and femininity. It is the core definition of sexuality derived through the dynamics of the Oedipal conflict that Hocquenghem and that Deleuze and Guattari attack. Hocquenghem's argument is relevant here in that he was concerned with the impact of society on the unconscious mind, but he presented an oversimplified view of society and of mental functioning. A problem arises in trying to compare men and women: Nowhere in Hocquenghem's text is there mention of female homosexuals, so we do not know the extent to which this analysis fits female homosexuality. In addition, social class is unspecified. We have seen in the Kinsey reports that sexual behavior varies with social class; specifically, Weeks (1978) reported that men's consciousness of themselves as homosexuals varies with class. In Hocquenghem's analysis, the social system is undifferentiated and the economic system – that is, capitalism – is invoked instead.

A more penetrating analysis is provided by Foucault (1979), who argued that, rather than being repressive, the bourgeois society that developed with the rise of capitalism has exploited sexuality. The effects, he suggested, are not undifferentiated but influence at least four aspects of sexual knowledge. The objects of this knowledge are the hysterical woman, the masturbating child, the Malthusian (procreative) couple, and the perverse adult. More importantly, in suggesting that bourgeois society exploits sexuality, Foucault escaped the problem of repression. As we have noted, Hocquenghem accepted the older Freudian notion but turned it on its head. Rejecting the notion that homosexuals feel persecuted and are sick, he argued that so-called normal people who repress all but the heterosexual aspect of desire become paranoid. It is they who are disturbed and project their anxiety onto others.

In this discussion of some French theoretical approaches to homosexuality, and more generally to the impact of society in determining sexuality, we have come a long way from the description of Omani *xanith*. The discussion has allowed us to link the social and the unconscious, but it has lost track of the comparison between women's and men's sexuality. This appears to be the cost of achieving a broad social perspective.

Before concluding this section on social uses of sexuality, we should note the work of Gagnon and Simon (1973). They saw sexuality as being extremely susceptible to cultural patterning. Sexuality can be defined by the rules a particular society imposes on social interaction and uses to determine positions in society. Gagnon and Simon stressed that individuals can create their sexual identities through a vast potential variety of sexual scripts that the interactive rules allow. This view elaborates and formalizes the relativist tradition of such eminent anthropologists as Margaret Mead, and it poses important questions about the development of sexual identities. The questions it ignores are those raised by psychoanalytic explanations – why a particular individual chooses one identity rather than another, or why the genitals are the focal point in all societies' constructions of sexuality. Each of these approaches make a contribution, even though each leaves many questions unanswered. Masters and Johnson's (1980) most recent research on homosexuality still reflected their physiological bias, but by providing information on the sexual behavior of homosexuals they may have helped combat a common prejudice in our society. To begin to understand the nature of women's and men's sexuality we need to know more about what they do, why they do it, and how it is viewed by their society.

5

Aggression, violence, and power

"Most violence, most crime . . . is not committed by human beings in general. It is committed by men." So wrote the columinist Jill Tweedie in the British newspaper the *Guardian* (April 27, 1978). Similarly, organized groups that use violence in the name of "the people," the state, or their country – such as the army and the police – consist largely of men. Violence is seen as the masculine way of reacting to the difficulties and frustrations of life. The feminine way, as we shall show in the next chapter, is typically viewed as a more passive response.

Feminist writers who claim that violence is a *male* problem rather than a human problem are undoubtedly correct in the sense that most overt acts of violence toward other adults are now and were in the past committed by men. They neglect to mention, however, that a great deal of female encouragement has fanned the flames of male violence. The idea that toughness and aggression are admired masculine features, the sending of white feathers to those men who rebelled against this masculine stereotype, the direct encouragement given to wrestlers by women from ringside seats, and offers from prostitutes of free sex for U.S. soldiers going to Vietnam are all examples of different ways in which women have played their part in perpetuating male violence. Many others could be mentioned. Germaine Greer (1970) went so far as to claim that "violence has a fascination for most women." Although this may be an overstatement, it does describe one side of an ambivalent attitude that women have toward male aggression.

Whether or not we would want to portray women as inciting

124

men to violence or as discouraging them, it is clear that when it comes to committing overt acts of violence this is generally left to the men (although there has been a recent trend toward female violence that we shall mention later in this chapter). Are minor acts of violence, losing one's temper, and verbal abuse also characteristically male, or are such lesser acts of aggression more nearly equally distributed between the genders? We pose this question because there is the possibility that the two genders have the same degree of motivation to be aggressive but that men are more likely to act out such violent impulses than women. Most people do not believe this: It is generally thought that on average, men *are* more aggressive than women, as well as being more violent. This widespread belief is detected in the reports of social psychologists' descriptions of gender stereotypes, and the notion of masculine aggressiveness has been incorporated into our language in phrases such as "fiercely masculine." So people *believe* that men are aggressive, but is this really true? It is, if we take the findings of psychologists who have measured aggression in the two genders as our evidence. In this case, therefore, lay opinion and the psychologists' measures agree that men are more aggressive than women.

When we say that men are more aggressive than women, we could mean that men are more aggressive to one another than women are to other women; alternatively, we could be concerned with aggression between the genders – why men commit more aggressive acts against women than women do against men. Research on these two questions has been pursued along different lines, with different explanations being offered in each case. The respective "levels" of aggression within each gender have been studied by psychologists – generally under rather artificial conditions – and have been explained in terms of either biology or socialization. Aggression by men toward women has only recently been recognized as a problem and has been studied more by sociologists. There have been some attempts to explain this aggression in terms of the family backgrounds of violent men.

So far we have employed the terms *aggression* and *violence* rather loosely. *Violence* usually refers to acts involving great physical force and is often used of events in the animate and inanimate world alike. When using the word *violence* to apply to human actions, emphasis is placed on the physically damaging nature of the act itself rather than on the person's intentions. *Aggression* is a more difficult word to define, because it has a number of partially overlapping meanings. It can refer to active ambition or assertion of the self or to forcefulness; in the latter sense, it describes a way of acting or a personality characteristic and is closely related to aspects of the male stereotype described in Chapter 2, such as "active," "assertive," and "confident." *Aggression* can also refer more specifically to the motivation behind acts of violence, and in this sense it can be thought of as consisting of three aspects, the injury inflicted, the intention behind the act, and the emotion accompanying it. In practice, aggressive acts tend to contain different combinations of these three aspects. *Aggression* meaning "assertiveness" and *aggression* meaning "motivation to commit a violent act" can be linked if we regard an assertive person as being more ready to commit violent acts if his intentions are frustrated.

The measures psychologists use to study aggression take various forms. For children, they consist of observations of fighting and other aggressive acts in nursery school and school playground settings, measures of destructiveness and fantasy aggression in play, and ratings of aggressiveness by parents, teachers, and peers (Oetzel, 1966; Maccoby and Jacklin, 1974). For adults, a variety of different laboratory methods are used by social psychologists. These include providing opportunities for verbal aggression and criticism and measuring a person's willingness to administer (what are believed to be) electric shocks to another individual (Baron, 1977). Various "hostility scales" involving self-appraisal ratings and questionnaires are also used for measuring aggressiveness as a personality characteristic.

In this chapter we first describe research on gender differences in aggression and violence, addressing the question "Are men really more aggressive than women?" We then discuss the possible explanations offered by psychologists for the gender differences in aggression and violence outlined above. Finally, we consider the wider subject of power relations between the genders.

Are men really more aggressive than women?

The general impression given by many reviews on aggression is that, irrespective of the measure used, men are generally more aggressive then women. In some studies no gender differences have been found, but reports of greater female aggression are rare (Maccoby and Jacklin, 1974, 1980). Greater male than female aggression is generally found from an early age; it has been reported during play in children as young as two and three years of age (Maccoby and Jacklin, 1974). Despite one attempt to argue that measures of the gender difference are unreliable below six years of age (Tieger, 1980), a high degree of consensus is apparent when all the available evidence is reviewed (Maccoby and Jacklin, 1980). Let us now take a closer look at some of these studies.

Studies with children

The majority of studies dealing with young children were carried out in nursery schools. It is relatively easy for psychologists to gain access to these schools, but the results of such studies will reflect any biases that may exist in the types of children attending them. For example, in the United States, most of the children observed in older studies were middle-class. In more than twenty investigations published before 1966, boys were observed to be more aggressive than girls (Oetzel, 1966). More recent reports, which include a greater proportion of British studies, are generally in agreement with the earlier results (Maccoby and Jacklin, 1980). For example, one study carried out in fifteen different nursery schools, day nurseries, and playgroups found that conflicts between boys were more frequent than those between girls or between girls and boys (Smith and Green, 1975). Another study, which compared English children with Kalahari San children, found more aggressive actions and facial expressions in boys than in girls in both samples (Blurton-Jones and Konner, 1973).

There are fewer observational studies on school-age children. In a combined sample of three- to eleven-year-olds from six different cultures observed during free play, there was more physical and verbal aggression by boys than by girls (Whiting and Edwards, 1973; see also Maccoby and Jacklin, 1980). In an English study of boys and girls in the classroom, eleven-year-old boys showed more physical aggression than girls of the same age (Archer and Westeman, 1981).

A related gender difference often reported in these observational studies is that boys' play involves more "play-fighting," particular wrestling and tumbling, than does girls' play (e.g., Smith and Connolly, 1972; Blurton-Jones, 1972). This gender difference was also observed in the Kalahari San study of Blurton-Jones and Konner (1973). Play-fighting differs from "real" fighting in that any aggressive acts such as chasing, wrestling, or hitting out are usually accompanied by laughing, making a face, or some other sign that "it is all in play or fun" (Garvey, 1977).

There are very few exceptions to the general pattern of more frequent aggression by boys than girls in preschool and school-age children. The occasional study (for example, Blurton-Jones, 1972) may report no gender difference, but there is little sign of any apparent reversal of the usual gender difference (Maccoby and Jacklin, 1980). If we are to look for possible cases of such a reversal, a distinction between verbal and physical aggression must be made – an important distinction, particularly in relation to gender differences. Indeed, there is a common belief that girls and women make up for their lack of physical aggression by verbal hostility, often referred to by such terms as *cattiness* and *bitchiness*. Some psychologists, notably Bardwick (1971) and Feshbach (1970), also suggest that girls show more verbal and "prosocial" aggression than boys (*prosocial aggression* refers to rule enforcement, such as saying, "You mustn't do that" or "I'll tell the teacher if you don't stop"). Although the evidence for greater male aggressiveness is weaker in the case of verbal aggression (Maccoby and Jacklin, 1974), there are few actual instances of girls being more verbally aggressive than boys, as Bardwick and Feshbach suggest. In one study of the level of fantasy play with a doll, girls were more verbally aggressive than boys (Durrett, 1959), and in another study of eleven-year-olds in the classroom, girls were again found to show more verbal aggression (Archer and Westeman, 1981). There are, however, other reports in which boys are found to be both physically and verbally more aggressive than girls (e.g., Whiting and Edwards, 1973). Altogether, there is relatively little evidence for the suggested reverse gender difference in verbal aggression.

Studies with adults

In studies of aggression in adults, rather different measures are used. Laboratory studies typically involve measuring how willing someone is to give an electric shock to another person in a contrived situation. Measures of aggression outside the laboratory include questionnaires about aggressive and hostile feelings and the analysis of the aggressive content of daydreams. Generally these measures indicate either a higher level of aggression in men than in women or no gender difference; only occasionally is the reverse gender difference reported.

Maccoby and Jacklin (1974) reviewed research on gender differences in aggression and confidently concluded that the major fact highlighted by studies of aggression in young adults and in children is that "males are consistently found to be more aggressive than females." Have other psychologists agreed with Maccoby and Jacklin's conclusion? Baron (1977), for one, did not. He suggested that laboratory studies published in the early 1960s did show a gender difference in aggression, but that this had largely disappeared by the late 1960s and mid-1970s. Two possible explanations were offered to account for this trend. The first involves a procedural difference: Studies reporting a large gender difference do not expose the subjects to provocation, whereas those finding no difference often involve provocation. Baron therefore suggested that at low levels of provocation men are more likely to behave aggressively than women, but that when provoked both react in a similar manner. Baron's second explanation was that there has been a change in female roles in recent years, including a lessening in passivity. This explanation is more consistent with his emphasis on a relationship between the date of the study and the appearance of a gender difference. It is, however, based on very few studies, and there have been many earlier reports of no gender difference in aggression. Baron's conclusions should therefore await assessment in the light of further evidence.

Another review has challenged the generality of a gender difference in aggression. Frodi et al. (1977) concluded that in most laboratory studies the occurrence of the expected higher levels of male aggression is variable and depends on a number of more specific gender differences. More recent studies are generally consistent with these conclusions (White, 1983). A gender difference is more likely to occur in studies where the subjects are not angered. There is also an indication that women are more likely to shy away from physical aggression (as represented by willingness to administer electric shocks). Frodi et al. suggested that women generally experience greater anxiety about aggressive feelings than men and that this provides a powerful inhibiting factor on their level of aggression. They pointed out that aggression and anxiety about aggression are inversely related for women but not for men and that several other studies show that women are more anxious after being aggressive then men. A study of Richardson et al. (1979), showing that women were more aggressive when they were not being observed, is consistent with this suggestion.

Another factor is that women may generally have more empathy for their victim than men. Thus the presence of a justification for aggression may increase female aggression and hence abolish the gender difference. Finally, there is some evidence that certain aggressive cues, such as guns or knives, may provide a stronger instigation to aggression in men than in women.

Frodi et al. (1977) also concluded that studies of self-report measures of "general hostility," analyses of aggressive content in dreams and daydreams, and interpretation of projective tests all indicate that men are more aggressive than women. But this contrasts with the less consistent pattern found in laboratory studies, apparently because these other measures are based on the subjects' own reports of their behavior and consequently may reflect the influence of gender stereotypes.

How representative are the studies of aggression we have described so far? The ages of those observed in these studies reflect the ready availability of children, adolescents, and young adults (usually university students) as subjects for psychological research. Maccoby and Jacklin's review of gender differences in aggression contained no studies of subjects over twenty-four years of age! On these grounds alone, any conclusions drawn from psychological research must be limited. Another major limitation of psychological studies is their reliance on artifical measures of aggression produced in laboratory experiments and on self-report measures. If we look at sources outside social psychological research, such as violent crime statistics and cross-cultural surveys, we can obtain evidence from a wider age range in real-life conditions. Such sources generally show that men commit the vast majority of violent acts. According to statistics for the United States up to 1969, men heavily outnumbered women in committing violent crimes, and five times more men were arrested in connection with murder (Johnson, 1972). Similarly, in the United Kingdom, almost ten times more men than women were convicted for violence against other people (*Social Trends*, 1984).

According to these statistics, therefore, violent crime is clearly a male problem. Some commentators suggest that this pronounced gender difference has diminished in recent years, and the subject of female violence has received a fair amount of media publicity, particularly in relation to adolescents and young adults. A number of youth subcultures have encouraged certain forms of violence in both genders, and it is now fairly common for women to be involved in acts of violence reported by the media, although at one time this was almost unknown. For example, a British newspaper report of women muggers quotes an Old Bailey judge as saying that he was "terrified" by this new aspect of crime – simply because it was carried out by women (*Guardian*, October 28, 1977). Another British newspaper report referred to a "new strain of violence emerging among our young girls" (*Sunday Times* [London], May 1, 1977) that had caught the attention of the British National Union of Teachers. However, the violent crime statistics for this age group show only a very small increase during the years 1975–7, when this violence was supposed to have emerged; it is therefore difficult to decide whether these specific cases have been exaggerated. But some research shows an increase among women in typically "male" crimes, such as robbery, burglary, assault, and vandalism, during the late 1960s and early 1970s (e.g., Thompson and Lozes, 1967). Other research has documented violence among British adolescent girls (Campbell, 1982). One point to bear in mind in assessing media reports is that female violence is particularly noteworthy, because of its departure from the stereotype of the passive woman. Men in contact with female terrorists view them as more ruthless, more cruel, and more calculating than male terrorists, but this opinion is not shared by women commentators (BBC radio program, "More Deadly Than the Male," 1978).

There are few observational studies of real-life aggression in adults, as opposed to that in children, for it is much more difficult for a psychologist to witness contexts in which adults are violent to one another. There are, however, some exceptions: A study by Depp (1976) in a mental hospital in Washington, D.C. found that aggressive incidents occurred predominantly among male patients.

Cross-cultural comparisons of aggression also show that it is a predominantly male characteristic. For example, a comparison of reactions to bereavement, which often involve feelings of anger and aggressive actions (Parkes, 1975), revealed more instances of violence among men than among women (Rosenblatt et al., 1976). Women, on the other hand, are more inclined to self-injury and attempted self-injury.

Generally speaking, a more clear-cut gender difference is revealed from these studies of real-life violence than from the laboratory studies. This suggests that although overt violence is a predominantly male characteristic, less intense incidences of aggression show a less pronounced gender difference.

Domestic violence

The research we have discussed so far is generally about aggression or violence carried out on someone of the same gender. Violence by a member of one gender toward the other, as between a husband and wife, has until recently not been considered a subject for academic research. Nevertheless, violence by men toward their wives has been known for millennia and has usually been condoned by the law. Many men still regard assaulting or physically "punishing" their wives as a right, and this attitude is supported by Jewish and Christian beliefs about the subservience of women (Davidson, 1977). For example, it is only during the last century that statutes in the United States have appeared outlawing even the most severe forms of wife beating.

These forms of private violence by men toward women have existed at the same time as a more public disapproval of violence toward and by women. This dual standard persists today and is epitomized by the attitude that it is ungentlemanly for a man to strike a woman unless she is his rebellious wife. Research on violence between men and women reflects the dual standard. On the one hand, laboratory studies of willingness to aggress show that male subjects are more likely to direct a higher intensity of aggression to a male than to a female victim. On the other hand, the few – and comparatively recent – studies of violence in the home indicate that some men exercise few such restraints in hitting their own wives or lovers in private.

Studies of domestic violence suffer from one obvious drawback: The violent act occurs in private, and in most cases it is not even in the victim's interest to admit that it has occurred. Consequently, evidence is most readily obtained from extreme cases where the violence has ended in murder or where the victim has sought refuge outside the home. A wife's escape from a violent husband is made very difficult through society's reluctance to acknowledge that this form of violence is a social problem. Ninety percent of a sample of 150 women entering a women's aid center in New York State (Abused Women's Aid in Crisis – AWAIC) reported that they would have left their violent relationship earlier had the resources been available (Roy, 1977). Two-thirds had already sought police help, and of these women 90 percent reported that the police had failed to make an arrest, while over two-thirds said that the police had been unhelpful.

Studies carried out at women's aid centers tell us about the circumstances of those women who have experienced extreme domestic violence and have been able to leave home. Roy (1977) obtained figures for the frequency, onset, and form of violence, the type of help sought, the involvement of drugs and alcohol, and the reasons for remaining in a violent home. The frequency of violence varied from less than once a month in 20 percent of the cases to more than once a week in 25 percent of cases. More frequent violence was associated with the use of a weapon and with sexual abuse. Violence often began early in the relationship. In 90 percent of cases it was associated with alcohol or drug problems, although it was not necessarily confined to the period of intoxication.

In some cases it is the husband who is the victim of his wife's violence, but this form of violence is almost totally unrecorded, and there is little public recognition that it exists. If a man is a victim of his wife's violence, the stigma and the expected ridicule would provide ample reason for hiding what has happened. It is only from studies of divorce proceedings and from some fairly recent survey studies of domestic violence that evidence has been obtained for this form of violence.

Survey studies normally either concentrate on families for which incidents of violence have been reported to the authorities or try to assess the frequency of unreported incidences of violence in a typical cross section of families. Gelles (1972) did both by interviewing two small samples of families in which violence had been reported to a social work agency and to the police and then comparing these with neighboring families. There were eighty families altogether, and in most instances only the wife was interviewed. Over half the respondents reported the occurrence of at least one violent incident, and about a quarter reported regular violence, defined as between once every two months and every day. As expected, families obtained from the police records manifested the highest proportion of violent incidents (85 percent); those from the social work agency, rather less (60 percent); and neighbors' families the least (30 percent).

The frequency of violence committed by husbands against wives was greater than that by wives against husbands, but the percentage difference was not very great (47 percent vs. 32 percent). More repeated violence – defined as over six times a year – was committed by a quarter of the husbands and by 11 percent of the wives. The methods of violence were different, husbands tending to use forms that require physical strength such as pushing, choking, punching, and kicking, and the wives more often using hard objects. Husbands more often made violent threats by punching or kicking an object such as a door or by firing a gun and implying that this was what they would next do to their wives. Wives more often used a knife or a heavy object, saying that this was "protective" – to stave off the possibility of more severe violence by the husband.

Gelles's respondents gave a variety of reasons for these acts of violence: Some involved the notion of the husband punishing his wife or "knocking her to her senses"; others involved frustration that evoked aggressive feelings directed toward the wife because she was the nearest available target; still others resulted from conflicts within the family over disciplining children or over sexual relations. Gelles's study has a number of shortcomings, some of which he acknowledged: For instance, the sample size was too small, it was not random, and the information was derived from wives' accounts of the domestic disputes. One drawback he overlooked was the lack of any statistical tests carried out on the results: Thus one cannot be sure about which differences were chance variations. Gelles's research also provided very little information about the dynamics of the violence – how it fitted into other aspects of the relationship between husband and wife – and the extent to which husbands and wives differed in their readiness to use violence as a solution to family problems. By providing only percentage occurrences for various categories of violent acts, it is difficult to tell how many of the acts were responses to previous violence and how many represented the initiation of violence.

A more recent study of domestic violence, carried out by Steinmetz (1977), obtained information from husbands, wives, and their children in fifty-seven families and found some incidence of marital violence in 60 percent of these. This high figure probably results from the author including throwing objects as a form of violence, since this was the most common form of violence reported. The frequency of violence exhibited by husbands and by wives was very similar; as in Gelles's study, however, such a simple tallying of numbers of incidents provides only a superficial picture of domestic violence. Steinmetz reported that men generally did more damage as a result of their violent acts, and he regarded this as a consequence of their greater size and strength. Occasionally this may be reversed, and he cited an example of a husband who was beaten by his younger wife.

These studies show that both husbands and wives may commit violent acts against each other in the home and that these differ in terms of their form and in the degree of resultant damage. But little is revealed about possible differences in the context and meaning of violent acts committed by husbands and wives.

Explaining gender differences in aggression

We now turn from considering the nature and extent of gender differences in aggression to the explanations psychologists have offered for greater male aggression and violence. We consider these under the headings of biological and environmental explanations. The first links men's aggression to their biological makeup, an example of biological reductionism (see Chapter 1). The alternative comes from developmental psychology and emphasizes the learning experiences of boys and girls. It includes the influence of commonsense views – in particular, the approval of "toughness" and aggression in boys.

Biological explanations

Can male aggression be explained in terms of biological differences between men and women? Research on animals has shown that the male is the more aggressive sex in many species. This aggression is often associated with organs specialized for fighting, such as the antlers of stags and the spurs of cockerels. These weapons and the greater aggressiveness of the male are both dependent on the male hormone testosterone and are greatly reduced in castrated animals, one of several reasons why farm animals such as bulls are easier to manage and less likely to injure one another when they have been castrated. What could be simpler, therefore, than to explain the greater aggressiveness of human males in terms of the action of testosterone? This is essentially the viewpoint of those psychologists who favor a biological explanation for male aggression (e.g., Gray, 1971a; Hutt, 1972a; Maccoby and Jacklin, 1974).

In considering this explanation, we first outline the evidence from animal studies for the claim that males are generally the aggressive sex and briefly discuss the role of testosterone in animal aggression. We then consider research aimed at discovering whether there is a link between testosterone and aggression in men. Finally, we discuss briefly the importance of size and strength differences between men and women as factors contributing to greater male violence.

What are the animal sex differences in aggression? In a wide range of animal species, the male is more aggressive than the female – more ready to fight or threaten. But there are many exceptions and qualifications. First, male aggression is seasonal in many species, occurring when the males are in breeding condition. It is associated with the establishment or holding of particular areas or "territories." This is commonly the case in fish and birds. In many mammals, seasonal breeding, accompanied by male aggression, occurs without territory formation – for example in the red deer and the elephant. In other mammals, such as rats and mice, the male is more consistently the more aggressive sex.

Females also show a form of "seasonal" aggression. This is typically associated with defense of a nesting site, eggs, or young and occurs in a wide variety of species. Unlike male aggression, it has only recently been studied either in a natural setting or in the laboratory, and most studies have been on rodents. Thus, female mice who are suckling their young become just as aggressive as males. In other species the female is as aggressive as the male (or more so) even when she has no young: Examples include European voles (several species of *Microtus*), hamsters and gerbils (Frank, 1957; Payne and Swanson, 1970; Swanson, 1973). Even in species where the female is supposedly "nonaggressive," such as the house mouse, this description is not quite accurate: Laboratory-reared females derived from wild mice will attack another mouse after being housed in isolation for a period of time (Ebert and Hyde, 1976). Primates, the order to which humans belong, show great variety in their social structures. Male dominance is common, but direct conflicts between the two sexes is often prevented by their having limited contact with one another. In a minority of species males defer to females during either part or all of the year (Hrdy, 1981).

The evidence for the contention that the male sex is the predominantly violent one among other mammals is, therefore, not as overwhelming as is often suggested. Psychologists who make generalizations from animal to human aggression tend to concentrate their attention on laboratory species, such as the rat or mouse, in which the male is typically more aggressive than the female and to ignore other species, such as the hamster or the gerbil, in which the two sexes are similarly aggressive.

What is the role of sex hormones? Experimental studies using rats and mice have shown that testosterone, which is present during early development and after the age of puberty, is necessary at both these times for the typically higher level of aggression in the male. Some psychologists (e.g., Hutt, 1972a; Maccoby and Jacklin, 1974) have relied on such research to provide a model for hormonal influences on human aggression. They suggest that in human beings, as in rats and mice, testosterone causes the male to be more aggressive than the female. We are skeptical about this conclusion, since it ignores the variability and the complexity of the relationship between hormones and behavior in animals. As we have already pointed out, in some species the male is more aggressive than the female, but in others—such as the gerbil and the hamster—he is not. In the hamster, female hormones are implicated in affecting aggressive behavior. Why should psychologists choose rodents such as the

rat and the mouse for their speculations about human aggression and ignore these others where the pattern of hormonal
control is different? We could also ask why rodents are regarded
as relevant to human beings at all. Primates – the order to which
the human species belongs – and rodents diverged from a common ancestral stock relatively early in mammalian evolution and
have followed different courses of evolution both within and
between their respective groups ever since. Much is known
about hormones and behavior in rats and mice simply because
of their convenience for laboratory experiments and because of
the tradition of using them for behavioral research. But whether
such information is relevant to human beings can only be assessed by actually studying human beings and comparing the
findings for the two species. Let us look at research on the
possible relationship between testosterone and aggression in
men.

There are two stages in the life of a human male when androgens such as testosterone could exert a direct effect on parts
of his brain and hence on his behavioral predispositions: during prenatal development and at puberty. The major source of
evidence for the first is the work of Money and Ehrhardt
(1972), which we referred to briefly in Chapter 3. Money and
Ehrhardt studied girls who for one reason or another had been
exposed to androgens during their prenatal development, and
they compared their behavior with that of a group of normal
girls, obtaining their information from interviews with parents
and with the girls themselves. Although they found evidence
of rougher, more energetic play in the hormonally affected
girls, there was no indication of increased (or decreased) aggression – that is, in terms of real fights – during childhood.
(There are many problems in interpreting their studies, and
these are discussed more fully in Chapter 9. Principally, these
are the difficulties in separating effects that might have arisen
from the action of androgens on the brain from those that
might have arisen as a result of parents' reactions to their girls'
genital abnormalities.) A more recent study of girls exposed to

androgens during their prenatal development (Reinisch, 1981) does show a higher level of potential aggression, assessed by the girls' written response to conflict situations. To determine how reliable this finding is requires further studies of a similar type.

Several studies have sought to relate aggression to testosterone secreted at puberty or during adult life. The first of these was carried out by Persky et al. (1971), who found in a group of young men that the higher the rate of testosterone production, the higher the score on questionnaire measures of aggression and hostility. Olweus et al. (1980) found a similar relationship, but two other studies (Kreuz and Rose, 1972; Doering et al. 1974) did not.

Meyer-Bahlberg et al. (1974) used a slightly different method: They selected "aggressive" and "non-aggressive" groups of subjects on the basis of questionnaire scores and compared rates of testosterone secretion and blood levels of testosterone; they found no differences between the two groups. Kreuz and Rose made a similar comparison, this time involving prisoners convicted of either violent or nonviolent crimes: Again, no differences in testosterone levels were found, although ten prisoners with histories of violent crimes *in adolescence* showed higher plasma testosterone levels than eleven prisoners lacking such histories. Kreuz and Rose suggested that testosterone may have played a part in predisposing individuals to be aggressive in adolescence but that it had a less pronounced effect thereafter. Another positive finding is that of Ehrenkranz et al. (1974), who reported that twelve prisoners with a history of chronic violent behavior showed higher blood levels of testosterone than a group of nonviolent prisoners. A study of a group of sex offenders (rapists and child molesters) also showed that those judged to be most violent according to questionnaires had higher testosterone levels than the other sex offenders, whose testosterone levels were in the normal range for the general population (Rada et al., 1976).

One study (Ehlers et al., 1980) found a correlation between

testosterone and aggression in young women attending a neurobehavioral clinic, those with histories of violence showing higher testosterone levels.

It is clear from this research that a correlation between testosterone and various indicators of aggression, past and present, is often found, particularly in studies comparing people with and without histories of violence. What exactly does this mean? Does a high testosterone level cause aggression, as would be predicted by those who favor a biological explanation for gender differences in aggression?

One of the pitfalls in inferring a causal relationship from this type of evidence is that we cannot rule out the possibility that a person's psychological state may have *produced* measurable changes in body chemistry (see Chapter 1) – that being or feeling aggressive raises testosterone levels. This is certainly known to occur in other primates: In a newly formed group of rhesus monkeys there is usually fighting that results in the establishment of a "dominance hierarchy." Rose et al. (1972) found that defeated or "subordinate" males showed an 80 percent fall in blood levels of testosterone under such circumstances, whereas the dominant monkey showed a progressive rise. A male from an established breeding colony also showed a large increase in testosterone levels (over 200 per cent) twenty-four hours after he had dominated strange males who had been added to his group. Other studies, both on monkeys and on human beings, indicate that testosterone secretion is generally lowered by stressful situations (e.g., Mason et al., 1969). There is also some evidence that conditions associated with anger may increase the secretion of the hormone (Archer, 1979). Mazur and Lamb (1980) carried out studies on achievement and testosterone levels in young men and found that both winning a tennis doubles match for a monetary prize and receiving an M.D. degree were associated with a rise in testosterone. In view of these findings, the higher levels of testosterone in certain violent prisoners (Kreuz and Rose, 1972, Ehrenkranz et al., 1974) and aggressive young men (Persky et al., 1970) could represent a *consequence* of their aggressive actions.

Furthermore, the view that testosterone simply *causes* aggression in human males represents a narrowly conceived reductionist approach that neglects the complex interaction between hormones, mental state, behavior, and new environments. We have indicated one example of this complex interaction – the consequences of environmental events and their associated mental states affecting hormone levels. The understanding of the mechanism that links testosterone and aggression in humans must await more sophisticated research designs than the present ones, which are largely based on simple cause-and-effect notions.

Ellis (1982) has suggested a more complex, hormonally based explanation of sex differences in aggression that takes account of environmental influences on testosterone secretion. He suggests that in mammals (including humans) of both sexes, androgen levels are increased as a result of positive, exhilarating experiences and successful achievement of sexual, aggressive, or status-related goals. Decreased androgen levels result from frustrating experiences, such as social isolation, defeat, denial of access to sexual outlets, and loss of status. Ellis goes on to suggest a threshold effect for androgenic action on aggression, so that the hormone only affects behavior below a certain level. In normal males, this threshold is exceeded, so that no influence on aggression is apparent. This influence is, however, apparent in females (cf. the study by Ehlers et al. described above), in males at puberty, and as a result of castration. There is, unfortunately, little evidence on these last two points, which are crucial ones for deciding whether male and female differences in androgen levels can explain gender differences in aggression. However, even if a link between aggression and testosterone secretion could be established in these two instances, it would not provide a complete explanation for gender differences in aggression. As we have seen, the greater aggressiveness of the human male can be first observed at about three years of age – long before the rise in testosterone levels at puberty.

The causes of the gender difference in aggression are likely to be varied and complex. So far we have considered one possibility – that testosterone might have a direct effect on the brain and so increase the likelihood of aggressive behavior in the male. We are considering here the possibility of a difference in aggressive motivation between the genders. A less direct biological contribution might result from sex differences in size and strength. These are, of course, only average differences; but they are sufficiently marked to suggest they affect the likelihood of success in physical violence and to assume particular importance in relation to violence between a man and a woman. For example, in the study of domestic violence by Steinmetz (1977) described in the previous section, similar types and incidences of violence were found to be committed by men and women, but greater damage generally resulted from the men's acts. Steinmetz even suggested that men and women have an equal potential for committing acts of domestic violence and initiate similar acts of violence, but that husbands have the capacity to do more damage. She also suggested that the situation may occasionally be reversed when the usual size and strength differences are reversed.

Sex differences in size and strength also play an important part in occupations that involve the possibility of violence. Until recent years, size and strength have been regarded as essential for active service in police and armed forces, and women have been relegated to nonoperational roles apparently for this reason. Nevertheless, modern weapons – even hand-held ones such as the gun and the grenade – have proved effective equalizers of size and strength differences, and in recent years women have come to play increasingly active roles in paramilitary operations such as politically motivated terrorist groups. The United States Army has also included a larger proportion of women during the last decade, and they have even been trained for combat roles (Davidson, 1978). We shall return to this subject in the final chapter on social change and the future. We now turn to psychological explanations for the gender difference in aggression.

Environmental explanations

Explaining differences in aggression between boys and girls in terms of their different upbringings forms part of a more general explanation of gender differences, often referred to as the socialization view. One influential psychological approach has concentrated on two forms of the learning process whereby cultural stereotypes are transmitted to children. These cultural stereotypes about aggression include the following: Throughout childhood, violence and aggression are strongly disapproved of in girls. Girls are not expected to respond aggressively even if they are attacked: They receive more sympathy and approval – and ultimately their own way – if they cry and attract the attention of an adult or an older brother than if they hit back. Boys, on the other hand, are often encouraged to be tough and to stick up for themselves. They receive a double message about violence, one facet of which is that it is appropriate in certain circumstances and acceptable if not taken to extremes: In particular, it can be an appropriate way of "looking after yourself" and is an important component of social status in boyhood (Hartley, 1957). One of the most important messages that boys learn regarding aggression is that they must not be regarded as afraid to fight. These cultural stereotypes about aggression are transmitted to children through their parents, their peers, the educational system, and television and other media images (Tieger, 1980).

Although there is considerable agreement among psychologists about the broad outlines of such an environmental explanation, there is disagreement on the details – for example, whether such a view provides a complete explanation of gender differences or whether hormonal factors also play a part, whether learning influences operate at younger ages, and what is the role of conscious selection and monitoring of gender-appropriate behavior by children (Maccoby and Jacklin, 1974, 1980; Tieger, 1980). The evidence relating to these issues is at present complex and conflicting. Rather than pursuing

them here, we shall instead describe some of the more traditional research on *how* boys and girls come to learn different
messages regarding aggression. Some studies are concerned
with rewards and punishments, others with imitation learning
and boys' identification with aggressive people.

Although it is generally believed that parents, peers, and
teachers react differently to the aggression of boys and girls,
boys receiving more encouragement and less restraint than
girls, there are few studies that have actually assessed whether
this is so. Serbin et al. (1973) found that teachers of preschool
children reprimanded or restrained girls more than boys for
their aggressive acts, but other studies have found little difference in the responses to boys and girls of this age (Maccoby
and Jacklin, 1980). Psychologists have studied how children
imitate aggression by setting up controlled experiments. One
study that appears in most child development textbooks is that
of Bandura et al. (1961), who allowed children between ages
three and six years to watch an adult "playing" either aggressively or peacefully with "Bobo Doll," a large, inflatable doll
anchored to a solid base. The children were then taken into
another room and given toys to play with, and it was found
that in their own play the boys imitated aggressive behavior
more than did the girls.

It is interesting to note the remarks of the children in this
study about the appropriateness of the adult's aggressive behavior. When performed by a man, it was generally regarded as
appropriate, whereas aggression was seen as inappropriate for
a woman. Some of the children remarked that the woman's
aggressive behavior was "not the way for ladies to behave"
and that she was "like a man." Male aggression met with more
approval, with comments such as "He's a good fighter like
Daddy" and "I want to sock like Al," (Al being the man's
name). The man also influenced the children's behavior to a
greater extent than the woman did, presumably because her
behavior was inappropriate for her gender. Other studies of
imitation show that the important feature in determining

whether a child will imitate an adult is whether the activity is regarded as appropriate for the gender of the child watching it, regardless of the gender of the adult (Barkley et al., 1977). Thus, if a girl already regards aggression as unfeminine or inappropriate for her gender, she will not imitate a woman who behaves aggressively. In our society and in many others, female aggression is seen as highly inappropriate and undesirable, so that the misgivings about female aggression expressed by the children in Bandura's study are merely reflections of a more widespread stereotype prevalent in our culture.

Cultural stereotypes about female aggression can be further illustrated by considering women's boxing. On a British BBC radio program ("Today," January 18, 1977) the boxer Joe Bugner talked of his refusal to fight on the same bill as women boxers. He said he had seen a women's boxing match and had been appalled by it because it "seemed like real fighting." These remarks were made by a man who had a very successful career in precisely the same activity that he disapproved of for women. Clearly, it was not boxing that had appalled him but rather that female boxers had violated a commonsense view about how women should behave. Women's boxing is restricted by law to a few states. When describing a successful American woman boxer, a reporter from the *Sunday Times* of London (March 12, 1978) went out of his way to emphasize her femininity: Not only did Cathy "Cat" Davis "fight like a man," but she was also "desirable, . . . blonde, blue-eyed, and 25." The readers had to be convinced that she really was a woman, since her chosen activity involved a fundamental violation of most people's view of femininity.

Women's boxing illustrates the strength of attitudes against female aggression. Of course, this does not represent a universal reaction, since women's boxing matches are in fact held in some places. But the usual attitude would be to regard it as a deviant activity, and the majority of adults and children who exhibit aggressive behavior, both in real life and in books, television, and films, are men. It is not surprising, therefore, to learn that males tend to respond positively to television violence more than do females and that boys imitate television and film violence more than do girls.

The social-learning explanation has been applied to domestic violence by men toward women. Several studies have reported that husbands who beat their wives often come from homes in which they were beaten or witnessed their fathers beating their mothers (e.g., Roy, 1977). Men and women who observed their parents being violent are more likely to be violent to their marriage partner than those who did not (Gelles, 1972). There is also evidence that parental violence influences the *type* of aggressive act that is favored. Gelles's explanation of family violence is that the experience of a violent domestic background makes a person more prone to react violently to later stresses. We have discussed the various reasons why men show more acts of aggression than women, taking into account the possible influence of hormones, of size and strength, and of the different learning experiences of men and women. These involve influences which reflect attitudes and beliefs about violence derived from the wider society in which the person lives. As such, they represent more than an individual's personal views and preferences. They are ultimately related to the nature of the wider society, and in particular to the power relations between men and women.

Power

We have taken a primarily psychological or personal view in reviewing gender differences in aggression and violence. Power is usefully examined by expanding our horizons to include sociological and anthropological explanations. Unfortunately, sociologists themselves do not agree about the definition of *power*. In his analysis of power and authority, Lukes (1975) provided several distinctions useful in classifying major differences among social theorists. One approach has been to construe power as the collective exercise of communal and consensual will; here emphasis is on belief systems and ideology. Another, more recent approach is to analyze power in terms of an imbalance or asymmetry in relationships. Both approaches can be seen in commonsense views of gender. The first is represented by the notion of "the natural order." Within this belief system it is held that men and women recognize their differences but also their shared needs; for these reasons both are content, men to pursue their careers and women to look after children. The emphasis on asymmetric relationships can be seen in the contemporary argument that women have been denied equal opportunities by men. Legislation designed to correct this inequality arises from a recognition and disapproval of it.

According to Lukes, there are three different ways of looking at asymmetric power relations. All usually involve conflict and resistance. The first view is in terms of compliance: The powerful person or group can impose its decision or will on the less powerful. This definition is commonly employed in psychological research and results in an emphasis on outcomes. In biological accounts, the larger size and greater aggressiveness of men is used to explain the subjugation of women. A second view sees power as being exercised through dependence: Power relations that arise from conditions of economic dependence between industrial nations and producers of raw materials are of this type. This view can also be applied to the economic dependence of women on men and to the psychological training of boys and girls: Males are trained to be dominant and females to comply. The third view of asymmetric power relations is in terms of inequality: Those in positions of power have greater access to material and social rewards. Feminist anthropologists and sociologists have pointed out numerous ways in which women are kept in low-paid jobs, encounter difficulty in career advancement, are excluded from certain occupational roles, and are assigned primary responsibility for child care (Mead, 1935; Polatnick, 1973; Walum, 1977). Inequality of access to rewards is seen in all these examples.

Even among anthropologists of a feminist persuasion there are different views about the exercise of power by men and women. One group recognizes a universal division of labor and power asymmetry: It is acknowledged that women are located in the domestic sphere with responsibility for child care and food preparation and that men are properly the hunters, fighters, clearers of the land, or workers in the public domain. These analysts view authority as held by males but do not accept the inevitability of patriarchy. Instead, they are puzzled by the failure of women to struggle and resist.

A second group has begun to reexamine the relative power of men and women in particular societies and to question the appropriateness of the conclusion that there is a universal asymmetry in which men are more powerful. In some Middle Eastern societies, for example, women's power in the domestic sphere entails considerable control of material and social rewards through female solidarity groups. In a similar vein, it is noted that in certain peasant societies women may gain considerable informal power through the control of information. Within this discourse Rogers (1978) argued convincingly that much anthropological analysis is not only male-centered but is also biased in terms of our own society's values in that the public and formal sectors of society within which men operate are held to offer greater rewards. From such an analysis the universal power of men and the inevitable inferiority of women follows.

Rogers presented an innovative theoretical framework that provides a new approach to the analysis of power relations. The notion that men and women may construe the world differently is central to her model, and she described this as "ideological differentiation." The kinds of differences we have noted in earlier chapters – the different roles filled by men and women and the specific actions expected according to gender – were labeled by Rogers "behavioral differentiation." Bearing in mind that in any particular society men and women may or may not be expected to behave differently and may or may not be expected to construe the world differently, Rogers constructed a classification of societies in terms of four types of gender differentiation. The two clear cases are, first, societies in which gender is ignored both behaviorally and ideologically, and second, those in which men and women are clearly differentiated along both dimensions. Reports have suggested that in the pioneering days on some *kibbutzim* a total absence of gender differentiation existed (Tiger and Shepher, 1975), although this was difficult to maintain. The definitions of male and female in Oman, which we described in Chapter 4, provide an example of a society with behavioral and ideological differentiation.

Of the two mixed types of societal gender differentiation, Rogers asserted that our own society offers an example of a culture in which behavioral differentiation is expected but in which there is no clear expectation of ideological differentiation. Men and women are expected to act differently but to inhabit the same conceptual world. The other type is difficult to imagine: societies in which men and women are expected to behave in a similar fashion although they are believed to be fundamentally different by nature and to live in different conceptual worlds. The example Rogers cited was that depicted in *Lesbian Nation: The Feminist Solution*, a fantasy world based on gender segregation in which men and women have completely separate power hierarchies, women do everything that men do, but the two genders are viewed as different species (Johnston, 1973). It is interesting to ponder the four types of societies, but even more fascinating to consider their meaning for the distribution of power between men and women in our own culture.

We can now ask how Rogers's four types of behavioral and ideological differentiation relate to the distribution of power. For Rogers power involves both ideology and relations of asymmetry. If resources can be shown to be distributed equally between men and women, we would conclude that there was no inequality in the distribution of power. Rogers urges that we look at both the domestic (informal) and public (formal) sectors of society in our analysis of power. If we acknowledge that men and women inhabit different worlds, the public and domestic, then each can be seen as providing unique rewards. Thus in the presence of ideological differentiation, relations between men and women may be symmetric rather than asymmetric.

Rogers's analysis can be applied to the Omani to produce a view that differs from our usual impression of gender inequality in Islamic societies. When we apply Western values, Omani men appear to exercise vast power over Omani women. They determine their movement and company. Yet if we use Rogers's framework and accept the Omani world view, with gender differentiation in both behavior and ideology, the power relationship between men and women is called into question. Since each inhabits a separate world and has a distinct nature, they are not to be compared – each gender is necessary for the other's survival.

As our discussion has indicated, behavioral differentiation occurs in our society along a variety of dimensions. But the question of whether ideological differentiation also occurs is more problematic. One alternative is to view men and women as fundamentally different. This is represented by the commonsense notion that differences between men and women reflect the "natural order" and by the view of those scientists who have tried to explain behavioral (and role) differences by arguing that men and women are fundamentally different. The alternative view is that men and women live in essentially similar conceptual worlds and that theories that seek to explain the behavior of men are also adequate to explain the behavior of women. This is represented by the commonsense notion that behavioral differentiation results from "conditioning" and by a parallel scientific view held until quite recently by most psychologists and anthropologists. In psychology this view has been called into question, for example, by Carol Gilligan (1982), who doubts whether the same developmental theory is applicable to boys and girls. In anthropology it has been challenged by the observation that male and female anthropologists have different models of the world (Ardener, 1972). We believe that although there is behavioral differentiation between men and women in our society, their conceptual worlds can be viewed as essentially similar, particularly when we contrast our society with others that show marked ideological differentiation between men and women, such as the Omani.

According to Rogers's analysis, when behavioral differentiation is associated with ideological similarity, this should result in a hierarchical relationship between men and women and in inequality in the distribution of material and social rewards. In Chapter 2 we discussed the considerable inequalities in men's and women's earning power. What other evidence is there for the accuracy of Rogers's analysis? Nancy Henley (1977) argued that there is ample evidence of a power imbalance between men and women in our society and that it can be seen in their behavior. She studied the nonverbal messages exchanged through smiles and frowns, glances and gestures, movements toward and away from others. Some scientists have used such observations to determine information about friendship, sexuality, and emotions. Henley believed that they are indicative of the dominance of men and the submissiveness of women. As part of her argument she demonstrated that the gestures described as those of dominance are those that bosses make to their employees regardless of gender. Examination of the behavior she observed (Table 5.1) and a moment's thought should confirm her contention that staring, touching, interrupting, and pointing – the gestures of dominance – are also gestures men characteristically make when they interact with women.

When these differences in nonverbal behavior are first pointed out, they come as a surprise. Men are usually not aware of their assertiveness or women of their compliance. One of Henley's aims has been to help people become conscious of the inequality their gestures indicate. Although men and women could claim that their actions follow only the dictates of convention and common courtesy, their interaction, at

Sex and gender

Table 5.1. *Gestures of dominance and submission*

Dominance	Submission
Stare	Lower eyes, avert gaze, blink
Touch	"Cuddle" to the touch
Interrupt	Stop talking
Crowd another's space	Yield, move away
Frown, look stern	Smile
Point	Move in pointed direction, obey

Source: Henley (1977), p. 187.

an unconscious and unintended level, has been shown to reflect the inequality of power between genders in our society. This is true whether we examine touching, gazing, personal space, or the use of time. These power relationships are also expressed in language (Spender, 1980).

The naturalistic study of communication leaves little doubt about the unequal distribution of power in our society and the widespread, though perhaps unconscious, recognition of male authority. Laboratory studies of power provide a less revealing picture of behavioral gender differentiation. Nonetheless, it has been suggested that the differences that do appear reflect inequalities in the structure of society (Eagly, 1983).

In laboratory studies of power, asymmetric relationships have been conceptualized primarily in terms of compliance, whether the particular variable is labeled "competition," "dominance," or specifically "compliance." Many laboratory studies use a game format in which one player can impose a decision upon another. Children have been studied using a device that breaks apart if both children pull it but that will yield a marble to the noncontender if only one child pulls. Competition leads to joint failure, whereas cooperation produces success for one person. Although Maccoby and Jacklin (1974) were skeptical about the use of this game – in which competition is clearly maladaptive – they reviewed twelve studies involving children between three and eleven years of age. Gender differences occurred in only some of the studies; but when they did occur pairs of boys tended to be more competitive and pairs of girls more cooperative. When boys were paired with girls, the boys became more cooperative; and girls paired with boys became more competitive.

"Prisoners' Dilemma," a more abstract and adult game, is also used to measure competition and cooperation. In this game both players are hypothetical prisoners accused of a crime. They may make one of two moves: either confess to the crime or deny it. If both refuse to confess, they must both be set free for lack of evidence. The prosecutor (experimenter) bargains and offers to be lenient if both confess, or, if only one confesses, to let him go free and give him a reward while his partner receives a stiff sentence. It is assumed that if a player chooses to confess he is more concerned with his own welfare (competitive motive), whereas if he refuses he is concerned about the welfare of his partner (cooperative motive). The game is usually played a great many times consecutively, and the resulting complexity in the payoff probabilities has led Nemeth (1973) to question whether the players are aware of the allegedly competitive and cooperative consequences of their choices.

Reviewing twenty-three studies based on "Prisoners' Dilemma," Maccoby and Jacklin found little evidence of consistent gender differences. Although Deaux (1976b) noted differences in players' strategies, she recognized the theoretical ambiguity that surrounds the identification of their motives. A competitive choice may reflect a desire either to gain a reward or to defeat an opponent. Similarly, in a cooperative choice the motive may be to maximize personal payoff, to disregard rewards altogether, or to strive to appear generous. In an attempt to disentangle these different motives, Wyer and Malinowski (1972) designed a variant of "Prisoners' Dilemma" in which it was possible to distinguish *competitive responses* – winning at a partner's expense – and *individualistic responses* – getting as much for oneself as possible. Although the direct comparison of men's and women's perfor-

mances revealed no gender differences, the gender of one's opponent was important, as it had been in the studies of children.
Men were more competitive against other men and against
highly successful players irrespective of gender, and women
were more competitive against low achievers of both genders. In
other words, men appeared keener to win at the expense of men
and winners, and women were more motivated to win when
faced with a loser. The position of men and women in society at
large appears to influence their signal value as challenging or
less challenging opponents within the confines of the laboratory
game.

Another way in which power has been conceptualized in
psychological experiments is in terms of leadership. When
gender differences in leadership ability are investigated, power
is often measured as a psychological trait and called "dominance." Deaux (1976b) reviewed leadership studies of adults in
groups. Two of her questions are of particular interest: "Do
women emerge as leaders as often as men?" and "Do men and
women cope with the role of leader with equal success?" Even
the election of women as national leaders in Israel, Britain, and
India cannot deceive us into believing that women are called or
rise to positions of leadership as often as men.

Deaux reported a study by Megargee (1969) in which men
and women were assessed for dominance by means of a questionnaire and then formed into pairs each containing one person high and the other low in dominance. Each pair was then
asked to chose a leader. When two women or two men were
paired, the more dominant person was chosen as leader 70
percent of the time. In mixed pairs that contained a more dominant man, he was chosen 90 percent of the time; but in mixed
pairs in which the woman was the more dominant person, she
was chosen as leader only 20 percent of the time. In the discussion prior to the choice of leader it was observed that it was the
dominant woman who usually decided that the man would be
the leader. The failure of a dominant woman to become leader
is difficult to understand if we consider only the final decision.

But if we look at the interaction that led up to it we can readily see that the dominant women were exercising power and control by choosing men as leaders. This study highlights the problems of research on dominance, in that there are observable differences between dominance as measured by a questionnaire and its behavioral manifestation in women's unwillingness to assume positions of leadership. Part of the explanation may lie in the position of men and women in society at large, as authority is expected to reside in men – they are employed as symbols of power, even when the decision is made for them by a woman.

The exercise of leadership has been shown to be influenced by symbolic power relationships in the wider community in a study by Jacobson and Effertz (1974). They set up all-male and all-female groups, groups with two men and a female leader, and groups with two women and a male leader. Individuals in all four types of groups evaluated the performance of their leader and fellow members after completing a difficult problem-solving task. The problem-solving performance of the four differently composed groups was considered equally poor by the experimenters. Despite this view that the groups had performed in a similar fashion, the male leaders were rated poorer by their fellow group members than were the female leaders. Leaders themselves, however, rated the performance of female group members below that of male group members. Commenting on these results, Deaux (1976b) suggested that they reflect gender stereotypes in that men are supposed to be good leaders and women good followers. According to this interpretation, groups that fail must have poor male leaders, while women in groups that fail must be poor followers. Not only are men expected to assume authority, but they are expected to exercise it with skill. Similarly, the submission of women is expected to be well practiced and successful.

Despite the ease with which we have fitted studies of competition and cooperation and of dominance and leadership into a framework of inequality in power relations between men and women in our society, it should not be assumed that the psychological picture is unambiguous. Maccoby and Jacklin's comparison of dominance in boys and girls was thwarted by the emergence of same-gender play groups in school-age children (see Chapter 9). These groups dominate the social life of boys and girls throughout middle childhood, and it is largely the awakening of sexual interest that results in some mixing of boys and girls in adolescence. Another difficulty in studying gender differences in dominance is a failure to differentiate between toughness, aggressiveness, and dominance. It is also difficult to measure dominance itself, as one must decide whether to measure only success in influencing others or intentions as well. As we have already noted, these problems occur both in examining the psychological power motive and in trying to conceptualize the exercise of power in society.

Restricting the definition of *power* to those acts that are successful in achieving compliance is an approach that has been used in laboratory games and in some naturalistic studies of decision making in situations of conflict. It ignores those aspects of asymmetric relations that Lukes (1975) identified as dependence and inequality. He labeled this the "one-dimensional" view. It has also been criticized by other social theorists who argue that power can be exercised by those in authority to keep conflict out of the decision-making arena, ensuring that there is no outcome to be observed. As an example of this "two-dimensional" approach to power, it could be argued that male interest in keeping the birth rate up prevents open discussion of abortion. In suggesting his own "three-dimensional" view, Lukes would argue that there was a further exercise of power by men to be seen in their ability not only to keep the issue of abortion out of public debate but also in shaping women's consciousness so that they did not question whether to have children. In response to this more subtle exercise of power based upon the control of consciousness, only recently has the issue of control over their own bodies been raised by feminists.

Given the very real complexities attached to the definition of *power*, it is hardly surprising that psychological studies appear partial and incomplete. In Lips's (1981) recent monograph on gender differences in power, the limits of a psychological approach are apparent. The headings under which she examines power are primarily psychological. The first four are "power as a quality attributed by one person to another," "power as a source of motivation to act," "power as a process of social influence," and "power as a trait or state of individuals" (in part reviewed earlier as dominance). Although she included a fifth approach to power, viewing it as an aspect of social structure, and concluded that power is more than an individual characteristic or trait (the first, second, and fourth definitions) but depends upon the control of resources, her predictions about power inequality were distinctly personal. Lips recognizes that men have greater access to and control of resources as the result of their position in the social structure, and she acknowledges that this status difference is socially constructed. Nonetheless, she also points out that men are, on average, larger and stronger than women and that this gives them an advantage in the pursuit of power. Seeking to avoid biological determinism, she suggests that women's current efforts to improve their physical fitness and strength may result in a change in the power relations between men and women. This curious conclusion may be a function of her narrowly psychological account of power. As we have already noted in examining other behavioral domains, in the absence of a well-articulated theory, explanations will reflect commonsense notions about the nature of gender differences.

6

Fear, anxiety, and mental health

Aggression, the subject of Chapter 5, and fear, the subject of this chapter, are closely linked emotional states. The same type of external conditions will often produce one or the other, and the switch from fear to aggression and vice versa can take place rapidly (Archer, 1976b). Fear inhibits aggression, and aggression inhibits fear.

If we consider the masculine and feminine stereotypes in our society, it is apparent that men are regarded as responding aggressively in the face of life's frustrations and difficulties. A closely related attribute, and one that more strongly and consistently prescribes male behavior, is that men are supposed to be brave and not show fear. Women, on the other hand, can show that they are afraid but are not supposed to behave aggressively. In modern Western society and in many other cultures, boys begin to learn early in life that they should not show fear and that they will be ostracized and ridiculed for doing so. This reluctance to show emotional "weakness" is maintained and strengthened throughout adult life, although many men will display such emotions in the privacy of their homes.

Male "bravery" is an integral part of many professional sports. Reporting on the reluctance of professional cricketers to wear helmets, the British sportswriter John Arlott wrote, "Batsmen were for long reluctant to take any steps to protect their heads from assault, for fear of being branded 'unmanly,' or even as one test player put it 'afraid' " (*Guardian*, June 12,

1978). In a similar vein, the phrase "to take your punishment like a man" means to accept it without undue complaint or emotional upset, or bravely.

Bravery is related to the masculine stereotype and as such is an ideal that is difficult to realize. The discrepancy between actual behavior and stereotypical demands may lead to difficulties. What happens if a man *is* afraid and cannot assume the confident aggressive manner that one of his gender is supposed to achieve? There are ways of making a frightened man feel tough. The use of drugs, alcohol in particular, is one. It is no coincidence that alcoholism has been mainly a male problem, because "Dutch courage" is needed more by men than by women. A song about Scottish drinking habits sums up the change of heart induced by alcohol: "Stone cold sober they come in like Mickey Rooney, / Three pints later they go barging out like big John Wayne" (Billy Connolly, in a British BBC television program, "Checkpoint," August 17, 1978).

How to get over feelings of fear and inadequacy can be seen as a recurrent male problem. Alcohol and drugs may provide one kind of (temporary) answer; presenting a tough, aggressive exterior is another.

Women, on the other hand, are much freer to express feelings of fear and inadequacy, and such responses usually get sympathy and comfort from others, particularly men. It is socially more acceptable for a woman to be fearful and timid than to be an alcoholic or too aggressive.

A partial explanation of the pattern of gender differences in aggression, fear, and mental health in terms of social attitudes is provided later in this chapter. It differs from the approach taken by those who suggest that there are biological differences in the emotional makeup of the two sexes and who argue that our social attitudes merely reflect these differences. Before discussing these and other explanations, we examine evidence for the claim that women are more fearful and anxious than men.

Are women more fearful and anxious than men?

There are relatively few studies that will help us to answer the question of whether women show a greater degree of fear and anxiety than men. Books on fear usually contain little or no information on the subject: For instance, in Rachman's (1978) book there is no entry for "sex differences" or "gender differences" in the index, and in Sluckin's (1979) their coverage is restricted to about half a page. More attention was paid to gender differences by Gray (1971b); he suggested that women show more pronounced fear and anxiety than men as a result of their hormonal constitution. We shall return to this explanation later.

Broadly speaking, there are three types of studies of possible gender differences in fear that we could consider relevant: those carried out on animals, on children, and on young adults. We are concerned here with gender differences in adult humans, and therefore studies of animals or children will be relevant only if they show clear parallels with adult differences. Such parallels were apparent in the case of aggression we discussed in Chapter 5. But on the subject of fear, Maccoby and Jacklin argued that the parallels with studies of rats and mice are slight and that there is little point in considering these studies in relation to human gender differences. Gray (1971a, 1971b) took a different view, which we shall outline later.

Maccoby and Jacklin (1974) reviewed studies of the development of fear responses in infancy. In some studies, girls first showed a fear of strangers at an earlier age than boys did, but this finding was not a consistent one, and it may indicate girls' intellectual maturity. Kagan (1978) reviewed several studies carried out subsequent to Maccoby and Jacklin's survey and argued from these that girls do generally show an earlier onset of fear of strange social situations than boys. Girls' fear response also wanes at an earlier age than that of boys. Kagan regarded this particular gender difference as part of the generally earlier maturation of girls than of boys, and he claimed that girls come to recognize strange and unfamiliar events and people at an earlier age. Is this early gender difference relevant to adult sex differences in fear? Kagan believed that it is not, and he argued that differences in the age of onset of the fear response in infancy are unlikely to have any long-term significance.

Maccoby and Jacklin (1974) also reviewed studies of older children's fears. They concluded that there is some evidence that girls are more fearful than boys, but this is not a consistent finding. The measures in these studies were either direct observation or parent's records. In older children and in adults, the most common measure is a questionnaire inquiring about the person's fears. Interpretations of questionnaire findings often fail to distinguish between how fearful people think they are and how fearful they actually are when confronted by something frightening. Thus most of the evidence on older children and adults has been obtained by asking people to rate how fearful they are rather than by assessments of their behavior. In the case of aggression, such self-report measures were seen to exaggerate gender differences along stereotypical lines (see Chapter 5). We can expect what people say about their fearfulness to reflect gender stereotypes about fear and courage as well.

Gender differences, when reported in questionnaire studies, tend to show females displaying greater intensity of fear than males (Maccoby and Jacklin, 1974; Block, 1976b). Since we have no experimental or observational studies to compare with these ratings, we cannot estimate the extent to which they reflect men's unwillingness to admit their fears. Maccoby and Jacklin also pointed out that many of the questions are biased toward items more likely to be related to girls' than to boys' fears: For instance, items include fear of animals and of walking home alone at night, but not fear of failure or appearing cowardly.

Klorman et al. (1974) found that specific fears of small animals, such as snakes and spiders, were reported more often by a sample of British women than by men. In a study that supports the conclusion that such reports may be better indicators of behavior for women than for men, Speltz and Bernstein (1976) set out to differentiate between willingness to admit fears and actual expression of fears: Male and female undergraduates who had reported either high or low fear of snakes (assessed by a fear questionnaire) were given a behavioral test that involved being asked either to enter a room containing a snake or to pick up a snake. Among people who reported a high degree of fear, men were generally more often able to enter the room or go near a snake than women. These results indicate that men who described themselves as highly fearful were more able to overcome their expressed fears when confronted with a real snake than were highly fearful women.

Although we should be cautious about generalizing from a single study of a particular type of fear, Speltz and Bernstein's results do suggest that even when men and women are matched for equivalent levels of reported fear, women actually show more avoidance of the feared object. There may be a different relationship among stereotypes, self-reports, and actions than we have so far considered. The stereotype may influence men's actions more than it does their verbal reports. Does this mean that it is easier for a man to say, "I'm scared of snakes" than to appear frightened?

This discussion is highly speculative, since there are comparatively few experimental studies of gender differences in fearfulness. Another possible source of information is clinical evidence, but again we have the problem of the discrepancy between what people say and what they do. Women apparently report more phobias—extreme fears that interfere with their everyday living—than do men (see the later section on mental health).

Anxiety is an emotional state similar to fear in many of its physical manifestations; it is not, however, directed toward specific objects or people and is usually more prolonged. Self-report questionnaires based on symptoms such as difficulties in sleeping or headaches are available for assessing anxiety states in both children and adults. The consensus from available studies of children is that girls report greater general anxiety than boys. Similarly, clinical anxiety states are found more frequently in women than men; these are discussed later in the chapter in the section on mental health.

How can we explain these findings? We first consider a biologically based viewpoint. In a wide-ranging article, Jeffrey Gray suggested that there are biologically based gender differences in both aggression and fear (Gray, 1971a). His argument on aggression is reasonably straightforward: The male is the more aggressive sex in the animal world. However, animal sex differences in fear have not been so widely studied, and there is no clear pattern to compare with human gender differences. Gray based his particular argument almost entirely on laboratory tests of fearfulness, or "emotionality," in rats and mice (Archer, 1973). These tests mainly involve assessing the extent of an animal's "emotional" defecation and its reluctance to move when it is put into an unfamiliar, brightly lit, enclosed area. On the basis of such tests, Gray suggested that male rodents are more fearful than females. Although his interpretation of the rodent tests is in dispute (Archer, 1971, 1975; Gray, 1979), this particular issue is not essential to Gray's theory of human gender differences. He did not base his argument about human gender differences directly on evidence from rats and mice; rather, he used the studies to show that some animals display sex differences in fearfulness and that these are under the control of their sex hormones. He then suggested that although the human gender difference is in a direction opposite to that suggested for rats, it nevertheless has a similar biological–hormonal–basis. Gray cited no direct evidence that sex hormones are involved in the human gender difference, but speculated whether the difference he identified between rodents and human beings exists between primate and rodent groups or between human beings and other mammals (Gray and Buffery, 1971). There is very little evidence on which to evaluate his hypothesis, and until information is available from a much wider range of animals there is very little that can be derived from such a forced and speculative comparison of laboratory rodents and human beings. The argument for a biological basis to human gender differences in fear is therefore a particularly weak one (Archer, 1971, 1975).

An alternative explanation is one that seeks to show how stereotypical beliefs about gender are transmitted to children throughout the process of "socialization" (see Chapter 9). Boys and girls receive different messages from adults and other children about when they can show fear, anxiety, and similar emotions. Early in life, boys come to realize that they must avoid certain "feminine" types of behavior (David and Brannon, 1976). Among these are too open an expression of emotional upset, such as crying or whining, or readiness to display particular fears. Boys and girls show some knowledge of masculine and feminine stereotypes even at early ages. One of the characteristics that young children of two to three years of age attribute to a "boy" doll is that he "never cries" (Kuhn et al., 1978). Children between five and eight years old know many of the adult stereotypical personality descriptions, including the "feminine" characteristics of emotional and weak (Best et al., 1977).

We can only provide the broad outlines of such an explanation for gender differences in fear and anxiety. In contrast to the well-studied subject of childhood aggression, there has been little or no research into the degree to which boys and girls imitate emotions such as fear or anxiety shown by people of the same and of the opposite gender; nor have we found any research documenting the degree to which the expression of emotional upset and fear is encouraged or discouraged in boys and girls.

Are women moodier than men?

The question of whether women are moodier than men is often asked in relation to the more pronounced and regular fluctuations in reproductive hormones that occur throughout a woman's life. Thus the question becomes "Do women's hormones make them moodier than men?" More specifically, women are said to be particularly prone to emotional outbursts or depression prior to menstruation, immediately after childbirth, and at the menopause, and changes in hormonal levels at these times are held to be responsible. What is the evidence for such claims? Let us look first at the menstrual cycle.

A variety of psychological changes have been reported during the different phases of the monthly cycle. The best known of these are negative mood changes, such as anxiety and irritability, reported by many women just before menstruation. These are generally measured by a self-assessment health and mood questionnaire, the Menstrual Distress Questionnaire (Moos et al., 1969). Although similar changes have been shown in some laboratory studies (e.g., using behavioral measures of frustration: Schonberg et al., 1976), there is little experimental evidence for general changes in task performance across the menstrual cycle (Ruble and Brooks-Gunn, 1979; Sommer, 1982). Although there are some positive findings (e.g., Vila and Beech, 1978), overall there is little conclusive evidence of increased physiological arousal or reactivity during the premenstrual phase (Sommer, 1982; Strauss et al., 1983).

Dalton (1969, 1979) had claimed that there is evidence of poorer examination performance and increases in antisocial or "neurotic" activities, such as shoplifting, accident proneness, and attempted suicide, prior to menstruation. However, her claims have been dismissed on the grounds of methodological inadequacy and have not been replicated in other studies (Parlee, 1982; Sommer 1982).

In the medical literature, the behavioral and mood changes are commonly linked with physical changes such as water retention and changes in the balance of mineral salts. These are referred to as the "premenstrual syndrome," a term that was first used in the 1930s (Janiger et al., 1972; Clare, 1979) and that carries the connotation of a specific illness. The medical view of premenstrual symptoms has several consequences, two of which have been pointed out by feminist writers such as Birke and Best (1982): First, it can provide a rationale for occupational discrimination; second, because it implies physiological malfunction, alleviation of symptoms is sought through drug treatments. Several specific hormonal explanations have been offered for the premenstrual mood changes by medically qualified researchers (Clare, 1979; Green, 1982). Perhaps the most common one involves progesterone deficiency or imbalance (Hamburg and Lunde, 1967; Dalton, 1969, 1979), although the hormone aldosterone, which affects mineral salt balance, has also been implicated (Dalton, 1969).

Evidence for hormonal explanations of premenstrual mood changes is, at best, indirect and unconvincing. Direct measurements of progesterone, aldosterone, and prolactin have all failed to support hypotheses implicating these hormones (Clare, 1979, 1983). Most of the evidence cited in support of hormonal theories is derived from the putative therapeutic effects of hormonal intervention – for example, through injections of progesterone (Dalton, 1979) or oral contraceptives containing synthetic progestogens and estrogens (Bardwick, 1971, chap. 2). Assessments of these and other forms of premenstrual treatments (Clare, 1979; Green, 1982) reveal little or no evidence for any improvement when the treatments are subjected to double-blind trials (i.e., where neither doctor nor patient knew the nature of the treatment). Green (1982) concludes, "At present, positive attitude appears to be the most potent item in the premenstrual treatment armamentarium."

In the early 1970s, several women psychologists in the United States (e.g., Parlee, 1973; Sommer, 1973) argued that the widespread negative attitudes to menstruation in our culture could explain both the occurrence of mood changes and the severity of distress occasioned by physical symptoms. Such a viewpoint often provokes hostility from women who suffer badly from premenstrual symptoms, since they regard any psychological explanation as implying that they are neurotics or hypochondriacs. Despite specific assurances that this is not intended or implied (Paige, 1973; Birke and Best, 1980), it remains a common reaction.

Supporters of the psychological view of premenstrual mood changes have marshaled considerable evidence for their case for more than a decade. Findings that crimes or accidents tend to occur during the premenstrual phase (Dalton, 1969, 1979) have been shown to be inadequate on statistical grounds (Parlee, 1973; Sommer, 1973; Tavris and Offir, 1977) and have not been replicated (Parlee, 1982). Furthermore, such traumatic events may themselves bring forward the time of menstruation, so that the event only appears to be premenstrual in retrospect (Birke and Best, 1982; Parlee, 1983). Similarly, Dalton's (1969) claim for poorer examination performance in English schoolgirls during the premenstrual phase was dismissed as statistically unreliable and has not been replicated either in earlier or later studies (Parlee, 1982; Sommer, 1973, 1982).

Evidence from self-reports of mood changes is consistent with the view that such reports are strongly influenced by knowledge of the phase of the menstrual cycle, which, combined with negative beliefs about menstruation, leads to exaggerations of the extent of the negative changes. The strongest evidence for marked mood changes is found in restrospective studies, where women have to remember what they felt like at previous phases of the cycle. In prospective studies, where present mood is assessed at different times, mood changes were reported less frequently, their magnitude was less pronounced, and a smaller proportion of women reported severe symptoms (Ruble and Brooks-Gunn, 1979; Parlee, 1982). In a further two studies, where the purpose of the questionnaire was disguised, no evidence of premenstrual mood changes was found (Englander-Golden et al., 1978; Vila and Beech, 1980).

One intriguing study has even shown that knowledge of the phase of the cycle is *by itself* sufficient to produce symptoms. Ruble (1977) informed young women that it was possible, through a new scientific technique, to predict the exact date of menstruation. All the women were in fact about a week before their next period, but some were told that they were immediately premenstrual, others that they were one week before, and a third group that they were ten days premenstrual. Ruble found that those women who *thought* that they were premenstrual reported experiencing a higher degree of "premenstrual" symptoms, such as water retention, than did those who though they were intermenstrual.

Other types of evidence for the psychological view include a study by Clarke and Ruble (1978), who found that premenarcheal girls (and young boys) have a well-defined and mostly negative set of attitudes and expectations about menstruation, believing that it will be accompanied by physical discomfort, increased emotional feelings, and disruption of normal activities. Paige (1973) discovered that the severity of menstrual symptoms was related to cultural attitudes and reflected different religious beliefs. Among Jewish women, adherence to menstrual taboos prescribed by their faith was most likely to be strongly correlated with severe physical and emotional symptoms. For Catholic women, traditional views about a woman's role – that a woman's place is in the home – were more likely to be linked with severe menstrual symptoms. Since it is unlikely that the severity of physical symptoms could have caused these particular social and religious beliefs, and since religion provides the main source of negative attitudes about menstruation and sexuality in our culture, Paige's study provides evidence for the importance of specific negative attitudes to menstruation in determining perceived menstrual distress.

On the basis of the type of evidence we have just described, Ruble and Brooks-Gunn (1979) put forward a social psychological theory of menstrual symptoms as an alternative to what they see as the more widely accepted (but poorly supported) hormonal theories. Social context and cultural beliefs are increasingly being taken into account when considering the perception and meanings of medical symptoms (e.g., Melzack and Wall, 1982, in relation to pain perception). Ruble and Brooks-Gunn discussed menstrual symptoms in terms of a process that links perception of the body's psychological and physical state with knowledge of the phase of the cycle and with beliefs about premenstrual symptoms. Such beliefs are, they argued, well known and almost universally perceived in a negative way and will bias every stage of attributing meaning to symptoms that occur premenstrually. The authors discussed in some detail the possible mechanism through which such biases might operate.

A slightly different interpretation of menstrual distress is given in a British study by Clare (1983). On the basis of questionnaire evidence, he concludes that some form of premenstrual change is widespread (but see above for some reservations about such evidence). Since he finds that the magnitude of such complaints increases with poor health and with marital dissatisfaction, he also concludes that many women tolerate menstrual symptoms until they have additional problems. This view – that symptoms are present all the time but are not complained about – contrasts with Ruble and Brooks-Gunn's view that the symptoms themselves arise from a woman's perceptions of her bodily state (including general health) and her social context (which includes marital satisfaction).

We have discussed premenstrual mood changes in some detail since the subject is a controversial and comparatively well-researched one. Emotional changes of a more severe kind have often been reported after childbirth. These include depression, fearfulness, and irritability, and various surveys carried out in the 1950s and 1960s in the United States found some form of emotional upset in as many as 30–60 percent of women (Sherman, 1971). It has again been suggested that hormonal changes, such as the sudden fall in progesterone levels, cause the negative mood (e.g., Hamburg and Lunde, 1967) and that susceptibility is linked to premenstrual symptoms (e.g., Dalton, 1971). Although the subject has not been so well researched as premenstrual changes, alternative psychological explanations have also been offered to account for these emotional changes. Paige (1973) suggested that a woman would have good reason to react emotionally to all major reproductive events, since they represent her main avenue of achievement and self-expression. Thus, reacting to the reality and the responsibility of looking after a baby after the excitement and anticipation of pregnancy and to the realization that freedom, mobility, and social contacts are curtailed could well cause depression. These suggestions are speculative since very little research has been carried out on this subject. One exception is a study by Breen (1975), who sought to understand the meaning of a woman's first pregnancy and childbirth. Good adjustment was related to factors evident during pregnancy and after the birth. Successful mothers saw themselves as active both before and after the child was born. If women are deprived of a feeling of control by obstetric practices, this may place them at risk at a time when their hormones are changing dramatically.

In a book on postnatal depression, Weldburn (1980) argued that hospital deliveries can significantly increase the risk of depression by removing a woman's feeling of control. Further, she suggested that factors such as tiredness, a sense of social isolation, and loss of independence, status, and money can also be important determinants of emotional changes when a woman becomes a mother.

Anxiety, irritability, and depression have also been reported as accompanying the menopause (e.g., Sherman, 1971; Tavris and Offir, 1977). Again, these have been attributed to a direct effect of hormonal change – in this case the decline of estrogen (Dalton, 1979) – but there is no convincing evidence for this view. A more plausible explanation is that menopausal mood changes represent a response to the physical symptoms of the menopause and to the significance of the menopause as a sign that reproductive life and the younger years are over. A woman may also be subject to outside stresses at this time. A well-known study by Bart (1971) found that depression in a sample of middle-aged women was related to the loss of the maternal role that often occurred at about the same time as the menopause. Greene (1981) found that several types of stressful life events that tend to increase at this time (e.g., the death of a close relative or friend) were more potent influences on supposedly menopausal symptoms than the menopause itself.

What can we conclude from this survey about the theory that a woman's hormones are directly responsible for mood changes before menstruation, after childbirth, and at menopause? First, we can conclude that the evidence is certainly not as convincing as it might have appeared at first sight. Secondly, there are plausible alternative explanations in terms of the attitudes, beliefs, and expectations surrounding significant changes in a woman's reproductive life. A more comprehensive explanation of the mood changes would have to include consideration of both the physical changes and their significance for the women concerned.

Although it has been common to ask whether a woman's emotions are linked to her reproductive hormones, the same question has seldom been asked for men. It is of course easier to tell when a woman's hormones are changing owing to their more regular fluctuations and external manifestations. Men undergo quite large fluctuations in testosterone levels, but these neither are accompanied by obvious external signs nor follow an identifiable and regular pattern. One study (Doering et al., 1974) investigated the possible relationship between what men said about their emotions and their testosterone levels. A sample of twenty young men were used, and the measures were obtained every other day for two months. A relationship between the two was found for some individuals but not for others. The precise relationship between emotional state and hormone levels also varied across individuals. The strongest overall relationship of testosterone and mood was with depression, but again there was a great deal of individual variation.

Are there gender differences in mental health?

So far we have considered fear, anxiety, and related emotions experienced by men and women. When we look at the more extreme states of fear and anxiety, those that interfere with normal living and are viewed as mental illness, we find that gender stereotypes are again important. As we saw in Chapter 5, crime statistics reinforce our notions of the aggressive male. Similarly, when we look at reports on mental health or psychological disorders, the stereotypical description of women as more emotional than men is echoed by the greater number of women in many categories of mental illness. So striking is this comparison that one modern observer has offered a new twist on Freud's dictum that the neuroses are the negative of the perversions by describing the neuroses as the "negative of criminality" (Zerssen, 1976).

Despite the problems that gender stereotypes raise in a comparison of mental health in men and women we will consider the extent to which various types of disorders occur in the two genders. We begin by looking at statistical reports and then consider possible explanations for differences in mental health. As with many other comparisons of men and women, different types of explanations have been used to account for the same findings. Theories may stress biological differences; they may seek to explain vulnerability by looking at the world of inner experience; or they may indicate different sources of stress in the daily lives of men and women.

Psychiatric diagnosis is often problematic, and the very concept of mental illness has been attacked (Laing, 1967; Szasz, 1970). As we noted when discussing suicide in Chapter 2, the statistics do not speak for themselves. Unless issues concerning classification are analyzed critically, the numbers presented under various headings may have little meaning.

In a series of lectures considering the problems of modern medicine, Kennedy (1980) showed that the difficulties in the diagnosis of mental illness are not unique to it. The decision to label an individual ill requires that a judgment be made irrespective of whether the illness is physical or mental. The decision that physicians, sufferers, and others who are concerned must make is whether the condition (be it physical or behavioral) is sufficiently different from the norm to be considered an illness. In the field of psychiatry there are particular problems that relate to the dual focus on mind and body. Many experts believe that behavioral symptoms will eventually be reducible to physical, usually biochemical, malfunctioning. It is this as-yet-unproven hypothesis that Szasz (1970) attacked when he argued that mental illness is not the result of biological difficulties but that madness is a product of society. Laing's (1967) argument that those labeled mentally ill are victims of the norm subverts the entire diagnostic process, which rests upon some implicit notion of mental health as a norm.

Defining the norms of mental health is undoubtedly a more hazardous undertaking than estimating the normal range of glucose in the blood or of pulse rates. Knowledge of what constitutes appropriate behavior and feelings is important, as experts, usually psychiatrists, are called upon to judge whether particular behavior and feelings deviate from the norm.

In a classic study, Broverman and her colleagues (1970) investigated the impact of gender stereotypes on the norms of mental health. They asked professional clinicians to describe a healthy person, a healthy man, and a healthy woman. The verbal portraits of a healthy man and a healthy person were very similar; a healthy woman, however, was seen as more conceited, excitable in a minor crisis, submissive, and emotional and less adventurous, aggressive, competitive, independent, and objective. The work of Broverman et al. (1970) demonstrated that very different standards are used in making judgments of mental health and illness in men and women.

Kaplan (1983) takes their conclusions farther. In the context of the 1980 revision of the American Psychiatric Association's *Diagnostic and Statistical Manual of Mental Disorders* (DSM-III), she argues that the norms applied in judging women's behavior as indicative of illness are biased according to the feminine stereotype. To illustrate this she suggests that only those aspects of dependence typical of women's behavior are classified as symptomatic; the dependence of men is ignored. Her critics have marshaled evidence to show that there is no overall bias against women – in some categories there are more male patients – but in total, more women are reported to suffer as the result of mental illness (Kass et al., 1983; Williams and Spitzer, 1983). Her critics maintain that results based upon the DSM-III are not artifactual. These issues are controversial and not readily resolved by debate. As in Chapter 2, we again need to approach official statistics with considerable caution.

Official statistics

In this section, which deals primarily with official statistics, our figures are based upon established psychiatric practices in the classification of mental disorders. The diagnosis and categorization of English mental-hospital admissions are based on the *Manual of the International Statistical Classification of Disease, Injuries, and Causes of Death* (1967). In the American studies the 1968 and 1980 editions of the American Psychiatric Association's *Diagnostic and Statistical Manual* was often used. These systems rely on the appearance of crucial index symptoms or constellations of symptoms for the diagnosis of specific disorders.

A few definitions may usefully be kept in mind while examining these statistics. Full definitions that involve a theory about mental illness are beyond our brief. It is generally agreed that the most severe disorders are the various *psychoses*, which involve loss of contact with reality, self, or other people. Those behavioral disturbances with a recognized biological component, such as alcohol poisoning or severe infection, are grouped together and described as *organic psychoses*. The many psychoses with no known pathology of the central nervous system are usually termed *functional psychoses*. This category includes the *schizophrenias* with observably bizarre behavior, certain *paranoid states*, and severe *affective disorders* such as *manic–depressive psychosis*, with its altering moods of intense elation and despair.

The *psychoneuroses*, which include anxiety attacks, irrational fears such as agoraphobia, hysteria, and various obsessions and compulsions, are considered milder disorders. This does not mean that individuals necessarily experience less distress; but they may be able to function at work and in the family, and some may never seek treatment. Clearly it is difficult to estimate the number of psychotics and neurotics who never seek treatment, though community surveys provide some indication of the number of people who are ill but have not sought treatment.

With these general distinctions in mind we can examine some statistics. We begin by considering first admissions to all mental hospitals and units in England in 1979. Table 6.1 shows the actual number of first admissions according to standard diagnostic categories and the proportions of men and women in the various categories.

The only diagnosable categories in which men predominate are alcoholic psychosis, alcoholism, and drug dependence. The categories with the highest proportions of women are depressive psychoses, psychoneuroses, and senile and presenile psychoses. The greater life expectancy of women contributes to their predominance in the last-named category. The overall picture to emerge from these statistics is one of more frequent first admissions of women (58%), particularly in the categories of the functional psychoses and psychoneuroses.

A similar pattern has been reported in the United States (Gove and Tudor, 1973). Again women predominate; 52 percent of first admissions diagnosed as suffering from functional psychoses are woman, while 59 percent of those described as psychoneurotic are women. These percentages rise for people discharged from out-patient psychiatric clinics and reach their peak in general hospital treatment, where women comprise 59 percent of those treated for functional psychoses and 65 percent of those treated for psychoneuroses.

Studies of communities and analyses of treatment by general practitioners produce similar statistics (Gove and Tudor, 1973). A study of doctors in New York City found that women were more frequently diagnosed as suffering from psychological disorders (Locke and Gardner, 1969). These figures were analyzed by age

Table 6.1. *First admissions to mental hospitals and mental-health units in England, 1979*

	Men	Women	Total
Schizophrenia, schizo-affective disorders, and paranoia	2,000 47%	2,238 53%	4,238
Depressive psychosis and involutional melancholia	1,342 35%	2,488 65%	3,830
Alcoholic psychosis	136 68%	63 32%	199
Senile and presenile	1,906 35%	3,559 65%	5,465
Other psychoses	1,826 38%	3,020 62%	4,846
Psychoneuroses	2,274 34%	4,401 66%	6,675
Alcoholism	2,559 72%	997 28%	3,556
Drug dependence	237 69%	108 31%	345
Personality and behavioral disorders	2,253 49%	2,350 51%	4,603
Other psychiatric conditions	5,367 38%	8,799 62%	14,166
Undiagnosed	467 51%	446 49%	913
All diagnoses	20,608 42%	28,629 58%	49,237

Source: Based on Department of Health and Social Services (1982).

as well as by sex and showed that the period from thirty-five to forty-four years of age was that of the greatest vulnerability for women: 25 percent of their problems were diagnosed as being of a psychiatric nature. The peak decade for men was between forty-five and fifty-four years, but even then only 16 percent of their symptoms were considered evidence of psychopathology.

An English study of general practitioners reported related though not strictly comparable findings. All visits to a group of

Table 6.2. *Patients leaving treatment in 933 outpatient clinics in the United States, 1961*

	Men over 18	Women over 18	Total
Total patients	33,046	44,966	78,012
Psychoneurotic disorders	6,543	14,302	20,845
Phobic reactions	169	452	621
As a percentage of total	.5	1.0	
As a percentage of psychoneurotic disorders	2.6	3.2	

Source: Based on Frazier and Carr (1967).

London doctors were monitored for a year. For every 1,000 women registered with a particular doctor, 175 visits during the year involved diagnosis of a psychiatric illness, while only 98 visits per 1,000 registered male patients involved a similar diagnosis (Shepherd et al., 1966). Within these groups, women were more likely to be described as suffering from some form of psychoneurosis – 67 percent as compared with only 57 percent of men so diagnosed.

So far we have focused on functional psychoses and psychoneuroses generally, but other disorders may furnish clues to experiences of unusual fear and anxiety – namely, phobias and physical illnesses with an origin in psychological distress. Few surveys report phobic reactions alone. Frazier and Carr (1967) used statistics based upon reports from out-patient clinics in the United States. Looking at their findings in Table 6.2, we see a familiar pattern. Not only were there more women among all patients leaving the clinic after treatment, but there was also a higher percentage of women in the psychoneurotic and phobic reaction subcategories.

Illnesses such as stomach ulcers and backache are believed to reflect an emotional conflict, though their symptomatology is somatic. Men and women show different patterns here: Men are more likely to develop gastric and duodenal ulcers and skin disorders, while migraine, high blood pressure, and insomnia

are more common in women (Garai, 1970). It has been suggested that women more often react to emotional conflict by
developing a psychological disorder, whereas men more often
display physical symptoms; but Gove and Tudor (1973), using
hospital statistics, community surveys, and studies of general
practitioners, reported a higher incidence of psychosomatic disorders among women. Although we cannot provide a defini-
tive conclusion, it appears most unlikely that the psychosomatic illnesses, taken as a group, are more common among
men; in fact there is some evidence that more women report
suffering from these complaints (Mayo, 1976).

Suicide is included in this discussion of mental health even
though the meaning of each act is not clear. We assume that
people who succeed have been deeply distressed; and even if
we interpret unsuccessful suicide attempts as cries for help,
some fear, anxiety, or depression is undoubtedly present. The
statistics are unequivocal: More men than women commit suicide, and they use more violent methods (Stengel, 1964). However, the reverse is true of attempts at suicide: In 1970 Garai
reported that four women attempted suicide for every man
who made an attempt. A more recent summary of worldwide
studies reported a female-to-male ratio of two to one in Australia, Great Britain, the United States, and Israel, a nearly
equal ratio in Poland, and almost two men attempting suicide
for every woman attempting suicide in India (Weissman and
Klerman, 1977). In all these countries suicide attempts have
increased in recent years. Rates of successful suicide among
women have also been rising, and the once-prevalent notion
that male suicide is related to career difficulties while female
suicide reflects interpersonal problems no longer seems ten-
able. In a study of suicide among American women the rates
for those who were medical doctors and psychologists was
reported to be almost three times as high as that of other
women (Schaar, 1974). From this last study we can conclude
that career difficulties are producing intolerable strains on
women. Loneliness and isolation, usually factors in the suicide

attempts of women, have been implicated in the suicides of elderly men in a British study (Whitlock, 1973).

The picture we have drawn is necessarily incomplete, but before we intepret these limited findings it is important to consider the impact of marriage on the mental health of men and women. Returning to suicide, we note a study by Gove (1972) that showed that marriage seemed to protect men from suicide even though across all categories – never married, divorced, widowed, and married – men committed suicide more often than women did. At an extreme, divorced men committed suicide four times as often as divorced women.

Marriage has a different effect on the mental health of women. Returning to the statistics for mental illness, single, divorced, and widowed women are comparatively free of psychological disorders, whereas married women seem to make up the bulk of women among the mentally ill (Williams, 1977). Among men we are more likely to find that the seriously ill, the schizophrenics, are single, perhaps because psychotic men find difficulty in establishing and maintaining a stable relationship and in providing a home. Speculation about the effects of marriage and its relation to mental health leads readily to a discussion of the demands of gender roles and their impact on psychological well-being. But before we examine this or any other explanation, we need to consider the reliability of the data we have presented.

Are gender differences in mental health reliable?

We have already discussed problems in both the diagnosis and the reporting of mental illness in men and women. These are complex issues, and we wish here to alert the reader further to possible sources of bias.

A reluctance to treat official statistics as evidence of a greater female susceptibility to mental illness has led to a variety of criticisms and attempts to challenge the evidence. As we already noted, Kaplan (1983) argues that the rules that determine

the judgment of mental illness are biased against women. Chesler (1972) asserted that mental illness is a career into which
women are pushed and that hospitalization may provide a
haven when role pressures become too demanding. Lipshitz
(1978) claimed that the problems of diagnosis are magnified by
the fact that the overwhelming majority of hospital doctors are
men, who may well expect women to be overemotional. The
willingness of physicians to ascribe psychological disturbances
to women is indirectly verified by the large numbers of American women who are prescribed psychoactive drugs – specifically, tranquilizers, sedatives, and stimulants (National Commission on Marijuana and Drug Abuse, 1973). This controlled
and legitimized form of addiction among women has been
compared with men's use of alcohol and illicit drugs (Stoll,
1978).

Adding to the tendency of male physicians to see women as
psychiatric patients may be women's own tendencies to seek
help. Studies have shown that women more frequently seek
help for emotional problems (Phillips and Segal, 1969). In addition, once individuals come to psychiatric clinics, doctors are
reluctant to admit that treatment is not required: They tend to
diagnose and prescribe for those seeking help (Ingham and
Miller, 1976).

Although it is difficult to measure directly distress or the
need for treatment, we can look at research on men's and
women's willingness to reveal intimate details about themselves. More than twenty years ago American studies suggested that women were more willing to reveal intimate details of their lives to close friends (Jourard, 1964). Since then,
there has been a general shift toward greater popular interest
in psychological phenomena. One of our undergraduates
compared letters to *Jackie,* an English magazine for teenage
girls, and found that the problems posed in 1978 were of a
more intimate, sexual, and interpersonal nature than those in
1968. A greater concern with the world of emotion and inner
experience may also be occurring in men, and it may be re-

flected in a greater willingness among men to reveal intimate details.

A greater willingness to reveal personal experiences and emotional problems is probably not the whole explanation for the higher reported incidence of mental illness among women. A study that systematically explored bias in reporting concluded that women did, in fact, experience more symptoms (Clancy and Gove, 1974). Despite the many methodological problems in this field, the evidence suggests that there is something other than women's greater willingness to seek help that results in the differential incidence of mental illness in men and women. We have noted already that surveys of mental health in the community at large avoid a help-seeking bias, and even these surveys suggest greater mental illness among women.

The reporting of high rates of depressive illness in women – 65 percent in Table 6.1 – has also come under attack. Again, it has been argued that the same underlying emotional condition more often produces physical symptoms in men. The possibility that alcoholism and crime may mask depression in men was considered in an exhaustive review of research reports, but the authors concluded that the greater incidence of depression among women is a reliable phenomenon and not a methodological artifact (Beck and Greenberg, 1974). On the basis of a thorough epidemiological survey, Weissman and Klerman (1977) concluded that depression is more common among women throughout Western society. Byrne (1981) offered support for their conclusions by providing evidence from a survey of both physical and psychological symptoms of depression in a nonpatient sample in Australia. He argued that the gender difference was not artifactual and that further search for the origins of the gender difference in depression was required. He asserted that his results could not be explained away by gender differences in the social sanctions that allegedly prevented men from reporting their symptoms, nor by claims that the specification of gender-appropriate behavior for women established them in the patient role.

How are gender differences explained?

Our discussion of mental illness in men and women has already drawn attention to a link between gender roles and stereotypes and the more frequent diagnoses of mental illness in women. Let us look more closely at this type of account and then move on to psychological and biological explanations.

Our statistics for mental illness in the United States are derived largely from the research of Gove and Tudor (1973). They approached the issue of gender differences in mental health from a sociological perspective and attempted to link the greater frequency of mental illness in women to gender roles. In particular, they examined the role of the housewife in order to show the risks inherent in it. Although their statistics were presented only as incidences of illness in men and women, their explanation hinged upon the role of the housewife. This gives it a middle-class bias, since working-class women are often forced by economic necessity to work as well as keep house. Gove and Tudor summarized the sources of stress for the housewife under five headings: (1) restriction of possibilities of gratification to home and family to the exclusion of work satisfaction; (2) frustration of needs for competent performance and achievement, as child minding and housework appear to require little skill and command little prestige; (3) lack of demands or structure, allowing time to brood over troubles; (4) limited satisfaction for working wives who view their careers as secondary, who experience discrimination in opportunity for advancement, and who carry a double load, working as well as keeping house; and (5) lack of specificity of demands in that women are required to adjust to their husband's and children's needs and expected neither to formulate nor to afford priority to their own aspirations.

Besides marshaling evidence for the different effects of marriage on men and women, Gove and Tudor considered historical and cultural factors. They pointed to different rates of mental illness in different communities, and they related co-

hesiveness of traditional communities to an overall lower incidence of mental illness, with even lower rates for women.
Economic stress and unemployment were reported in communities in which there was more mental illness, and in these
men outnumbered women in the ranks of the distressed. The
limits of sociological explanations become clear when we attempt to account for social change. Not only have women's
roles changed in recent years, but so too have men's roles,
and these changing gender roles undoubtedly influence each
other and incidences of mental illness. One example of such
change is provided by data from the Midtown Manhattan
study (Srole and Fischer, 1980). In a comparison of the incidence of mental illness in 1954 and 1974 it was shown that for
men and women of comparable age the rates for women had
declined while those for men had remained the same.

Psychoanalytic theory and learning theory have each been
combined with a sociological perspective to explain the higher
incidence of depression among women. Psychoanalytic theories of the causes of particular neuroses or psychoses do not
elaborate the theme of gender differences. Rather, this issue is
considered in the developmental theory of infantile sexuality
and is most clearly specified in terms of the Oedipus complex.
In Chapter 4 we noted that this aspect of the theory has come
under considerable attack because it posits that women, as a
result of their resolution of the Oedipus complex, are typically
more narcissistic, lower in self-esteem, and more dependent
than men. We saw that its critics, including psychoanalysts,
have sought to emphasize the influence of society on the development of women.

In a psychoanalytic account that considered societal influences on mental health and examined the increased incidence
of phobias in successful women after marriage, Symonds (1971)
argued that marriage and its implications of dependency may
act as a trigger when internal conflicts are already present and
unresolved.

Chesler (1972) followed a different strategy and related societal factors to Freud's classic work on depression, *Mourning and Melancholia* (1971). Here Freud differentiated real loss and its resolution through the mourning process from melancholia, in which the failure to come to terms with real or imagined loss leads instead to feelings of lower self-esteem and self-worth. In normal mourning the loving and destructive feelings toward the lost object are integrated, whereas in melancholia the destructive feelings are turned toward the self. Chesler argued that the same dynamic mechanism operates in depression in women, but that the loss – that of status as potent, mature members of society – is real. Women, she suggested, are socialized to accept loss, not to seek a strong ideal self. To deal with the anger this frustration induces, they turn it inward, with resulting depression. Chesler quoted the study by Bart (1971), which we discussed earlier in this chapter, linking depression in middle-aged women with their children leaving home; she noted the greater incidence of depression in women who had a large number of children. Chesler maintained that continuing satisfaction is denied even to women who accept the feminine role. This occurs because the role becomes superfluous when children grow up and leave home and because satisfactory performance is usually prevented when the family is large.

Another line of theorizing that has distant roots in psychoanalytic explanations of psychopathology views depression in terms of the feelings of helplessness that characterize it (Bibring, 1953). This approach has been developed by Seligman (1975) within a learning-theory framework. He has shown that individuals who repeatedly find themselves in situations in which their behavior cannot control unpleasant stimulation do not attempt to gain control later in manageable circumstances. In a laboratory experiment this effect was heightened when people were told that their problem-solving outcomes were determined by chance and among individuals who believed that luck determined their fate. Seligman argued that depression is characterized by helplessness specific to beliefs about one's ability to influence events, and he demonstrated this in comparisons of depressed and nondepressed people. In one study he showed the different effects of success and failure on the performance of these two groups in tests involving both skills and chance. His manipulation affected nondepressed people's expectations of success in tests of skill; but depressed people's expectations of performance on tests, both of skill and of chance, were unaffected.

We can only touch upon the thought-provoking results that Seligman's approach has yielded. The overall picture that emerged from laboratory studies of learned helplessness has led to the characterization of depression in terms of passivity, lack of observable aggression, and reduced effectiveness in solving problems. It has been suggested that the gender-role socialization of women leads to a similar outcome and that the adult role of women is one in which there is little opportunity for effective control (Litman, 1978). From similarities observed between the experimental induction of learned helplessness and an analysis of female life histories, Litman constructed a plausible account of the greater incidence of clinical depression among women.

Explanations of mental illness that draw heavily upon biological differences between men and women, although diverse, share a common starting point, linking female psychology and female physiology. What the psychoanalyst Helene Deutsch (1945) saw as the passive and masochistic tendencies of women she explained as adaptations to their reproductive functions in menstruation and childbirth. Her account is typical of theories that Osofsky and Seidenberg (1970) described as confused, fuzzy, and prejudiced in that they link female psychology to female biology but manage to separate male psychology from male biology. Gray's suggested hormonal account, considered earlier in this chapter, of why greater numbers of women experience fears and anxiety states is another example of this kind of thinking. We also examined the proposition that women show more marked mood fluctuation than men as a result of the hormonal changes associated with their reproductive lives. Some psychiatrists have focused on the use of oral contraceptives, childbirth, and menopause and have tried to relate these events to gender differences in psychopathology.

Evidence concerning the influence of hormonal factors on depression was examined in a scholarly review by Weissman and Klerman (1977). On a number of points the evidence was incomplete, and the authors concluded by suggesting closer collaboration between endocrinologists and psychiatrists in order to document the precise effects of hormones on depression, but they doubted that these factors would account for the large difference in male–female incidence. Evidence that mood variations during the menstrual cycle or oral contraceptives account for a greater incidence of female depression was inconclusive: Premenstrual tension could be found to contribute only slightly to the numbers of women among depressives, and particular physiological explanations could not be offered nor specific hormones implicated. Weissman and Klerman's conclusions are consistent with those based on other evidence, presented earlier in this chapter.

The search for an understanding of the impact of oral contraceptives has been impeded by serious methodological problems. It would not be ethically possible, in an effort to disentangle the psychological and physiological effects of the pill, to employ control groups who would receive inert placebos offering no hormonal protection from conception. Although the evidence of an increase in depression following childbirth is clear, a precise biological explanation is not forthcoming. We already noted that the notion that women are at risk as the result of extreme hormonal changes is called into question by the lower-than-average rate of mental illness during pregnancy. It is likely that the changes in life circumstances that the birth of a child entails are as important in relation to depression as the sudden changes in hormonal levels at birth.

Perhaps more surprising is the conclusion that the menopause is not characterized by an increase in mental illness generally or in depression in particular (Weissman, 1979). Life events such as the "empty nest" phenomeon described by Bart (1971) were seen to be of at least as great importance in accounting for continuing risks of mental illness as any hormonal changes triggered by the end of menstruation, a conclusion supported by other studies discussed earlier (e.g., Greene, 1981).

We have drawn upon only some of the biological explanations examined by Weissman and Klerman. They considered psychosocial accounts in an equally thorough fashion and concluded that it was most unlikely that any one of the explanations they had examined would provide an adequate account of the various illnesses described as depression.

The explanations we have considered, be they sociological, psychological, or biological, do not attempt to predict individual instances of mental illness. The approaches we examined leave unanswered the question "Why are relatively more women treated for certain mental disorders, especially depression?"

Even though it is not yet possible to offer an adequate explanation for the greater incidence of depression, psychoneuroses, and functional psychoses in women, we close this discussion by considering some research that constitutes a step toward a more complex and inclusive type of explanation. It also suggests why particular women may be at risk. It is a methodologically sophisticated and sensitive study reported in a volume as long as this one (Brown and Harris, 1978). We can only outline the theory, which was presented to account for clinical and subclinical depression among English women in Camberwell, a district of London.

Brown and Harris's study is not a treatise on gender differences per se. They only investigated depression in women and sought to explain the higher incidence among working-class than middle-class women in Camberwell. They were able to show that the differences occurred only during particular life stages – when working-class women had either one child younger than six years of age or three or more children under the age of fourteen years at home. Furthermore, they were able to account for class differences in depression in the face of equally stress-provoking life events involving long-term loss or disappointment, such as the death of a parent, grown children moving away, the discovery of a husband's infidelity, or the severe illness of a close friend. True, stressful life events were more common among working-class women with children, but even this does not account for the fact that the rate of clinical depression was four times greater in these women than in middle-class women who experienced the same degrees of stress.

Role identities and interpersonal and intrapsychic elements are each given a place in Brown and Harris's account of depression. The important intrapsychic elements are the absence of feelings of self-esteem and mastery. These echo Seligman's notions of learned helplessness. Inner feelings of self-worth are shown to be protected or exposed by role identities. Women able to maintain a positive outlook despite a distressing life event would typically have employment outside the home, an intimate relationship with husband or boyfried, and fewer than three children at home under the age of fourteen. No outside employment, lack of intimacy, and three children under fourteen were vulnerability factors associated with general feelings of hopelessness and clinical depression. The relationship between depression and a fourth vulnerability factor, loss of one's mother before one was eleven, has been specified more closely in recent years (Brown et al., in press). The importance of the experience of loss for enduring personality characteristics is not denied, but evidence has also been marshaled that showed that women who experience early loss and who deal unsuccessfully with premarital pregnancy are more likely to be women who subsequently find themselves in a marriage that locates them in the working-class. The greater likelihood that one or more of these vulnerability factors figured in the background of working-class women was invoked by Brown and Harris (1978) to explain the class difference in depression. We have chosen to conclude this chapter with their studies because they point the way toward a meaningful integration of some of the factors that may be invoked in future accounts of the different rates of depression and other mental illness among men and women.

7
The family

In this chapter and the next, we consider the worlds of home and work, the domestic and public spheres of social life. It is widely believed that a woman's place is in the home and a man's in the world outside the home. In Chapter 5 we considered the argument advanced by some feminist sociologists and anthropologists that it is male power that keeps women in their place – the home. Even when women are engaged in full-time employment, they are expected to clean, cook, and shop – to keep house for their families. Time-budget studies undertaken in the 1970s showed that the amount of time husbands spent doing housework was not influenced by wives' employment outside the home (Feldman, 1982). So pervasive is the view that it is proper for women to do housework that even among single employed Americans the time women reported spending on household tasks was twice that reported by men (Robinson and Converse, 1966).

Examination of the family and the world of work provides information about the typical behavior of men and women, their gender-appropriate roles and psychological dispositions. We challenge accepted beliefs by asking whether men can keep house and provide satisfactory care for young children and whether women have the abilities and motivation to fill skilled jobs and meet professional demands.

We begin our discussion of the family by picking up a major theme in comparisons of mental health in men and women – the impact of marriage on each gender. This emphasis on the family should not be interpreted to mean that we believe that the only legitimate unit within which to raise children is a family formed by a man and a woman in a legally sanctioned relationship. Yet marriage is a major institution in our society. An English study showed that in 1974 some 93 percent of women and 90 percent of men between the ages of forty-five and forty-nine had been married at some time in their lives (Leete, 1976). Nonetheless, with more frequent divorce, marriage at later ages, and widowhood, a significant part of adult life may also be spent living alone or in relationships outside legally sanctioned marriage.

The demographic data we reported in Chapter 2 noted household types besides those of married people with children and those of single adults. We saw that 11 percent of single-family households in England are composed of one adult and one or more children. As men remarry more quickly after divorce, and children usually live with their mothers, the majority of one-parent families are headed by women.

We begin our examination of the family by considering the impact of marriage on men and women and by examining the role of the housewife. Until quite recently sociologists focused on adult work roles outside the home, and that of the housewife was largely ignored. Female sociologists have sought to correct this omission (Gavron, 1966; Oakley, 1974). Again, in what may appear a biased manner, the contribution of mothers to child care has been carefully scrutinized by psychologists, while that of fathers has, until the past decade, been largely ignored. After examining the structure of the family, the roles in it, and its social function, we consider in detail one major function, that of child rearing. We first consider early attachment and the importance of the mother. After questioning whether women have a unique contribution to make to early development we compare the roles of mother and father in socialization.

Marriage and the family

In our society, when a woman is about to become a wife she usually expects – or is expected – to change her name and her residence, and sometimes her job may change as well. Women also change more than men psychologically as a result of marriage. A review of longitudinal studies reported that wives were likely to modify their personalities and their values in line with their husband's expectations (Barry, 1970). This study also noted that marital happiness was related to the husband's success both economically and at an interpersonal level. We have already seen that the loss of self-esteem and control in marriage entails psychological costs for women that are reflected in the greater incidence of mental illness, particularly depression, among married rather than single, divorced, or widowed women (Chapter 6). Being at work protects women from the full impact of marriage. Single women fare better than single men, for in our society men thrive on the care they receive in marriage whereas women are healthier living on their own. So, too, when a marriage partner dies, bereavement brings greater suffering to surviving husbands (Stroebe and Stroebe, 1983).

In theory at least, marriage brings changes for both sexes; a woman becomes a wife and usually a mother, while a man becomes a husband and usually a father. Indeed, it has been unusual for a man to assume the role of father outside marriage. In Table 7.1, adapted from one originally presented by Stoll (1978), we can see that the demands of marriage throughout the adult years are different for men and women.

Only as men reach retirement do their primary concerns shift from work to the family. In Stoll's five stages of female development, the primary focus for women is other people – their husbands, their children, their grandchildren, and finally, in widowhood, another partner. As Nancy Chodorow (1978) noted, the modern family, stripped of almost all the functions it had in earlier times, has become "a quintessentially relational and personal institution, *the* personal sphere of society."

In summarizing a topic as vast as the family in a few hundred words, it is easy to overlook differences of culture, class, and historical era. Sociological accounts, intent upon showing

Table 7.1. *Roles of men and women in a family household*

Stage of development	Men	Women
I. *Entry* Marriage or living together	Becoming a husband or mate: Change to responsibility status Redefine self as "mature"	Becoming a housewife: Change to dependent status Acquire domestic skills Redefine self as "mature"
II. *Expanding circle* Childbirth	Becoming a father: Increased support responsibilities Change in self-definition Readjustments in spouse role	Becoming a mother: Acquire child-care skills Restrictions on many activities Major self-redefinition Change in spouse role
III. *Full-house plateau* Completed family	Self resignation: Major redefinition of self Acquire fathering skills	Self-development: Increased community involvement Return to work part-time Acquire child-rearing skills
IV. *Shrinking circle* Departure of children	Self-change Change in self regarding sexuality and "masculinity" Disengagement from work Acquire leisure pursuits	Search for new roles: Becoming a grandmother Return to work or education full-time Reorient to spouse Change in self regarding sexuality and "femininity"
V. *Disengagement*	Widowed, divorced: Becoming a potential spouse Change to independent status Acquiring domestic skills	Widowed, divorced: Becoming a potential spouse Change to independent status Increased economic responsibility
(*Remarriage*)	Becoming a husband, stepfather: Change to responsibility status	Becoming a wife, stepmother: Change to dependency status

Source: Adapted from Stoll (1978).

that family roles are socially constructed, take care to point out the time-boundedness of views of family roles and functions that have been based upon the modern, middle-class family (e.g., Walum, 1977). The complete separation of production and reproduction – the economy of child rearing, as we know it – is only a few centuries old. Before the rise of modern industrial society, the family was often a social and commercial center. In rural areas women might work the land, look after livestock and poultry, make clothes, process and store food, as well as bear children and rear them. In cities the homes of the mercantile class were centers of trade and production. Passing merchants along with apprentices were housed and fed; children were trained; food, clothing, and household articles were made in the home. In the poorest families female labor extending beyond child care was necessary for survival. With the onset of the Industrial Revolution women and even young children were often found working in mines and mills. It is often forgotten that the professions have also undergone great changes. Two and three centuries ago women were active medical practitioners, functioning not only as midwives and nurses but generally providing care in the community (Mitchell and Oakley, 1976).

Urbanization and the concentration of production in factories relocated production; the rise of formal education weakened the apprentice system and education in the home; the manufacture of food and improved storage methods contributed to reducing dramatically the functions of married women. Baking bread and cultivating a garden have today come to represent a nostalgic quest for meaning and purpose in the life of married middle-class women, alongside the remaining functions of childbirth and child rearing (French, 1978). The idealization of housework is not restricted to women. One male author writes, "Household work is the last area of preindustrial craft work that we have left. . . . [It] should be held up and praised as a way of escaping the estrangement to which many are subject in modern life" (Beer, 1983). Neither the author nor the fifty-six men he surveyed were full-time househusbands; this may have allowed them to find pleasure in tasks that are obligatory for many women.

We already noted in Chapter 2 the growing numbers of married women working outside the home. The middle-class and upper-class Victorian ideal of women restricted to the home has been eroded. Indeed, it was never attainable for working-class women who in the past went to work before they reached puberty and who even in marriage worked to supplement the low wages of their husbands.

Insofar as the family has been stripped of most functions other than that of reproduction, it is tempting to seek in biology explanations of its continued existence. So alluring is this approach that even an avowedly feminist sociologist, Alice Rossi (1977), recently espoused it. Her assertation of biological necessity is noteworthy in that she had previously argued for sexual equality in the same journal, *Daedalus*. It is easy to discuss her affirmation of a biosocial approach to the family as reflecting the general retrenchment that the women's movement began to undergo in the late 1970s, but to do so would be to ignore the seriousness of her contribution to our understanding of the family. For this reason, we consider her current position at length and examine two critiques of it.

In her original paper Rossi (1964) adopted the view that women become mothers as the result of their socialization. From this position, she proposed an undifferentiated education for boys and girls – a stance that many enlightened parents adopt but have difficulty maintaining when it is undermined by the gender-stereotyped gifts of well-meaning friends and relations or the gender-differentiated world of formal education. From her later biosocial perspective, Rossi questioned the wisdom of striving for equal participation by men and women in the public sector and in the home; in particular, she expressed doubts about the quality of child care that can be provided by men and even by those women whose lives are committed equally to their families and to their work outside the home. This is certainly a radical change. Let us examine the argument Rossi put forward to support her new position.

Rossi's fundamental assertion is that sociological theories that ignore "the central biological fact that the core function of any family system is human contiguity through reproduction and care-rearing" (p. 2) are bound to be inadequate. Though she holds no brief for the older view of the isolated nuclear family as the sole normal institution for reproduction and child care, neither is she sympathetic to the egalitarian approach, which she sees as an attempt to deny or obliterate all gender differences between the sexes.

In terms of Rogers's model, which we examined in Chapter 5, the egalitarian position implies no behavioral or ideological gender differentiation – a view that Rossi questions but that is, in fact, close to her own earlier position. Rossi then regarded as desirable not only equal participation by men and women in the worlds of work and home but also the transfer of parental obligations to institutional care. She traced her later unease to her awareness of a deep separation between parenting and sexuality and of the impact of institutional life on young children. Her strongest statement was that "communally reared children, far from being liberated, are often neglected, joyless creatures" (p. 25). These observations and much self-examination led Rossi to seek answers in our evolutionary history. She argued for sex differentiation at a behavioral level and sought to provide ideological justification for this differentiation by asserting that the nature of men's and women's sexuality is different, as are their respective commitments to parenting. To do this she drew on evolutionary and hormonal accounts of differences between men and women.

Theories drawing on human evolutionary history in hunting-and-gathering societies, already familiar from Chapter 3, were elaborated by Rossi in a new direction. So far we have encountered arguments that locate the origins of men's greater size and aggressiveness in the utility of these traits to primordial hunters. Her assertion that women's manual dexterity, persistence, and physical and emotional endurance similarly reflect the reproductive success of those females capable of combining the bearing and care of their young with gathering and small-game hunting was new. Rossi was careful to disclaim strict genetic determinism, but argued instead that men and women learn different skills with differential ease. She asserted that men would require greater training to be as good parents as women because their interests in reproduction are primarily sexual and lack the female's strong relational bond to the young. Similarly, she claimed that female cosmonauts and soldiers require special training to compensate for the absence of male musculature. Rossi saw *fathering* as being socially learned, whereas successful mothering, she posited, evolved over millions of years.

But Rossi sought biological accounts beyond genetic explanations. She also considered the importance of fetal hormones in organizing the brain to respond in a gender-appropriate fashion. She reviewed the arguments we summarized in Chapter 3 regarding the interaction of hormones and behavior, but again emphasized potentials for gender-appropriate behavior. From the genetic code that organizes male and female physiology to hormones that regulate behavior, the message is that each sex more easily acquires behavior appropriate to its gender.

Rossi is open to criticism, but we must not underestimate her scholarship and sophistication. In spelling out the consequences of considering biological factors in role learning, she was careful to distinguish rare from common roles. For example, to become a neurosurgeon requires delicate manual dexterity, and this is more common in women. Rossi noted that very few people become neurosurgeons, and although social pressure has barred women – who are most likely to have the requisite aptitudes – there are still a few men with sufficient manual dexterity. When large numbers of manually dextrous workers are required, as in the electronic industry, women predominate. So too with parenting; here Rossi believes that nature gives women the edge. She characterized men as essentially less interested in the young and efforts to train male nurturing as unlikely to be successful. The unisex pattern, she claimed, is a masculine pattern through which children are neglected owing to reduced interest in, and commitment to, nurturing.

Despite her plea for contemporary sociological theory to incorporate knowledge from biology, Rossi did not sanction the rearing of children by women in isolated nuclear families. She is aware of the hazards this poses for women, and she also stressed the costs of such isolation for children in terms of sibling rivalry. This awareness led her to suggest the establishment of growth centers where children can learn how to interact with age mates and be trained by child development experts. Her emphasis is on the child's social development rather than on providing alternative supervision aimed at giving mothers the freedom to pursue careers or find jobs. Given the cost of such programs, Rossi proposed that growth centers might evolve as self-help groups, providing a sense of community for parents and children alike.

Rossi was aware that her views would draw fire from feminists – and they have. Cerullo et al. (1977–8) assessed Rossi's paper in the context of a retrenchment that they defined as the return to favor of the isolated nuclear family. While appreciative of Rossi's feminist contribution to studies of the family, they nevertheless disagreed with her choice of strategy to employ in the face of the apparent failure of egalitarian socialization to counter existing maladaptive gender differences. One strategy they suggested was to reexamine and refine socialization theory rather than look to biology to explain the failure of educational efforts, as Rossi did. Cerullo and colleagues cited a number of phenomena for which alternative explanations are possible. Regarding the long period of physical dependence of the human infant, for example, they contended that, rather than leading to an inbuilt need for bonding to the mother, it only demonstrates the need for prolonged infant care.

Whereas feminist scholars have sought explanations for the

virtually universal division of labor by gender in terms of economic conditions as well as of the socialization process, Rossi has played down these efforts and sought to locate the source of present gender roles in our evolutionary history. The counterargument is that Rossi is assuming the necessity of social organization as we know it (Cerullo et al., 1977–8). Rossi's new position also places women firmly in nature, makes natural society's existing institutions, and in fact represents a form of biological determinism. Her critics have asserted that the very model Rossi sought to pursue, that of interaction, was lost as soon as she attempted to determine from current conditions absolute estimates of the relative contributions of biology and social learning to women's gender roles and women's parenting abilities.

Nancy Chodorow (1978) has attacked Rossi's biosocial model not only on biological grounds but also in the context of her own account of mothering. Rather than ascribing women's mothering to genes, hormones, or socialization, Chodorow claimed that the question "Why do women mother?" remains to be answered. Along with Rossi, she found a simple socialization explanation inadequate and so looked to modern psychoanalytic accounts, particularly those in the field known as object relations theory, to explain the role of the mother in men's and women's inner worlds.

Chodorow's arguments take us back to the psychoanalytic concept of the Oedipal conflict, which we first encountered in Chapter 4. Post-Freudian theorists have examined the child's earliest years and have outlined differences in the development of adult sexual aims and love objects based on pre-Oedipal relationships. The very demands of male and female development become clearer when the importance to an individual of the first year of life and of the relationship to the primary mothering agent is considered. In the process of growing up, a boy need not relinquish his feelings for mothers, though he must renounce his desires for his own mother, but a girl must turn away from her mother only to compete with her or other women for the love and attention of her father and men in general. Boys can carry over into adult heterosexuality the qualities of their first love, but adult heterosexuality for girls involves loss of the mother to some extent and feelings of jealousy and competition with the mother as well as love in relation to the father. Chodorow saw these early experiences as crucial, since in heterosexual relations men and women live in very different inner worlds, significantly determined by their different experiences of primary love in the pre-Oedipal period. These differences influence not only adult relationships between men and women, but also mothers' responses to their male and female infants.

Chodorow's account is considerably richer than this summary indicates, providing detailed explanations of each gender's struggle for freedom from primary love and dependence as well as of the fantasies each entertains about its recapture. Yet the essential point is that the struggle is different for men and women. For the male it may result in hostility toward women, while for the female it can lead to idealization of the male. At the risk of oversimplification, we can say that men potentially regain the mother through heterosexuality, whereas for women the consequences of post-Oedipal heterosexuality, tempered as it is by pre-Oedipal wishes, are that they can regain the mother only by becoming mothers themselves. Thus, according to Chodorow, men and women have very different needs and feelings about bearing and looking after children.

In this discussion of gender differences as they are realized in the family, our attention has centered primarily on adults. We presented Chodorow's psychodynamic theory not as an account of development, but as an explanation of the willingness of men and women to accept the traditional roles of husband and wife, father and mother. In the section that follows, our primary focus is the growth and well-being of the infant and child per se. In looking at psychologists' descriptions of the optimal conditions for development, we seek guidelines for the optimal distribution of child-care responsibilities. Rossi has taken a firm stand on the issue. She believes that human evolution has predisposed women to being better caregivers than men. In the section that follows we examine psychological theories that seek to explain how the needs of children in their early years are best met.

Mothering and attachment

In entitling this section "Mothering and attachment," we follow the conventional terminology of psychological research and in so doing wish to draw attention to the pervasive stereotype of women as mothers. As we have just noted, many scholars, as well as laypersons, believe that it is natural for women to mother and that women are better able to care for children. We will explore the extent to which psychological theory and research support this view.

Developmental psychology has undergone dramatic changes in the past twenty-five years. These changes reflect shifts in the theoretical outlook of psychologists generally and are not confined exclusively to theories of child development. In line with an attack on behaviorism, the view that the infant is a passive lump of clay to be molded according to the needs of society has also been abandoned. Changes in psychological accounts of development also reflect shifts in public attitudes about family roles.

One of the scholars most influential in changing the public's view of the nature of infant development was John Bowlby. An expert in adolescent and child psychiatry, he was asked shortly after World War II to undertake a study of homeless children for the United Nations. His report, which has been the focus of much research and controversy, contains the widely quoted conclusion that "mother-love in infancy and childhood is as important for mental health as are vitamins and proteins for physical health" (Bowlby, 1951, p. 158). Bowlby's report had an immediate impact; major improvements in the institutional care of children were introduced, and middle-class Western women examined their mothering function much more carefully. Critics of Bowlby held his ideas responsible for speeding the return of women to the home after demobilization (*Sunday Times* [London], July 9, 1976) and for encouraging the social seclusion of women with young children (Morgan, 1975).

By the time a second, summary edition of Bowlby's conclusions was published in 1965, a good deal of new research had been undertaken. In her contribution to this revised edition, Mary Ainsworth, a colleague of Bowlby's, identified eight major issues. We list them here to indicate the flavor of the controversies surrounding Bowlby's ideas, although obviously some are beyond the scope of our discussion. Stated in the form of questions, the issues Ainsworth noted are the following: (1) How is maternal deprivation (which Bowlby equated with absence of mother-love) to be defined? (2) Can mothering be provided in an optimal manner by more than one person? (3) Are the effects of maternal deprivation the same in all children? (4) Does maternal deprivation impair all aspects of a child's development? (5) Can different developmental impairments all be traced to maternal deprivation? (6) Are the impairments permanent, or can they readily be put right? (7) Is maternal deprivation implicated in juvenile delinquency? (8) Are the results of deprivation that are seen in children raised in institutions a particular reflection of their lack of mothering, or are they a consequence of the general impoverishment of their environment?

Bowlby's original report identified a problem – that of psychological and developmental impairment in children – and sought an explanation for it in the mother–child relationship. Research that followed, including much of Bowlby's own, aimed at understanding this relationship, especially the processes of attachment and separation. Though trained in psychoanalysis, Bowlby was dissatisfied with psychoanalytic accounts of the growth of mother-love. Freud held that the choice of the mother as the baby's first love object developed from the feeding relationship – from the breast that initially satisfied a physical need. Academic psychologists of a learning-theory persuasion offered an account similar in its emphasis on the satisfaction of physical needs. They believed that the mother acquires incentive value and comes to be a secondary reinforcer for the infant through her temporal and spatial contiguity with primary drive, physical need, and satisfaction.

A serious challenge to these "cupboard-love" theories came from Harry Harlow's experiments with infant monkeys (Harlow, 1958). He substituted inanimate objects for mothers and observed the development of baby monkeys. Harlow devised two sorts of surrogate mothers, each with a face and each able to provide milk. One was simply a wire frame, the other a frame covered with terry cloth. Offered the choice of the two, each of which provided milk, infant monkeys preferred the terry-cloth mother. When offered both the wire mother with milk and the terry-cloth surrogate without milk, the infant monkeys fed from the wire mother but spent much time clinging to the terry-cloth surrogate. The experience of feeding had not enhanced the attractiveness of the wire mother.

In a major work published in 1969, Bowlby presented a comprehensive theory of attachment, drawing heavily on ethological studies of animals in natural surroundings as well as on the experimental work of Harlow. We summarize his theory briefly as follows: First, the human infant is essentially social and predisposed by a number of instinctual response systems, which are primarily nonoral, to form an effective tie to its primary caregiver. Second, the affective tie develops in a regular manner and is usually well established by the second half of the first year. Third, in the normal course of development the mother is both the primary caregiver and the attachment figure to whom the infant is bonded. Finally, once the affective tie or attachment bond is well established, separation from the mother results in anxiety and protest. Prolonged separation results in an orderly sequence of protest, despair, and finally apparent detachment from the mother, so that upon her return the child may show no enthusiasm or interest. Total loss of the mother in the early years has a variety of long-lasting detrimental consequences.

Bowlby replaced orthodox psychoanalytic and learning-theory explanations with an evolutionary account of the origins of attachment. The various instinctual responses that lead to attachment – crying, gazing, grasping, and smiling, for example – are considered to enhance the infant's chances of survival by increasing closeness to the mother and protection from predators.

Recognition of the importance of the mother's attachment or bonding to the infant and of the infant's attachment to the mother has led to important innovations in infant care, but at the same time research has challenged many precise details of Bowlby's theoretical formulations (Klaus and Kennell, 1976; Rutter, 1981; Sluckin et al., 1983). Hospital deliveries in Europe and the United States increasingly include a period just after birth during which mothers and fathers are encouraged to look at their babies and to begin to get to know them. The care of premature and ill babies has been modified; mothers are now invited to stay in the hospital and take part in nursing their children.

The mother's attachment or bonding to the infant has not received a great deal of scholarly attention but has been publicized in popular works on infant care. Klaus and Kennell (1976) reviewed evidence from an infant-care center in Greece that suggested that nurses developed special relationships with particular infants and experienced loss and mourning when their babies left the institution to be placed in adoptive homes. Their account, typical of an approach that focused almost exclusively on an early period held to be critical for the development of maternal bonding, has recently been challenged, and more temperate suggestions for infant care have been offered (Sluckin et al., 1983).

Developmental psychologists have undertaken a great deal of research to investigate the sequence and objects in the development of the infant's attachment, to explore the consequences of individual differences in the strength of the attachment bond for other aspects of the infant's and young child's behavior, and to assess the consequences of brief separation and the introduction of strangers, as well as to determine the long-term consequences of maternal deprivation. We have selected a few issues that are relevant when considering the impact of gender differentiation in the provision of care for the young. The general issue most relevant to our concerns is that of *monotropism* – a term used to indicate that attachment occurs to only one person at a time and ideally to the infant's natural mother. Monotropism can be considered in terms of both the infant's attachment to one or more caregivers and the caregiver's ability to form a deep relationship with one or more infants.

The issue of a single object of attachment is often confounded with that of the biological mother as a privileged object of attachment. In a sense, we are back to the original question – the deleterious effects of the failure to receive sufficient mother-love, or maternal deprivation. The process of attachment and the objects of this attachment were investigated by Schaffer and Emerson (1964) in a pioneering longitudinal study of sixty infants observed during each month in their first year. Although their study lent general support to Bowlby, Schaffer and Emerson showed that the development of specific attachment need not be exclusively directed toward a single person. In the very first month in which a specific attachment was identified, 29 percent of the babies developed such a tie with more than one other person; indeed, 10 percent had ties with five or more other people. Even when the attachment object was a single person, the bond was not necessarily to the infant's mother. For a few infants, the sole bond was formed with a father or grandparent.

The *kibbutzim* of Israel have often been cited in arguments about child care in our own society, as they provide a unique kind of data on the issue of attachment. In a *kibbutz* the care of infants is shared between parents and *metaplot* (singular: *metapelet*), trained caregivers who live with the children in special "infant houses." Fox (1977) studied the reactions of infants to separation and reunion with their mothers and their *metaplot* using a variety of measures. In the seven *kibbutzim* in which he worked, primary care of the infant usually passed to a *metapelet* when the infant was three to four months old, and by the time the child was one-and-a-half years old the parents would visit once a day for three hours in the afternoon. Fox argued that as attachment figures, mothers and *metaplot* were interchangable and that each provided the infant with a secure base – one function of the attachment figure. The only measures that did discriminate between mother and *metapelet* were those based upon reunion, but the results were heavily influenced by the greater anxiety of first-born children on being separated from their mothers. In the *kibbutzim* study, infants were shown to form attachments to more than one person at a time, although in each case they were to women. In the work of Schaffer and Emerson we noted that, in addition to forming multiple attachments, a small proportion of infants became primarily attached to their fathers. From this it is reasonable to conclude that the object of initial attachment need not be the natural mother or even female.

We see in Fox's study that attachments may differ in subtle ways. Psychoanalytic writers have suggested that it may be more difficult both for an adopted child and for its new mother to form a secure bond (e.g., Reeves, 1971). The greater incidence of psychiatric disturbance in adopted children has been related to family background conditions as well as to breaks in the continuity of care (Hersov, 1977). When we examine fathers' participation in child care in the next section, we shall consider possible differences in the nature of children's attachment to mothers and fathers.

Even in this discussion of attachment, we appear to be focusing on parents or parent surrogates and neglecting to consider any differences in the ways in which boy and girl infants establish an affective tie with their primary caregivers. Information on this topic is scant. Fear of strangers, a phenomenon that has been observed after the attachment bond is established, has been studied in relation to the infant's intellectual development (Decarie et al., 1974). This work has shown a precise difference between baby boys and girls, a more frequent negative reaction being that of female infants in reaction to being touched by a stranger. Studies employing different measures of fear of strangers have confirmed a trend in this direction but have not yielded reliable results (Schaffer and Emerson, 1964; Tennes and Lampl, 1964; Morgan and Ricciuti, 1969). Decarie and her students suggested that the gender difference in fear reactions reflects a difference in the understanding of the situation rather than the kinds of differences in fear discussed in Chapter 6. Comparing infants of the same age and using the results of tests of intellectual development, object permanence, and the understanding of causality, they suggested that the negative response to being touched by strangers reflects girls' intellectual precocity. They noted that when infants of both genders are a few months older they generally show a negative reaction to being touched by strangers. Before considering further gender differences in the consequences of early experiences of mothering or in dependence and anxiety toward strangers, we shall look briefly at one further aspect of infant care – the optimal number of caregivers necessary to ensure satisfactory development.

Our discussion relies upon a review in which Peter Smith (1980) reexamined Bowlby's original material and surveyed a great number of research reports. Smith supported the general conclusion that there is little evidence that infants require an exclusive, warm, continuous relationship with a single person to develop emotional security (Rutter, 1981). At the same time, Smith considered the possibility that there exists an upper limit on the number of caregivers that a child can encounter and still develop satisfactorily. He concluded that although there may be no disastrous consequences when children are looked after by a few caregivers – perhaps as many as five – it is difficult to predict the result when fifty or more people take turns looking after a single child in the early years.

In support of his claim, Smith cited a study of children who lived in residential nurseries in London for at least four years from the age of four months (Tizard and Hodges, 1978). Tizard and Hodges considered anyone who had worked in one of these nurseries for at least a week a caregiver and estimated that the children encountered about fifty different caregivers in their four years' residence. When assessed at eight years of age, the majority of these children, whether they had returned to their natural parents, been placed in foster homes, been adopted, or remained in care, posed problems in school. Although their intellectual development appeared normal, teachers described them as antisocial, attention-seeking, and restless. We can conclude with Smith that there probably is an optimal upper limit on the number of caregivers in the early years. Even so, it may not be the number of caregivers per se that influences emotional development but the nature of the interaction between the infant and the changing caregivers. Smith suggested that the transient caregiver typically has difficulty understanding and predicting the behavior of the infant and hence fails to achieve a synchronous and mutually rewarding relationship. This, in turn, may adversely influence the caregiver's already fragile commitment to the infant. This may be why it appears inevitable that the quality of infant care suffers when the number of caregivers is great.

In the remaining part of this section we consider differences between girls and boys that may reflect their experiences of mothering and attachment. In a recent review Rutter (1979) notes that little effort has been directed toward assessing the different effects of maternal deprivation on girls and boys. In his own research on the Isle of Wight he has shown that short-term deprivation as the result of maternal illness or confinement is related to greater behavioral disturbance in boys than in girls (Wolkind and Rutter, 1973). But when children are in the care of another for a long time as a result of prolonged maternal difficulties, there is as much disturbance among girls as among boys. Rutter (1979) concluded that there is evidence of differences in mother–infant interaction and in boys' and girls' reactions to stress but that we cannot yet explain the nature of these differences and their long-term consequences.

It is a short step from consideration of the consequences of maternal deprivation to consideration of gender differences in the incidence of mental illness in childhood. Although the diagnosis of psychopathology in children is even more problematic than it is in adults, mental illness in childhood raises a number of important questions (Eme, 1979). Given the methodological drawback that the only available reports of incidence are based on treated cases rather than on community surveys, the evidence indicates that boys experience more problems than girls, more learning difficulties, more psychosexual disorders, and greater severity of antisocial behavior, as well as more neurosis and psychosis. These results are puzzling in the light of the adult incidences we considered in Chapter 6. There we saw that, with the exception of alcoholic psychosis, alcoholism, drug dependence, and personality and behavioral disorders, the incidence of women in all categories on first admission to mental hospitals is higher and that there is a higher incidence of mental illness among women generally. The discontinuity between childhood and adult psychopathology is striking.

It would be difficult to discount the importance of gender-role pressure in explaining the higher incidence of mental illness in women. An analysis of the strains of the boy's gender role – growing up both in the family and in early formal education in an essentially female world, but one with emphases on masculinity and achievements – may not be sufficient to account for the preponderance of boys in these categories of disturbance. Biological factors as well as social mediators of stress reaction in boys need to be examined. It is tempting to imagine that the greater vulnerability of the male from conception and his developmental immaturity can explain the differential male reaction to psychological stress and deprivation. Our argument by analogy does not so much explain as highlight the need, already pointed out by Rutter, to provide explanations for the differential consequences for boys and girls of variations in parental care. It appears that our scientific evidence echoes the old wives' tale that boys are more difficult to raise, though we are not much closer than they to understanding why this should be so.

The consequences of mothering and attachment that we have just considered are of a pathological nature. It is useful to ask whether in the normal course of development boys and girls acquire similar needs for other people and whether the strength of their attachment and dependence is generally the same. Psychologists have struggled to find satisfactory definitions and measures of dependence with which to approach the study of individual differences. Maccoby and Jacklin (1974) considered dependence by grouping together reports of behavior oriented toward the maintenance of closeness – proximity seeking, touching, and resistance to separation – and behavior oriented toward eliciting social contact – attention seeking, social skills, and social responsiveness. Maintenance and eliciting contact directed both at adults and at other children were each examined. The general picture that emerged was one of little differentiation by gender. No clear differences were seen in studies of the maintenance of closeness with parents or with other adults. Although studies in which one or the other parent left the infant did show more male disturbance, Maccoby and Jacklin generally subscribed to an ethological view and shared Bowlby's notion of the adaptiveness of attachment. The greater disturbance of male infants following parental separation may be viewed as another aspect of their differential response to stress. Thus when normal circumstances hold, male and female infants respond in a similar fashion, but fear or stress may differentially affect them.

The susceptibility of psychological research on dependence to the influence of prevailing stereotypes was noted by Maccoby and Jacklin. In observational studies of proximity seeking no clear differences between boys and girls appeared; but when children were rated by their nursery school teachers, girls were reported as being more likely to seek social contact. Given the evidence available, we conclude that under normal conditions, when undue stress or fear is not aroused, girls and boys are similar in their needs for efforts to maintain contact with other people.

Mothering and attachment in the normal course of development appear to result in no major differences in girls' and boys' capacities for social responsiveness or dependence. The greater male vulnerability to stress may mean that boys find some situations more damaging than do girls, but knowledge about the caregiving process does not yet allow us to identity these situations with precision. At best, we conclude that most infants develop satisfactorily when cared for by a few concerned people. The adults need not be female, but they must be sensitive to, and responsive to, the infant's needs.

Fathers and mothers

In this section we consider the contribution of men to the care of children. At one time psychologists concentrated on examining the effects of father absence, believing that by comparing the intellectual, emotional, and social development of children growing up with and without fathers they would learn about the influence of fathers. The past decade has seen the growth of fatherhood as an important area for psychological study (Biller, 1976; Lamb, 1976; Beail and McQuire, 1982). Unfortunately, as Martin Richards (1982) noted, research has been motivated more by issues of relevance than by a desire to test theories about the contribution of fathers in development.

Given that the two-parent family is the unit within which parental socialization usually takes place, it is difficult to understand what might be learned about the effects of the father in child care from an examination of families where the father is absent. Even if we believe such an enterprise to be profitable, trying to define father absence raises questions similar to those we encountered when discussing maternal deprivation. For example, is the father who leaves home before breakfast and who returns from work after the children are in bed to be considered an absent father? Are families in which grand-fathers and older male children fulfill the role of a father to be classified as fatherless? Even if we are given an adequate defi-nition of *absence*, it is also important to identify the age of the child and the length of the absence.

Rather than focusing on fatherless families in order to under-stand the role of the father, we first consider the general im-pact on children of growing up in one-parent families. These constitute a frequent alternative to two-parent families in mod-ern Britain and in many other Western countries. Second, we consider men's contributions to child care as described by their wives. Third, we compare the behavior of fathers and mothers, having already noted that infants form attachments to fathers as well as to mothers. We begin our comparison by examining the nature of the infant's bond with its father and mother and then look briefly at each parent's share in play and in routine infant care. Finally, we examine the effects of fathers' personal-ity on the development of their children.

We begin by understanding the effects on children of grow-ing up in a one-parent family. As we noted in Chapter 2, the majority of single parents are women, although there are more older children living in motherless homes. The National Child Development Study, which was based on all children born in England in a given week in March 1958, showed that at the age of seven there were six-and-a-half times more children living with only their mother than with only their father (Ferri, 1976). By eleven years of age the proportion had changed: There were four-and-a-half times more children living with only their mother than with only their father. Motherless families are usually the result of either death or marital disruption, as it is rare for a father to raise an illegitimate child. Fatherless families arise through the death of a spouse, marital breakdown, or illegitimacy.

Children who grow up in one-parent families show lower average performance and progress on educational tests and poorer school adjustment. These findings could reflect either the psychological effects of growing up in a one-parent family or general social differences between one- and two-parent families. The National Child Development Study showed that differences in the reading levels of seven- and eleven-year-olds from one- and two-parent families were greatly reduced when socioeconomic factors were taken into consideration. However, arithmetic ability still remained low among children from fatherless families. This particular effect has also been reported in a number of other studies of father absence (Lamb, 1976).

Teachers rate children from one-parent families as less well adjusted (Mack, 1976). Mothers who raise children on their own report that they have more problems with their children, especially with their daughters. These findings, based on adult ratings of children's behavior, may be influenced by teachers' and mothers' negative stereotypes about growing up in one-parent families or "broken homes" (Mack, 1976) and should be treated with caution.

We cannot ignore the financial hardships experienced in one-parent families. Although two-parent families show important differences related to the father's occupation or social class, these are further accentuated in one-parent families (Ferri, 1976). Among manual workers in Britain 6 percent of two-parent families receive government aid (supplementary benefits) to bring their income up to a specified minimal level. In motherless families in which the father is the manual worker this figure rises to 18 percent, and in fatherless families it reaches 52 percent. Even in families in which the father is a nonmanual worker there are great differences: 31 percent of mothers on their own receive supplementary benefits, in contrast to only 2 percent of intact families. Income is generally a problem in one-parent families, but the economic deprivation experienced by children who live alone with their mothers is greater.

There are difficulties other than those directly related to finances, but these differ little according to the gender of the single parent. For instance, 2 percent of children in two-parent families spend some time in the care of the state; even when divorced or separated men and women raise children on their own, the proportion rises to 12 percent. The difficult life conditions of the one-parent family are further reflected in the greater number of schools these children attend. Both care and schooling are also influenced indirectly by economic factors.

In mothers' reports of their husbands' contribution to child care we again see the influence of financial factors, even in two-parent families. The National Child Development Study provided information about fathers' contributions to child rearing. When the children were seven years old, and again when they were eleven, their mothers were asked to estimate the amount of help they received from their husbands in looking after the children. The mothers described more than half the fathers as taking an equal or a large share of responsibility for their children's care (Lambert and Hart, 1976); 10 percent were described as leaving everything to the mother – these men tended to be the fathers of younger children in larger families or to have experienced financial difficulties in the year preceding the data collection.

Since these findings are based on wives' accounts of their husbands' behavior, we may be tempted to dismiss them as subjective and biased. It is therefore important to find other evidence of the impact of fathers on their children's development. The National Child Development Study provided further data linking parental interest and performance at school (Lambert and Hart, 1976). When both parents visited school to discuss their child's progress with the teachers, performance on both reading and arithmetic tests was seven months ahead of that of children whose mothers alone visited the school. When neither parent took an interest in schooling, children were, on average, thirteen months behind on both tests. Parental interest is thus important, and fathers can make a sizable contribution to their children's school performance. Even from the viewpoint of a child, this study suggests that it is best to be one of few siblings or an older child in a family without financial problems in which the father takes an active interest in his children's development.

There can be little doubt from the evidence that comes from the National Child Development Study that an actively involved father benefits his children. Our next question concerns the nature of his contribution – more specifically, whether the affection offered and evoked by fathers and their play with, and care of, their children are very different from that of mothers.

In our discussion of attachment theory we concluded that there is abundant evidence that an emotional bond is established between the infant and one or more adults by the second half of the first year. Although research initially focused on the infant's attachment to its mother, Milton Kotelchuck and Michael Lamb have each carried out a series of studies on the father's place in infant social development (Kotelchuck, 1976; Lamb, 1976, 1977a, 1977b).

Kotelchuck's early research explored infant behavior in a laboratory playroom in which a mother, a father, and an adult stranger appeared and departed according to a fixed schedule. The activities he observed and measured can be divided into two classes; those related to attachment, such as crying, touching, and remaining close; and those related to affiliation, such as looking and vocalizing. This distinction is similar to that we already considered, in discussing dependence, between maintaining contact and eliciting it.

Kotelchuck observed that between the ages of nine and twenty-four months infants directed different attachment and affiliative responses to their parents and to a stranger. In addition, there was no easily interpretable difference in the pattern of responses to father or mother. These results have been replicated in cross-cultural studies in Guatemala and in infants' homes in the United States (Kotelchuck, 1976). Although the overall conclusion that infants react differently toward their parents and toward a strange adult may stand, it is still possible that there are differences in the interactions and types of emotional bond established between the infant and each parent.

Studies of infants' preferences for fathers or mothers when confronted with a stranger may furnish clues to qualitative differences in the emotional bond established with each parent. Different research settings yield different preferences (Lamb, 1977a) and produce conflicting results. When both parents are available, conditions of stress may produce a preference for the mother; but in less difficult circumstances no consistent preference is observed. The attachment and affiliative activities of infants were studied in their own homes in two longitudinal studies (Lamb, 1977a, 1977b). Infants studied between seven and thirteen months of age showed no preference toward either parent in their attachment behavior, but over this six-month period they developed a stronger preference for their parents compared to the stranger. Lamb suggested that this heightened attachment to both parents when faced with a stranger may be part of a focusing process that is also seen as a preference for the mother in conditions of stress. This process occurs at the end of the first year.

Lamb's study of infants in their second year provides a number of intriguing results. At home, attachment behavior can indicate preference for the father, although both parents are still preferred to a stranger. But when the amounts of activity of each of the three adults – father, mother, and stranger – are statistically equated, more affiliative behavior is found to be directed toward the stranger than to either parent. These results, and the general decline in attachment and affiliative behavior over the second year, highlight the importance of age in any discussion of the relationships of children with their parents. As the infant develops in the first two years, the bonds with father and mother develop and change.

Just as there are preferences for particular adults expressed by infants, so there may be differences in the ways in which fathers and mothers interact with their infants. We begin by looking at differences in parental behavior generally, and we then consider differences specific to the gender of the infant. The use of videotape recording in the past few years has allowed a much closer examination of the ways in which infants and adults interact, and studies have reported detailed analysis of sequences of behavior (Parke, 1979). From this finer analysis there have arisen suggestions of stylistic differences in fathers' and mothers' speech and touch. But when mothers and fathers were observed in their homes attempting to comfort the distress of their month-old infants, no differences were recorded; both parents appeared to accommodate their soothing techniques to the needs of their baby (Worobey et al., 1983).

We tend to think of routine infant care as the special province of mothers, knowing that many fathers have never changed their soiled infants. Fathers may be particularly important in a different way – in play. In the second half of the first year and in the second year many differences in parental play have been observed (Lamb, 1977a, 1977b). Until recently, few differences had been recorded in parental play patterns in the first six months of life. Mothers engage the young infant in conventional games such as peek-a-boo and pat-a-cake, and fathers tend to indulge in more rough-and-tumble play. In the second year fathers often play the games that their infants instigate and engage in physical play, whereas mothers read more to their infants. Even when the child is two-and-a-half years old, fathers still play in a physical fashion, whereas the play of mothers is of a more instructional and verbal nature (Clarke-Stewart, 1977). Parental play differs not only in quality but also in quantity, with fathers playing with their children more as the children get older.

As early as during the first year, infants respond more positively to play with their fathers than with their mothers (Parke, 1979). By the second year they respond more often to playful overtures from their fathers, and in a contrived laboratory setting two-thirds of children age two and a half chose their

fathers first as playmates. Parke concluded that each parent
makes a different contribution to their child's development, the
father by providing exciting physical play and the mother
physical care and verbal interaction. Although these comparisons have been made in two-parent families, they may provide
hints about the behavior that could be in short supply in one-
parent families.

So far in our discussion of parental behavior we have not
indicated whether the infant or child was a boy or a girl. In
fact, the infant's gender is important in determining the behavior of adults (Condry and Condry, 1976; Frisch, 1977). In a
laboratory study six-month-old babies were dressed up as boys
or girls. Mothers who themselves had six-month-old infants
were invited to play with them; in each case the mother was
told that the baby was a boy or a girl (according to dress)
(Smith and Lloyd, 1978). The perceived gender of the baby
influenced the mothers in that not only did they say different
things, but the same physical action of the baby evoked different responses. When the baby was presented as a boy, mothers responded with physical action; but they offered comfort
and soothing if the baby was presented as a girl. Mothers thus
responded to unfamiliar babies, in this laboratory setting, in
terms of gender stereotypes.

In daily life, stereotypes and parental influence also guide
fathers' and mothers' responses to their children. Both fathers
and mothers have been observed to look more at infants of
their own gender and to provide them with more stimulation
in play (Parke and Sawin, 1977). Fathers' preference for male
children has been shown in their greater involvement – talking
more and playing more with male infants (Rebelsky and
Hanks, 1971; Rendina and Dickerscheid, 1976). Fathers' preference for a male child can scarcely be doubted when we learn
that fathers talk more to a first-born baby shortly after birth if it
is a boy. Later-born males and all female infants are spoken to
less often (Parke, 1979). From the theories and evidence we
have examined, there can be little doubt that fathers and
mothers bring different expectations to child care and behave

in subtly different ways toward their offspring depending on their own and their child's gender.

The final issue that we consider in this brief examination of men and women's behavior as parents relates primarily to fathers. We look at the impact on children of personality differences among fathers. We begin by examining the masculinity of fathers and its influence on the development of boys. In this respect, two of the most influential theories of psychological development, psychoanalytic and social learning theory, agree that the model of masculine behavior that the father provides is important.

The methodological problems that we encountered in the measurement of masculinity and femininity in Chapter 2 reappear when studying the impact of the father on his children's development. If boys are first asked to rate themselves on a scale of masculinity and then asked to describe their fathers using the same scale, it is hardly surprising to find a similarity, because one person is making both ratings. One way around this problem has been to construct an artificial situation in which observers can rate fathers' and mothers' behavior in terms of their exercising or failure to exercise dominance, an important factor in differentiating masculinity and femininity. The assumption is made that in everyday family life the parents will display similar amounts of dominance. This technique has been used in studies in which parental dominance was related to preschool and school-age children's gender-role preference (Hetherington, 1965). The child's gender-role preference is measured using a stick figure called IT which is gender-neutral. The child is asked to choose from masculine and feminine objects those they think IT would like. Sons of dominant fathers tend to choose masculine objects.

Although the picture that at first emerges seems straightforward, later research has shown the process to be more complex (Biller, 1976). Boys' perceptions of their fathers' dominance have proved to be better predictors of their own gender preference and orientation than psychological assessment of parental dominance. In addition, when fathers who are rated high in dominance on the basis of their interactions with their wives behave in a restrictive and controlling fashion toward their sons, the boys tend to be less masculine. Furthermore, unless the father is dominant and active in the family, his masculine behavior in the world of work or leisure has little impact on his sons. Speaking again from the child's viewpoint, for a strong masculine identity to emerge in boys it is important to have a father who is actively involved in the home and takes a major role in family decision making. Fathers who seek achievement primarily in the world of work and who leave the home to their wives may find their sons do not share their masculine preferences.

The import of our discussion is that parental participation is important for masculine development in boys. The importance of the father in shaping a daughter's feminine gender identity has also been noted (Biller, 1976). Biller views femininity positively: Women are seen to be both independent and assertive as well as nurturant and sensitive. A masculine father is believed to facilitate his daughter's feminine development. Indeed, some psychologists have argued that fathers have the potential to play a more important part than mothers in their children's gender differentiation (Biller, 1976; Heilbrun, 1965).

This picture of masculine fathers dominating family decision making and thereby ensuring that their children are clearly differentiated as males and females requires a few reservations. First, a father may have views that are considered narrow and restricting by his family. His sons may show artistic tendencies and his daughters may pursue dangerous sports of which he disapproves. In such cases a father's efforts to impose his notions of gender-appropriate behavior could produce considerable family discord. On the other hand, a father who seeks to realize his own masculine ambitions through a daughter may encounter opposition. We cannot overlook the limits a child's own nature imposes on parental influence. Fathers make an important contribution to gender differentiation – but within the limits of their children's dispositions and their own natures and positions in the wider society.

8

Work, intelligence, and achievement

In Chapter 7 we discussed the family, traditionally regarded as a woman's sphere of influence and responsibility, and we considered why it is that women look after children. Here we examine the world of work, a man's sphere of influence, and ask why it is that men occupy the most prestigious and highly valued positions in it.

The first explanation we consider suggests that men and women possess different abilities and skills and that these suit them for the world of family or work or for different occupations within the world of work; furthermore, it is often claimed that gender differences in ability arise from biological sex differences. After examining the possibility that different abilities may underlie gender differences in work and achievement, we consider other explanations and discuss a number of related influences – stereotypes about women and work, opportunities, education and training, and aspiration and motives for occupational success.

We begin by examining some statistics on men and women in different occupations. Before discussing reasons for differences in occupational patterns, we must consider whether it is true that men achieve greater prestige and status in the world of work.

Do men get better jobs and earn more money than women?

In Chapter 2 we examined some British statistics on men's and women's occupations and found a number of differences re-

Table 8.1. *Median monetary income of people with income, by gender and education, 1980*

	Male	Female
Elementary school		
Less than 8 years	$7,035	$3,643
8 years	8,960	4,177
High school		
1–3 years	9,924	4,242
4 years	14,583	6,080
College/graduate school		
1–3 years	15,674	6,985
4 years	22,173	10,119
5 years or more	26,927	15,108

Source: Based on table 231 in *Statistical Abstracts of the USA* (1982–3).

lated to the world of work. For example, among school leavers who do not go on to higher or further education but instead enter into apprenticeship training, boys outnumber girls seven to one. Among those continuing their education, boys more often enter degree courses, although many girls train as secretaries or nurses. Girls are six times more likely than boys to enter a clerical occupation. These figures can be summarized by saying that men tend to enter higher-status and potentially better-paid occupations than women, are apt to receive more occupational training, and are more likely to be found in jobs with good promotion prospects.

We now examine statistics on male and female occupations in the United States. With regard to Table 8.1, which includes people with any monetary income, the lower median incomes of women are at least partly due to the higher proportion of women who work part-time. Participation in different occupations also explains some of the difference. Women account for 96.5 percent of private household workers, 80.5 percent of clerical and kindred workers, and 59.2 percent of service workers (89.3 percent of "waiters," a subcategory of service workers). These are all low-paid occupations (*Statistical Abstracts of the USA*, 1982–3, table 651).

The overall participation of women in professional, technical, and related spheres, where incomes are usually higher, is 42.9 percent, but this figure masks wide variation across specific occupations. Women account for 98.4 percent of preschool and kindergarten teachers, 98.8 percent of registered nurses, 83.6 percent of elementary school teachers, 82.8 percent of librarians, archivists, and curators, and 72.3 percent of health technologists and technicians. All these professions are generally lower-paid. Among the higher-income professions women account for only 4.4 percent of engineers, 4.6 percent of dentists, 14.1 percent of lawyers and judges, 13.7 percent of physicians, 38.5 percent of accountants and 35.2 percent of college and university teachers.

British figures for women's participation in the professions during the 1970s are similar (Mackie and Pattullo, 1977). Fewer than 5 percent of architects, engineers, scientists, and solicitors were women. About 10 percent of teachers and 27 percent of physicians were female, but within each of these professions a smaller proportion of women were found in higher-status positions. Only 1.7 percent of university professors and only 12 percent of medical consultants were women.

In other occupations we find a similar pattern in the United Kingdom. Fewer women occupy high-status positions than would be expected from their numbers in the work force as a whole. This is the case even in occupations where women are in a numerical majority, such as nursing and food retailing: Here a disproportionate number of the male minority gain promotion to the top grades. In food retailing, more than two-thirds of the labor force are women, and yet they occupy only 4 percent of management posts.

If there is a disproportionate number of men in higher-status occupations, where are most women workers to be found? The answer is that they typically carry out dull, repetitive, badly paid jobs that offer them few prospects for advancement. These jobs are concentrated in a relatively small number of industries, so that they are often identifiable as "women's work" and are considered less productive and important than other types of work. Women's work is found in service industries, in certain manufacturing industries such as food, drink, clothing, textiles, and footwear, and in shops and hairdressing. Women are also employed for cooking, cleaning, and serving food. Many women work part-time, and the hours they work often bear a close relation to the age and number of their dependent children. The lowest-paid of all women workers are those who work at home, again because of their dependent children; these include childminders and homeworkers for industry.

In Chapter 2 we observed that, on average, men earn more than women and that this cannot be explained by the numbers of hours that each gender works. A clear picture of the higher status, pay, and achievement of men emerges from our brief overview of work. In the remaining sections of this chapter we consider explanations for these findings. The first is the possibility that men and women possess different skills and abilities that suit them for particular occupations that just happen to differ in status and pay. Although this may appear an unlikely explanation to the politically and socially aware reader, nevertheless it is one that has been advanced at various times to explain partially or totally the occupational position of women. In our discussion we also consider the more general issue of psychological differences in intellectual abilities between men and women and how these might be explained.

Gender differences in intellectual abilities

In Chapter 1 we referred in passing to nineteenth-century biologists' explanation of men's allegedly greater intelligence. Although contemporary psychologists do not regard men as intellectually superior to women, many men still seem to believe that women are less intelligent or at least less rational and logical.

IQ tests were originally constructed so that, on average, men and women would score similarly (see Chapter 2); but it has often been claimed that there is a difference in the overall distribution of IQ scores, with more men at both the higher and lower ends and more women in the middle. Occasionally this has been referred to as the mediocrity-of-women hypothesis, and it has sometimes been used as an explanation for the greater scientific, artistic, and occupational attainments of men (Heim, 1970). We need to consider this claim as a possible reason for gender differences in occupational attainment.

In Chapter 2 we described various IQ tests and scales designed specifically to measure skills such as verbal ability, numerical reasoning, spatial ability, and memory. Consistent gender differences have been reported on a number of these subtests, and some psychologists have argued that these specific ability differences might suit men and women for different occupations. In particular, spatial ability has been linked to male preeminence in science, mathematics, and engineering. Biological explanations of gender differences in spatial ability have also aroused considerable interest. Several types of theory have been suggested involving genetic differences, brain lateralization, or sex hormones. Such theories suggest a direct link between the biological and the social and are used to argue that men are naturally *suited* to certain occupations (Archer and Lloyd, 1980), just as Rossi and others have argued that women are naturally suited to child care (see Chapter 7).

Are there more men with high intellectual ability?

A number of psychologists, beginning with Havelock Ellis (1903), have suggested that the range of mental ability is wider among men than among women. Accepting this hypothesis makes it possible to argue, even in the absence of an average difference in intelligence, that intellectual ability explains the greater scientific, artistic, and occupational achievements of men (see Shields, 1975, for a review of the origins of this theory). The theory has persisted to the present day, and recent versions have included speculations that gender differences in the range of IQ can be attributed to genetic factors. Thus Lehrke (1978, p. 193) has written: "It is highly probable that basic genetic factors rather than male chauvinism account for at least some of the difference in the number of males and females occupying positions requiring the highest levels of intellectual ability."

First we consider evidence for the claim that there are differences in the ranges of intellectual ability of men and women; then we examine some recent genetic explanations.

Statistics showing male preeminence in achievement over a wider variety of intellectual endeavors were used to argue the case at the upper end of the intelligence distribution. Surveys of institutions for the mentally retarded, which show a male majority in several different sets of national statistics, were used to document the predominance of men at the lower end. (Anastasi, 1958).

Critics of the variability theory question this evidence and offer other reasons for these findings. It has been suggested that sampling biases, where a higher proportion of male subnormals are cared for in institutions, while female subnormals are cared for by their families at home, may account for the differences reported (Anastasi, 1958). Critics also point out that in the classic study of gifted children by Terman (1925), which identified more boys than girls at the top range of intelligence, there was differential selection by teachers (Maccoby and Jacklin, 1974).

In studies of children's IQ scores there is no consistent tendency for boys to show a wider range of abilities than girls (Anastasi, 1958; Maccoby and Jacklin, 1974). When the upper and lower percentages of scores from various tests were examined in a large-scale investigation of mental abilities, little support was found for the variability hypothesis (Wilson and Vandenberg, 1978).

On inspection, the evidence for the variability hypothesis turns out to be weak; it rests on a few studies that may be biased in their sample selection. Despite the lack of sound evidence, however, there is no shortage of explanations for the alleged variability difference. Because males show greater physical vulnerability to developmental defects and illnesses, it has been suggested that their brain development may be less buffered from the environment than that of the female (Glucksmann, 1974; Maccoby and Jacklin, 1974). A similar theory of brain development has been used to account for the allegedly greater male variability in intelligence and to suggest that male intellectual development is more affected by the environment and female development more by genetic factors. This relationship was explored by Bayley and Schaefer (1964) using data from a longitudinal study. They linked IQ scores of children and various measures of maternal behavior. A reexamination of Bayley and Schaefer's study has questioned whether there exists a gender difference at all, and hence the need for an explanation of it (Kamin, 1978).

Corinne Hutt (1972a) related the supposedly greater male intellectual variability to a wider pattern of more advantageous and disadvantageous physical characteristics in men than in women. She also linked this general variability to the "Y chromosome theory" of Ounsted and Taylor (1972). These authors suggested that the Y chromosome of the male produces a slower rate of development and thus enables the environment to exert more influence on male development. A consequence of this greater environmental influence would be wider variability in male than in female characteristics. As we have already shown, the evidence for a wider variability in male IQ scores and for a greater environmental influence on male intellectual development is questionable. The Y chromosome theory is more usually invoked to explain the greater number of disadvantageous physical features that occur in male than in female animals – for example, their greater susceptibility to disease and their greater mortality rates. In the case of greater male mortality, an explanation in terms of a shorter (Y) chromosome producing slower development cannot apply generally, since the female possesses a shorter sex chromosome in many animal species in which male mortality is nevertheless greater (Trivers, 1972).

Another genetic explanation for greater male variability in intelligence suggests that there are genes on the X chromosomes that affect intelligence (Lehrke, 1978). In females, extreme forms of these genes are likely to be countered by effects from other cells, since the female body is a mosaic of cells with maternal and paternal X chromosomes; males possess only one type of X chromosome, that from the mother, so that the same gene will be active in every cell – resulting in more extreme forms of the genes being more readily expressed. The theory rests on the assumption that there are genes influencing intellectual development on the X chromosomes, but the evidence for these, taken from family relatedness of IQ, is indirect and inconclusive. This, together with the lack of evidence for the original intellectual variability hypothesis, makes confirmation of the X-chromosome theory unlikely. Despite the lack of firm evidence or convincing explanations, however, the notion that males are both more clever and more stupid than females lingers on.

Do specific abilities suit men and women for different occupations?

In Chapter 2 we considered the psychometric approach to measuring gender differences in specific mental abilities and described these differences. On average, men perform better than women on tests of spatial and mathematical ability, although women may perform better than men on tests of verbal ability (Maccoby and Jacklin, 1974). These and other results from psychometric tests are often used to explain and justify occupa-

tional gender differences. It is usually implied that the psychological ability is stable through time and is biologically based.
Thus occupational recruitment patterns are explained in terms
of differences in psychological traits, and these traits are in
turn explained in terms of biological differences between men
and women.

Explanations of this type have been offered to account for the
predominance of women in clerical occupations and of men in
scientific and technological occupations. The characteristics of
perceptual speed and verbal fluency are said to suit women
better for secretarial work (Broverman et al., 1968; Garai and
Scheinfeld, 1968); the higher spatial and mathematical abilities
of the male population are said to suit them better for scientific
and technological professions (Garai and Scheinfeld, 1968;
Heim, 1970). We shall restrict our detailed discussion of gender
differences in mental abilities and their explanations to spatial
ability, which has been used as an explanation for scientific
and technological occupations being predominantly male; we
also consider some biological explanations of the gender difference in spatial ability.

One obvious drawback in accounting for occupational gender
differences in terms of the specific abilities of men and women
is that differences in the latter are too small to account for
occupational differences (Archer and Lloyd, 1980; Hyde, 1981).
The proportion of women found in scientific and technological
occupations is less than 5 percent, and yet the overlap between
male and female scores for spatial ability is considerable (see
Chapter 2). It is a fairly simple matter to calculate the expected
proportion of women in such occupations if spatial ability were
the only factor involved. Hyde (1981) carried out such a calcu-
lation, making an initial assumption that it is necessary to be in
the top 5 percent of the overall range of spatial abilities in order
to be suited for occupations such as engineering. At this level
of ability, the ratio of men to women would be two to one – in
other words, far more women than the actual proportions
found in technological occupations. It is clear, therefore, that

gender differences in spatial ability could provide only a partial explanation for these occupational differences. Nevertheless, we now consider the subject of spatial ability differences and possible biological explanations in more detail, since they have been the subject of much research interest. We then discuss alternative explanations for occupational recruitment.

Spatial ability – or more correctly, visual–spatial ability – generally refers to success in solving problems that involve visualizing a spatial arrangement and carrying out mental operations on it. Related to the spatial ability tests are "field independence" tests, described in Chapter 2 (Witkin et al., 1962; Witkin, 1967). One of these tests, the Embedded Figures Test, involves the identification of a simple reference figure embedded or hidden in a more complex figure, thus providing a distracting background (see Figure 2.1). A second test, the Rod and Frame Test, involves matching a rod to the true vertical or horizontal in the face of a distracting background. As we noted in Chapter 2, Witkin and his colleagues (e.g., Coates, 1974) argue that the ability to perceive the simple figure or the rod as separate from the background or field – termed *field independence* – represents the perceptual component of a wider personality characteristic. It is claimed that field-independent people can separate the simple figure of the rod because they approach the world as if it were composed of discrete entities. They possess what Witkin calls an articulated cognitive style. On the other hand, field-dependent people, who have greater difficulty separating the figure or rod from the field, approach the world in a more global, less segmented manner. A major difficulty with Witkin's interpretation of performance on these tests lies in the close association between field independence scores and the ability to solve other spatial tasks. In Chapter 2 we noted that Witkin's interpretation conflicts with that of psychologists who emphasize the spatial ability component of field independence tests. These interpretations have different implications for explaining gender differences in performance on field independence tests and are discussed later in this section.

First, however, we consider the range of explanations that have been offered to account for the better performance of men than women on tests of spatial ability. There is again a choice of environmental and biological explanations, the latter involving heredity, brain function, and sex hormones.

A genetic explanation for spatial ability was first suggested by O'Connor in 1943 (DeFries et al., 1979), but it only stimulated research interest when elaborated by Stafford in 1961. Stafford suggested that a gene producing high spatial ability can occur on X chromosomes, and that this gene is "recessive" – that is, it can be overruled by a different gene on the other sex chromosome. If the gene occurs in a male, it will always be expressed because the Y chromosome carries little or no genetic material and hence cannot overrule genes on the X chromosome. In a female, a recessive gene on an X chromosome will only be expressed if the same recessive gene also occurs on the other X chromosome. This pattern of inheritance is termed *sex-linked,* and it is the accepted explanation of why conditions such as color blindness and hemophilia are more common in men than women.

The relationship between the spatial ability scores of parents and their children have been examined to see whether these fit the predicted pattern for sex-linked characteristics. In the first study of this kind, correlations were found in the expected direction, and hence it was suggested that gender differences in spatial ability might be attributable to a sex-linked recessive gene (Stafford, 1961). Later studies of family relationships have produced more variable results, and reviews of these studies have concluded that the sex-linkage hypothesis is unfounded (DeFries et al., 1979; Boles, 1980). Although other, more rigorous statistical tests of sex linkage are consistent with this conclusion (DeFries et al., 1979), Thomas (1983) urges caution before rejecting the sex-linkage hypothesis: He argues that it cannot readily be tested simply by comparing family relationships with the predicted pattern, as the existing predictions take too few variables into account.

A second type of biological explanation involves differences in the degree to which mental abilities are controlled by the right and left halves (*hemispheres*) of the cerebral cortex in men and women. This type of explanation has been applied to spatial and linguistic abilities (e.g., Buffery and Gray, 1972; Flor-Henry, 1974; McGee, 1979).

The basic idea is that the left and right cerebral hemispheres of the human brain are each specialized for different functions, the left or dominant hemisphere being the one in which language is usually processed, and the right or minor hemisphere being the one in which nonverbal, including spatial, processing occurs. Departures from this arrangement are supposed to (1) alter the efficiency of spatial (and possibly verbal) processing by the brain and (2) occur to a different extent in men and women.

What is the evidence that men and women show different degrees of hemispheric localization (*lateralization*) of function? McGlone (1980) reviewed the relevant studies and concluded that there was little support for the view of Buffery and Gray (1972), who argued that the female brain is more lateralized than the male brain. Where McGlone found gender differences, however, they were compatible with the opposite view – that the male brain is more lateralized, that is, more specialized for verbal functioning in the left hemisphere and for spatial functioning in the right hemisphere. It is important to emphasize that these are gender differences in the *degree* of lateralization and are small in magnitude compared to the extent of lateralization found in both men and women. The really striking finding is that the *human* brain shows hemispheric specialization.

Can these minor differences in the degree of lateralization of function account for higher male scores on tests of spatial ability? Levy (1969) has suggested that more pronounced lateralization is indeed associated with better spatial functioning (the opposite suggestion by Buffery and Gray, 1972, is rejected by most authorities). Although Levy's view has often been cited as an explanation for higher male spatial ability (e.g., McGlone and Davidson, 1973; Witelson, 1976), there is little or no direct evidence to test the possible link between hemispheric specialization and spatial ability (Siann, 1977). The limited available evidence suggests that gender differences in hemispheric specialization first appear at an earlier age than spatial ability differences (Fairweather, 1976; Witelson, 1976).

A third type of biological theory is that sex hormones may act on the brain to produce differences between men and women in spatial and other abilities (e.g., Broverman et al., 1968; Dawson, 1972). The evidence for these theories is poor, and the reader is referred to Archer (1976a) for a criticism of them.

Theories about environmental influences have usually been posed as alternatives to biological accounts. Although Witkin (1967) was careful not to exclude possible biological explanations, he explained gender differences as part of his general theory of "field independence" as follows: Children whose upbringing involves less parental control and more emphasis on self-reliance and achievement – male attributes in most cultures – become more field-independent, as shown by tests such as the Embedded Figures and Rod and Frame tests. The adequacy of his explanation of gender differences depends on the adequacy of his theory of field independence. This has been questioned by several psychologists, who have explained the tests either in terms of spatial ability (e.g., Sherman, 1967) or in terms of general intelligence (Vernon, 1969). Thus, evidence linking child-rearing influences and scores on field independence tests could alternatively be interpreted in terms of a link between child-rearing practices and spatial ability or a general intellectual characteristic.

Siann (1977) studied the development of gender differences in spatial ability in relation to environmental influences. Scottish children seven to sixteen years of age completed various spatial tests, including field independence tests, spatial tests of the type used in psychometric testing, and a number of specially designed tests, such as one that involved visualization and another that involved location of places and compass points. Gender differences were inconsistent in the younger children, but the twelve- to sixteen-year-old boys showed higher spatial scores than the girls of this age group. In general, gender differences increased with age, a finding largely attributable to the failure of girls' scores to increase with age.

Higher performance on spatial tests was associated with experience with certain activities, such as chess playing among the older children and drawing and painting out of doors among the younger age group. In older children there was a clear relationship between higher spatial performance and experience of three-dimensional forms – for example in woodworking, model making, or toys such as Lego and Meccano. Surprisingly, no relationship was found between map-reading experience and performance on the place location test, but cycling experience was associated with higher scores on this test.

One finding of particular interest in relation to occupational and child-care roles was that girls who viewed their future in terms of a career rather than primarily as a wife and mother showed higher spatial scores. In particular, girls who indicated that they wished to pursue careers in areas where understanding of spatial relationships might be helpful did well on spatial tests.

In view of these results, Siann offered the following explanation for the gender difference in spatial ability. Boys and girls engage in typically masculine or feminine activities, and boys' experiences are more relevant to spatial tasks, whereas girls view spatial tasks as inappropriate for their gender. This explanation provides a very different perspective from attempts to explain occupational choice in terms of spatial ability, and spatial ability in terms of biological sex differences. Instead, occupational choice is viewed as arising from a stereotype encompassing notions of which intellectual and occupational activities are appropriate for the two genders. Gender stereotypes are thus viewed as influencing the upbringing of boys and girls to give them different experiences of, and interests in, spatially related tasks – *and* different occupational interests.

Although Siann provided a plausible alternative to the bio-logical explanations, there is a weakness in the evidence on which her view is based. Most of this evidence consists of associations or correlations between various experiences and performance on spatial tasks. Logically, this could mean either that gender-related experiences influence spatial performance, as Siann suggests, or alternatively that spatial ability differences influence the child's experiences. Children with high spatial ability might choose to play chess since they perform well at it. But in other cases, where an experience is likely to be common to one gender rather than being chosen by a few individuals – for instance, woodworking and playing with construction toys for boys – this alternative explanation is less likely to account for differences in experience that relate to spatial ability.

Gender stereotypes and work

Siann's view of the importance of gender stereotypes for both ability and occupational differences leads us to the subject of gender stereotypes in the world of work. If we return to the main question of why men show greater occupational achievement than women, it is clear that there are several more likely answers than ability differences and that in one way or another these are all linked to gender stereotypes about women and work. The most direct influence is that stereotypes reinforce the idea that there is "men's work" and "women's work," thereby influencing gender differences in occupational training, opportunity, and levels of aspiration. Rather than showing a simple cause-and-effect relationship, stereotypes, opportunity, and aspiration all form part of an interrelated system. We have just considered the possibility that gender stereotypes influence the play activities, opportunities, and interests of schoolchildren and provide a foundation for gender differences in abilities and in occupational training. Different training opportunities, which are reflected in apprenticeships, profes-

sional training, and higher education, serve further to perpetuate gender stereotypes about work.

Stereotypes may exert a direct influence on women's occupational achievements by barring or strongly discouraging them
from entering a particular occupation, and they may strongly
affect the aspirations and motives of men and women in relation
to the world of work. We begin our discussion by considering
how gender stereotypes in relation to work might prevent or
discourage women from achieving in high-status occupations.
In later sections we discuss their influences on education and
occupational training and consider men's and women's aspirations and motivation for achievement in the world of work.

When we described gender differences in mental abilities, we
noted how frequently stereotypical beliefs derived from the
world of work influence descriptions of male and female abilities. For example, women were seen as being particularly
suited for the rapid, repetitive tasks of the assembly line
(Broverman et al., 1968) or for clerical occupations (Garai and
Scheinfeld, 1968). Stereotypes also exert a wider influence on
beliefs about the suitability of men and women for certain occupations. Some of the stereotypical adjectives we examined in
Chapter 2 may be used to justify male and female work patterns. For example, masculine adjectives such as *self-confident,
forceful, enterprising, assertive, confident, rational,* and *tough* are
those that are typically viewed as suitable for success in many
high-status occupations. Feminine adjectives such as *soft-
hearted, sentimental, talkative, gentle, fussy, dreamy,* and *emotional*
are generally regarded as unsuitable for high occupational
achievement. Such stereotypical beliefs form part of the attitude held by many men who fill positions of power in the
world of work. One North American study of managers' attitudes toward women workers revealed that they regarded
women as less dependable than men. In another study, of
male attitudes toward women executives, almost half the men
interviewed reported feeling that women were temperamen-
tally unfit for management (O'Leary, 1974).

Lists of adjectives typically used in describing men and women provide insights into beliefs about occupational suitability. There are also gender stereotypes specifically related to work. Broadly speaking, these beliefs reflect commonsense views of men and women as different and of men as superior. Men's work is generally valued more highly than women's, and occupations that shift from being male to female preserves generally lose status (Kipnis, 1976). For example, bank teller was once a fairly high-status male occupation in the United States, but it has since become a woman's occupation (93.5 percent) and has declined in status. If we take a broad look at occupations and their status in different countries, it becomes apparent that the higher status of men's occupations is much more consistent than the types of work carried out by men and women (Kipnis, 1976). In the United States, medicine is a predominantly male occupation and is highly valued, while in the Soviet Union it is mostly a women's occupation and has a lower status; but even in the Soviet Union senior consultants tend to be male. Schoolteaching is mainly a woman's profession in the United States, where it is less highly valued than in countries where it is a predominantly male profession.

These broad comparisons suggest that occupational status varies according to whether the work force is male or female. Touhey (1974), a social psychologist, has demonstrated in a laboratory study the effect of female participation lowering occupational prestige. He asked one group of male and female students to rate the prestige and desirability of five high-status professions such as law and medicine after they had been told that each one would show a substantial increase in the proportion of women over the next twenty-five to thirty years. A second group of students rated the occupations but received no information about the expected numbers of women. The students in the first group rated the occupations lower in status and desirability than did students of the second group. These findings are consistent with the view that the status of a particular occupation is higher when there are more men in the work force. In addition, they demonstrate that when large numbers of women enter an occupation, its status declines.

So far we have considered the status of occupations that are perceived as men's or women's work. We turn now to the evaluation of men's and women's work performance. Again, stereotypical beliefs held about women are essentially negative. We already noted that many men consider women to be unsuitable for positions of power and responsibility. Studies published in the 1970s report that male managers often regard women as making poorer supervisors than men, and they claim that workers feel uncomfortable with a woman supervisor (O'Leary, 1974; Hartnett, 1978). Surveys of male personnel managers also reveal a disapproval of women occupying senior posts, as well as a more general negative evaluation of women applicants (Hartnett, 1978).

Associated with negative judgments about women and their work performance is the notion that women are less motivated or interested in their work. It is claimed that women are less concerned with getting ahead in the world of work, that they are more content with intellectually undemanding jobs, and that they are more interested in the social ties they establish with other workers than with their work. Studies of the occupational aspirations of men and women, however, suggest that they are much closer to one another than such stereotypical views indicate (Cowley et al., 1973).

Attribution is a term used by social psychologists to describe people's interpretation of the behavior of others – for example, the reasons they put forward to explain another person's performance on a problem-solving task. Several attribution studies have been concerned with the reasons people give for successful and unsuccessful task performance by men and women. These studies are of interest to us in relation to stereotypes about men's and women's work performance. In one study the task consisted of matching labels to tools that were stereotypically either masculine, such as a screwdriver, or feminine, such as a whisk or a colander. Observers were informed about the quality of individual performances using these tools, relative to a hypothetical average, and then asked to rate actual performances. For the masculine objects, a good performance by a man was more often attributed to ability than was a good performance by a woman. Several other studies of this type have found that ability was more often used to explain male achievements and causes such as effort or luck to explain women's success (Deaux, 1976a). Failure was also judged differently according to gender: In women, it was more likely to be attributed to lack of ability.

Kay Deaux suggested that gender stereotypes affect people's expectations about performance. In particular, the idea that men are competent and that women are not is brought to bear in attributing success or failure. Thus a successful man confirms most people's expectations, and the cause of his success can be attributed to a stable characteristic – namely, ability. A successful woman contradicts most people's expectations, and a temporary reason for success is more likely to be sought – for instance, the woman has made a greater effort. Similarly, failure is more often expected for a woman and hence is more likely to be attributed to a stable characteristic, particularly lack of ability.

In this way, stereotypes about the competence of men and women affect expectations about their performance and influence attempts to explain it. Although this research was carried out in an academic setting far removed from the world of work, it demonstrated that the same level of performance can be judged to have different meanings when achieved by a man or a woman. Other studies have shown that the same piece of work may be rated more highly when attributed to a man than to a woman (e.g., Goldberg, 1968). If judgments such as these are widespread in the world of work – and there is no obvious reason why they should not be – they suggest a further important way in which stereotypical beliefs contribute to the higher occupational achievements of men. A woman may perform as well as a man and still have her achievement regarded as being less valuable.

So far we have examined the influence of gender stereotypes on occupational status and on evaluations of the work performance of men and women. Perhaps the most pervasive stereotype is the belief that a man's main responsibility is to go out to work and a woman's is to look after her family. One consequence of this belief is that a working man is seen as the breadwinner and a woman as merely working for "pin money." This view may also be used as a reason for undervaluing the contribution of women workers, for justifying lower pay for women, and for regarding men's careers as being of greater importance than women's. Despite this belief in both the United States and Britain, a large proportion of women workers were the chief economic supporters of households in the 1970s (Frieze, 1978; Hartnett, 1978).

The view that the man must necessarily be the breadwinner is still a widespread one, and some indication of its influence can be obtained from the reactions of men with families to unemployment. A British study of unemployment in London and Merseyside in the 1970s found that many unemployed men carried out "feminine" activities in the home, such as doing the housework and taking the children to school (Hill, 1978). This change of role was one of necessity rather than choice, and it was typically accompanied by a feeling of lowered status. Many men said that they felt degraded because they believed that they should be the breadwinner and were not.

In this section we have been concerned mainly with the influence of stereotypes on the value and status of men's and women's work and have shown a variety of influences that can contribute to the lower status of women's occupations and to the lower evaluations of women's work performance. Rather than list again which occupations are viewed as male or female preserves, we consider instead below how ideas about occupational suitability have influenced the opportunities and vocational training open to boys and girls.

Opportunity and training

As a result of such legislation as the Equal Pay Act of 1963 and Title VII of the 1964 Civil Rights Act, there are few occupations completely barred to women (or to men) in the United States. Similarly, the British Sex Discrimination Act of 1975 outlawed the most obvious forms of occupational discrimination. Nevertheless, in both countries beliefs about men and women and the work suitable for them still effectively prevent the entry of women into certain occupations and retard their promotion and advancement in many other ways.

Structural constraints also prevent many women from pursuing the uninterrupted careers often necessary for achievement in the world of work. Career development is usually geared to the typical male life plan, so that there is little provision for the flexibility required if a successful career is to be combined with childbirth and child care. By 1973, a third of American mothers with preschool children were working outside the home (Tavris and Offir, 1977). Yet surveys carried out at this time indicated that only 10 percent of children with working mothers attended day-care centers (Kahne, 1975). Similarly, in Britain in the 1970s a third of the female labor force were responsible for dependent children, and yet there were few child-care facilities; indeed, in the twenty years after 1945 there was a decline in day nurseries and nursery schools. This was partly attributable to doubts expressed by some child-care experts about the wisdom of women with young children going out to work. As a result, the majority of employed mothers had to make their own arrangements for the care of their children (Mackie and Pattullo, 1977).

The lower levels of further education and training provide a further constraint on the work opportunities open to women. Again, stereotypical ideas about women and work play an important part. The belief that woman's place is in the home may channel many girls' aspirations primarily toward marriage rather than occupational attainment. In addition, the limited range of occupations regarded as suitable for women may exert a restricting influence on the occupational aspirations, education, and training of girls. Surveys carried out in Britain in the 1970s showed that boys and girls were still being taught different subjects from an early age; some school subjects, such as physics and woodworking, were perceived as masculine, while others, such as biology and home economics, were seen as feminine (Mackie and Pattullo, 1977). This difference in interests is reflected in the proportions of boys and girls who pursue such subjects to an advanced level (see Table 2.5). Interest in computers among children is also male-biased, and this is particularly encouraged by the nature of commercially available software such as war games (Kiesler et al., 1983).

Hartnett (1978) argued that the career guidance offered British schoolchildren was often strongly influenced by gender stereotypes about women and work and contributed directly to the perpetuation of these stereotypes. Traditionally, nursing and clerical work have been the two careers thought suitable for girls (Mackie and Pattullo, 1977). Further evidence from British studies shows that both male and female career counselors approved more of occupational choices that were consistent with gender stereotypes than of those that were not. Career information leaflets also showed men and women in traditionally stereotyped occupations; and measures of vocational interest, interview methods, and test techniques used by career counselors reflected gender stereotypes (Hartnett, 1978).

Earlier in this chapter we described gender differences in further education and occupational training. Not only do more boys than girls take degree courses in Britain, but they are more likely to choose traditionally male subjects such as engineering, architecture, and science. Girls are more likely to choose subjects such as languages, literature, social administration or business.

Aspirations and achievement motivation

Having examined the external constraints and influences on women's work opportunities, we now consider achievement aspirations. Given the wide-ranging stereotype that women's work is of lesser value and status, it would hardly be surprising to find that women's aspirations are more limited than those of men.

Earlier in this chapter we considered attribution research and discussed the judgments that people make about the performance of others. We can also examine the judgments that people make about their own behavior. Older research suggested that women had lower expectations about their own performance than men; in other words, they were more likely to view their own successful performance in terms of luck, and failure as a lack of ability (Deaux, 1976a). This was thought to be a further consequence of the gender stereotype of lower competence (Deaux, 1976a). A more recent review of the evidence (Frieze et al., 1982) questions this conclusion, concluding that there are no strongly supported gender differences in self-attributions. Many of the studies did find gender differences, but the findings contradicted one another. In an earlier article, Frieze (1978) commented that studies that did demonstrate lower expectations for women often used tasks on which they had little or no experience. Frieze et al. (1982) suggest that there may be no *general* differences between men and women in their self-attributions and that perhaps this factor is not, after all, a generally important one for explaining differences in achievement.

The levels of occupational aspiration of men and women may be more closely related to their perceived possibilities for advancement in a particular occupation than to expectations about success in specific work tasks. In a study of employees from a large corporation in the United States, it was found that women in management positions had achievement aspirations

similar to those of their male counterparts. But in the corporation as a whole, men were generally more eager for advancement than women. Nevertheless, those men who viewed their
achievement opportunities as being blocked showed attitudes
to work and advancement similar to the majority of female
employees (Tavris and Offir, 1977).

So far we have considered people's attributions of their own
ability and their aspirations for advancement. These are both
related to achievement motivation, an aspect of personality
that has been researched by psychologists for many years.
McClelland and his colleagues first investigated it in the 1940s
and 1950s using a test called the Thematic Apperception Test
(TAT), in which people were asked to make up stories, in
response to a series of pictures depicting ambiguous situations,
which were then scored in terms of various themes, including
achievement.

Only a few of the earlier studies of achievement motivation
included women as well as men. The effects of deliberately
stimulating people's interest in achievement was assessed by
asking people to carry out a task after being told that good
performance on the task indicated intelligence and the ability to
organize material and evaluate conditions quickly and accurately. For men, these sessions led to an increase in the number
of achievement-related themes in their TAT stories, but this was
not the case for women (Maccoby and Jacklin, 1974). Originally
these results were taken as indicating that women showed less
achievement motivation than men, although women had dis-
played more achievement fantasy prior to stimulation. Later
findings showed that by altering the nature of the session designed to stimulate achievement from one involving competence to social approval, women's TAT scores could be induced
to rise more than those of men (Maccoby and Jacklin, 1974).

The conclusions that we might draw from this research are
tempered by the use of male characters in the TAT pictures.
Even when female characters are used for women and girls,
there are problems. It has been found that both genders show

fewer achievement-related responses to stories with female characters. The use of pictures of a specific gender leads to confusion of achievement motivation and ideas shared by both genders about appropriate behavior for men and women.

We cannot conclude from research on achievement motivation that women show lower levels of achievement motivation than men. Not very much research has been carried out on women and achievement motivation since the work of McClelland and his colleagues. An offshoot of McClelland's work is research on "fear of success," originally carried out by Martina Horner. She asked samples of undergraduates at the University of Michigan to write stories in response to cue story lines. For example, "After first-term finals, Anne finds herself top of the medical school class" was the cue used for women, where for men the name John replaced Anne (Horner, 1972, p. 161). Horner devised a scoring system for what she described as fear-of-success imagery. This consisted of three main themes: (1) social rejection – for example, fear that success would be linked with losing friends or with sexual unattractiveness; (2) more general guilt and anxiety about success – for example, fear that the person would be unhappy or feel unfeminine; (3) bizarre or exaggeratedly hostile themes or denial of the cue altogether. Horner's main and widely reported finding was that 65 percent of women but only 10 percent of men wrote stories containing at least one fear-of-success image (Horner, 1972).

Horner also tested students on a timed task that consisted of unscrambling mixed-up letters, and she compared performance when tested in a group or alone. Women who wrote stories with much fear-of-success imagery also tended to show a lower performance when tested in a group than when tested alone. As a result of her findings, Horner suggested that women have a motive to avoid success and that this explains the inconsistent and unpredictable behavior of women found in many of the earlier studies of achievement motivation (O'Leary, 1974).

Horner's study was widely publicized. Many psychologists and journalists believed that it provided an explanation for women's low occupational achievement. It seemed to indicate to them that whereas men are motivated to achieve without too many conflicting motives, women's achievement motivation conflicts with a feminine self-image, resulting in an overall motive to avoid success. The idea of fear of success became so much accepted for a time that there was even a symposium entitled "Fear of Success: Is It Curable?"

There have, however, been many criticisms denying the adequacy of Horner's original experiment, of her concept of fear of success, and its ability to account for gender differences in occupational attainment (e.g., Levine and Crumrine, 1975; Tresemer, 1977; Frieze, 1978). Many follow-up studies were carried out and a variety of results obtained in terms of the proportion of men and women who write stories with fear-of-success themes (Tavris and Offir, 1977; Tresemer, 1977). In a reanalysis of the combined results of nine published studies similar to Horner's original one carried out between 1971 and 1973 no difference was found between the fear-of-success imagery of men and women (Tresemer, 1977). In one fairly precise replication of Horner's study undertaken in 1975, 70 percent of the stories written by both women and men contained at least one fear-of-success image. The stories of both genders also contained about the same proportion of sentences with negative remarks about success (Levine and Crumrine, 1975).

It has been suggested that Horner's findings reflect people's understanding of the meaning of achievement for a man and for a woman rather than, as Horner suggested, a deep-rooted personal motive (Tavris and Offir, 1977). Horner (1972) followed up her earlier achievement motivation studies by asking men to write about a successful man and women to write about a successful woman. An assumption here was that whereas responses would not necessarily reflect personal motives, they might be related to wider beliefs and attitudes about female success. In other words, the stories might often be realistic assessments of what it would be like to be at the top of the class in the circumstances described in the cue line.

The general idea that success is a mixed blessing and consequently arouses ambivalent motives is a widespread and old one. It can be found in Eastern philosophy, in Christian teachings, and in psychoanalytical theory. Jung put forward the idea that achievements are often constructed at the expense of other aspects of a person's personality. Most of these ideas are primarily concerned with male success, since it is usually men who are successful.

Although ambivalent feelings and motives toward success may be widespread in men and women, the gender difference found by Horner has not been clearly or repeatedly established, and supportive results are not very numerous or consistent (Tresemer, 1977). Even if Horner's original results had been replicated, the effect obtained was of insufficient size to explain the much larger gender difference in occupational achievement. We conclude that women's lower occupational achievement and status are not explained by a motive to avoid success, but rather that they are the result of a combination of the other influences. Widespread stereotypical beliefs form the basis for undervaluing female occupations and achievement. Stereotypes also prescribe the restricted and lower-status occupations regarded as suitable for women. These beliefs both influence and are derived from differences in educational and vocational training available to men and women. They may also affect men's and women's aspirations and ideas about their own abilities, as indicated by self-attribution studies, but they do not seem to affect the motive to achieve or the avoidance of achievement, at least according to the measures used by social psychologists.

9

Growing up male or female

In several preceding chapters our discussion was ordered in terms of specific topics such as aggression and occupational differences, and in each case we considered theories that might account for the origins of the gender differences we described. Such theories often paralleled the commonsense explanations we discussed in Chapter 1, in that they focused on either the biological properties of the individual or the social environment. For example, laypeople tend to view male aggression as rooted either in biology or in the upbringing of boys. Echoing this view, psychological theories explain male aggression in terms of either hormones or learning in childhood. In this chapter we again consider developmental theories – but as a whole rather than as related to specific topics – and we seek to go beyond these competing, and essentially commonsense, views (which amount to what is technically referred to as the *nature–nurture* controversy). We consider more complex accounts of how people interact with their environments during development, including the ways in which they make sense of (or structure) their external worlds and biological characteristics. (We referred briefly to this type of explanation in Chapter 1, under the heading "Research Strategies.")

One approach to theorizing in developmental psychology is represented in the commonsense biology-conditioning debate. Another major concern has been with charting the changes involved in a person's journey through life, either through the entire life span or until a point in young adulthood that is described as maturity. Although the notion of stages and the processes underlying them is less ingrained in the public consciousness than the nature-nurture issue, it is still reflected in parents' hopes that their children will "outgrow" unwanted habits. In the last part of this chapter we consider the stage approach in relation to the different developmental pathways of women and men.

The nature–nurture issue

When a baby is born, the first question people ask is whether it is a boy or a girl. The appearance of the infant's genitals usually provides the answer. This sex assignment at birth will have far-reaching consequences for the child's life: It determines which one of two very different developmental pathways the infant will follow. How can such a minor anatomical feature as genital appearance be so important for the future? It could be that genital differences are related to other biological features that are different in boys and girls and that control aspects of psychological and behavioral development. Alternatively, the genitals may simply provide signals that are elaborately interpreted in the social world. These two alternatives represent respectively the biological and environmental explanations of the development of gender differences, the nature–nurture issue, which we introduced above. We now consider the two views in turn.

Behavioral differences between boys and girls found early in life are often attributed to a biological cause because it is assumed that cultural influences do not begin to operate until a later time. This idea, together with the associated notion that later gender differences can be traced to these early differences, has been put forward in several articles and books about sex and gender (e.g., Garai and Scheinfeld, 1968; Bardwick, 1971; McGuinness, 1976).

A number of criticisms have been leveled at these arguments. First, the evidence for behavioral differences in newborn infants is inconsistent and unreliable from one study to another (Maccoby and Jacklin, 1974; Lewis, 1975; Birns, 1976). It has been suggested that a greater number of differences are reported in North American than in European studies because newborn American boys are much more likely to have been circumcised shortly after birth than their European counterparts (Richards et al., 1976). However, a later analysis failed to support this hypothesis, finding few consistent gender differences whether the male infants were circumcised or not (Brackbill and Schroder, 1980). A second criticism is that even if early gender differences did occur regularly and consistently, this would not necessarily indicate that they were of biological origin. Adults differentiate between baby boys and girls from birth onward (e.g., Rubin et al., 1974; White and Wollett, 1981), so that we cannot tell whether a particular behavioral gender difference observed during infancy is produced by different parental reactions or by different biological maturation (Lewis, 1975; Birns, 1976). We are also skeptical of the assumption that later masculine and feminine characteristics can be traced to early gender differences, since there is little evidence for such continuity in psychological development (Maccoby and Jacklin, 1974; Birns, 1976). In view of these criticisms, we do not support the view that gender differences found early in life are necessarily biological in origin.

More specific biological explanations have been offered to account for psychological gender differences. These have taken several forms – for example, the action of sex hormones on the developing brain before birth, the influence of sex hormones during adult life, and differences in brain maturation between boys and girls. We have considered some of these explanations in earlier chapters – for example, Dorner's theory of homosexuality in Chapter 3 and theories relating to aggression in Chapter 5, fear in Chapter 6, and specific abilities in Chapter 8. Here we consider two more general views that gender-role-related activities and interests are influenced by sex hormones acting on the brain either during prenatal development only or at this time with further effects at puberty.

In rodents such as rats and mice, testosterone secreted early in fetal development affects not only the maturation of the reproductive organs, as it does in human beings (see Chapter 3), but also later behavior: It influences play behavior in the young animal and mating patterns, aggressiveness, fear behavior, and eating and activity levels in the adult (Archer, 1975; Quadagno et al., 1977; Olioff and Stewart, 1978). Money and Ehrhardt (1972), by analogy, applied findings of this type to human gender differences – principally to play and maternal interests (but also to career choice and sexuality).

It is widely believed that boy's play involves more vigorous activities, such as wrestling and tumbling ("rough-and-tumble" play) than girl's play (Chapter 5), and this difference is observed in cultures very different from our own, such as the Kalahari San (Blurton-Jones and Konner, 1973). It is also observed in several mammals such as rats and rhesus monkeys, where it has been shown that treatment of females with testosterone during prenatal development leads to increased rough-and-tumble play (Goy, 1968; Phoenix, 1974; Olioff and Stewart, 1978). Money and Ehrhardt (1972) reported that girls exposed before birth to (androgenic) substances similar to testosterone also play more energetically than normal girls. The hormone-treated girls were more interested in athletic skills and sports and preferred playing with boys. They were known to themselves and their mothers as "tomboys." The girls also showed diminished maternal interests, which were indicated by their lack of interest in dolls and infant caregiving and by their infrequent daydreams about pregnancy and motherhood. Money and Ehrhardt explain both these findings by suggesting that the hormone has had a masculinizing effect on the girls' developing brains. In explaining rough-and-tumble play and the lack of maternal interest, studies of early testosterone exposure and later behavior in rodents are cited to support the argument, although no clear connection has been established between parental behavior and early testosterone treatment in rodents (Reinisch, 1976; Quadagno et al., 1977). Money and Ehrhardt suggested that, in the case of human beings, the hormone affects those parts of the brain that control play and maternal interests.

Money and Ehrhardt's studies have become well known, but their explanation is controversial. Alternatives have been suggested – in particular, that the parents of these girls may have treated them differently. The general belief that these children had in some way been "masculinized" before birth could have altered their parents' social perception and treatment of them. Ehrhardt and Baker (1974) concluded on the basis of interviews with the parents that although these possibilities could not be ruled out, they did not seem to provide an obvious explanation. An alternative interpretation is that although the influences are not obvious, they operated in a subtle way. There is evidence from other studies that parents treat newborns differently according to gender (White and Wollett, 1981) and that they describe them in gender-stereotyped ways (Rubin et al., 1974). Mothers also reacted differently in a laboratory setting to the same baby depending on whether it was presented as a boy or a girl, whereas they reported few differences in the handling of their own babies (Smith and Lloyd, 1978) and were unaware that they handled the babies in the laboratory differently according to gender (Culp et al., 1983).

Quadagno et al. (1977) have specifically criticized Money and Ehrhardt's conclusions on the following grounds. First, they pointed out that a high proportion of the girls received late surgical correction for genital abnormalities – in other words, they had malelike genitals for some time after birth. Second, since Money and Ehrhardt derived their evidence from interviews and questionnaires given to the girls and their mothers rather than from observations of play, this only shows that the girls were *perceived* as tomboys and lacking in maternal interests. The label "tomboy" may have preceded the behavior and may have been based on parental expectations or on the appearance of the malelike genitals.

There may be a more general difficulty in using the label "tomboy." A study of autobiographies written by women undergraduate psychology students found that a majority of them described themselves as having been tomboys during childhood. Another study of adolescent girls found that 63 percent reported that they were tomboys; and a large majority of yet another sample also reported being tomboys in childhood (Hyde et al., 1977).

In view of these findings, more direct observations of girls exposed to androgens prenatally are necessary before we can conclude that differences are attributable to hormone exposure before birth rather than to parental expectations. Even if genuine behavioral differences were found, we should still not rule out the possible influence of parental reactions.

Since Money and Ehrhardt's pioneering research in this area, further studies have been carried out. Some were concerned with the effects on the fetus of female hormones, which are regarded as countering the effects of androgens. The findings indicated a lessening of masculine interests and heterosexual experience in boys (Baker, 1980), and a lessening of tomboyish behavior in girls, as a result of the hormonal treatment (Ehrhardt et al., 1981). Since the girls' genitals were not masculinized and behavioral assessment was more carefully controlled than in earlier research, some of the questions we raised have been answered. Evidence from these studies, and from others such as Reinisch (1981), who found that early androgen treatment was associated with a higher incidence of aggression (see Chapter 5), make it clear that the last word has not been written on this intriguing subject.

We have covered this type of biological explanation in some detail, since it is widely known and relies to a larger extent than most on human rather than animal research. The various difficulties and methodological criticisms that we considered illustrate the pitfalls in trying to establish conclusively the existence of a biologically produced gender difference relatively independent of environmental influences.

Money and Ehrhardt viewed the social environment as being able to *modify* the degree to which biological factors influence play orientation, maternal interests, and career choices. In relation to "gender identity" – the child's understanding of whether he or she is a boy or a girl – Money and Ehrhardt viewed the social environment as being the sole or major influence, a conclusion generally accepted by psychologists working in this area. Gender identity is established early in life (Money et al., 1957; Lewis, 1981) and assumes crucial significance in subsequent gender development (see the later section on the cognitive developmental theory).

In contrast to this view, Imperato-McGuinley et al. (1974) suggested that hormones exert a far more powerful and all-pervasive influence – controlling not only gender-role–related activities but also gender identity. We described some aspects of their work in Chapter 3, concerning the occurrence, in Salinas in the Dominican Republic, of *guevedoces*, genetic males with an enzyme deficiency that leads to a feminization of their genitals that is apparent at birth. At puberty the *guevedoces* become masculinized – their genitals included. The controversial aspect of the work of Imperato-McGuinley et al. is their claim that since the *guevedoces* had been reared as girls and yet had no difficulty adopting the masculine role at puberty, their adult gender identity must have been achieved, *despite* their upbringing, by an influence of prenatal and pubertal testosterone.

Their conclusion runs counter to the widely accepted environmental view of gender identity we noted earlier and to all other evidence from the clinical literature (Money and Ehrhardt, 1972). It was, therefore, not surprising that this work received an initially hostile response from Money (1976). Money argued that after three generations of experience with such children, the townspeople had learned to distinguish them as a separate category and that parents who reared them would be aware that they would no longer appear feminine after puberty. Money also claimed that even before the *guevedoces* were widely known to the townspeople, they would have been reared – because of their slightly masculinized "female" genitals – as someone of ambiguous gender. This particular point was questioned by Imperato-McGuinley et al. (1976), who claimed that interviews with the original parents showed that they had reared their offspring as girls – without apparent signs of uncertainty or ambiguity.

More recent discussions of these findings tend to support Money's interpretation. First, genital appearance apparently is not normal at birth (in particular, the clitoris is enlarged), and this could have influenced both upbringing and self-image (Baker, 1980; Rubin et al., 1981). Second, the existence of *gueve-doces* was well known in the area before they were studied scientifically. Third, they occur in a highly gender-differentiated, traditional culture (Baker, 1980), where a change from girl to boy would most probably be viewed with favor by parents. Fourth, whereas in our culture the occurrence of an apparently spontaneous sex change at puberty would be rare and unexpected, in Salinas it is more common (one of every ninety males). It is also interesting to note that reports of individuals with a similar enzyme deficiency in the United States show that they maintained their existing female gender identity despite masculinization of the body at puberty (Rubin et al., 1981).

On the available evidence, we can conclude that rather than revealing general principles about the influence of hormones on behavioral development, this research illustrates the way one particular culture has reacted to the spontaneous occurrence of individuals whose appearance and development raised doubts about their gender category.

Socialization accounts

We now turn to the "nurture" viewpoint in the nature-nurture controversy – that the environment provides the dominant source of influence in psychological development. In this case, environment refers to the interpersonal and cultural environment. In psychology and the social sciences, the term *socialization* describes the acquisition of culturally appropriate behavior, attitudes, and values. Socialization can be studied at a variety of levels. It can take the form of studying the values and attributes that are widespread in society – in other words, the stereotypes and social representations available for transmission to succeeding generations. In earlier chapters we have often discussed the existence and impact of stereotypes, since they have influenced research on gender.

The dominant psychological approach to the study of socialization in the 1950s and 1960s sought to explain the childhood origins of general personality characteristics – in particular, aggression and dependence (Mischel, 1970). These two attributes were chosen to represent respectively the undersocialized and the oversocialized individual (Danziger, 1971). Aggression and dependence are also of interest in relation to gender roles because they are believed to represent core masculine and feminine characteristics (Mischel, 1966). Indeed, Kagan and Moss (1962) found that measures of dependence and passivity showed a degree of developmental continuity for girls, where they were gender-appropriate traits, but not for boys, where they were not. Regarding measures of aggression, boys but not girls showed developmental continuity. Overall, however, approaches to the study of socialization based on general personality characteristics have revealed few identifiable childhood antecedents of adult behavior.

One major difficulty with this approach lies in the use of global concepts such as aggression and dependence. We noted in Chapter 1 that the use of these terms often reflects commonsense preoccupations. The assumption that they are single stable personality traits has not been borne out by research, as different measures of aggression and of dependence showed low relationships to one another (Danziger, 1971).

The socialization research we consider in the remainder of this section is concerned with the following question: To what extent are boys and girls subject to different pressures from parents and from others? The major question that has been asked about parental influences is directly related to the nature–nurture issue. It concerns whether such influences are sufficient to account for gender differences in psychological development. Maccoby and Jacklin (1974) concluded that the evidence revealed surprisingly few differences in parental behavior that were determined by the gender of the child. However, in the previous section we noted studies, carried out since then, of parents' reactions to their newborn babies and to strange infants that revealed the influence of perceived gender. These results contradicted Maccoby and Jacklin's conclusions in that they demonstrated parents reacting differently to boys and girls *from birth* – but the generality of these findings is yet to be demonstrated.

One large-scale research project on the child-rearing practices of parents of school-age children showed considerable differences in parental treatment of boys and girls (Block, 1978). For example, parents of sons were more concerned with punishment and negative sanctions and with conformity to gender-stereotyped standards; fathers also provided more comfort to their daughters than to their sons. Block specifically criticized Maccoby and Jacklin's conclusions on parental socialization influences on the grounds that they had used concepts that were too global – such as aggression, independence, and restrictiveness. In Chapter 1, we noted some of the difficulties with these general labels. Block claimed that these terms have different meanings when applied to sons and daughters. She also stressed the role of the father, commenting that studies reviewed by Maccoby and Jacklin often combined data from both parents or lacked any evidence about the father. Block's study, on the other hand, indicated that mothers and fathers played different roles in socialization. Block pointed out that the children in her study were on average around twelve years old, whereas Maccoby and Jacklin were discussing evidence from younger ages. She rightly raised the possibility that if socialization practices become more marked with age, this might account for some of the discrepancy between their conclusions.

We have already noted, however, that there is some evidence that parents react differently to boys and girls even in infancy. Parents typically provide boys and girls with different toys, and again this begins early in life. In a study of the contents of one- to six-year-old children's rooms in a number of middle-class homes, Rheingold and Cook (1975) found clear gender differences in the toys provided. The contents of boys' rooms were more varied and contained more toy animals, vehicles, and live animals, whereas girls' rooms contained more dolls, dollhouses, floral wallpaper, fabrics, and lace. At eighteen months, provision of these different toys at home did not coincide with the children's play preferences as observed in the laboratory, where girls spent as much time as boys in a pursuit regarded as masculine, playing with a large plastic truck.

Of course, parents are not the only agents of socialization. According to Tieger (1980), Maccoby and Jacklin's conclusions about a relative lack of evidence for socialization influences also ignored sources from outside the family. Tieger referred in particular to the impact of the media. Television programs and commercials portray gender-stereotypical images (Sternglanz and Serbin, 1974). Teachers may respond in a gender-stereotypical manner to boys and girls (Serbin et al., 1973). Peer groups are yet another influence. Fagot (1977) observed that children playing at gender-inappropriate activities were criticized and ostracized by their peers. Pitcher and Schultz (1983) found that the peer group was a particularly important source of gender-related ideas for preschool children and that these ideas tended to be caricatures of adult stereotypes. There is, therefore, ample evidence that gender-stereotyped messages coming from a variety of sources are available to boys and girls from an early age.

In the rest of this section we consider how these stereotypical messages are transmitted to the child. Attempts to answer this question have usually followed one of two major theoretical perspectives. Here we consider one of these, social learning. The other, the cognitive developmental perspective, is considered in the following section.

The social-learning approach developed from the behaviorist tradition in North American psychology, which had been concerned with formulating general laws of learning. The principles of classical conditioning – learning through association of events in time – and operant conditioning – learning through receiving a reward for a specific action – have been widely applied to human learning, including the learning of gender-appropriate responses (Mischel, 1966, 1970). An important principle that has been added to modern accounts is learning through observing the responses of another individual. Imitation is clearly an important feature in human socialization, and it has played a prominent part in social learning explanations. The social-learning account of the acquisition of gender differences encompasses imitation as well as principles of reward and punishment.

Children receive parental approval for behavior appropriate for their gender and disapproval for inappropriate behavior (Fling and Manosevitz, 1972; Fagot, 1974, 1977; Snow et al., 1983). As we have already discussed, these parental reactions can be observed very early in life. Further examples can be found in a study by Lewis (1975), who reported that touching was discouraged in infant boys, whereas girls were freer to touch other children. Peer group pressure is another source of reward and punishment. Fagot (1977) found that three- to four-year-old children would criticize, and be less likely to initiate play with, other children whose play involved opposite-gender activities. Similarly, a three-year-old boy who said that he wanted to cook the dinner was told by his girl playmate that "daddies don't cook" (Garvey, 1977). Teachers provide yet another source. Fagot (1977) found that nursery school teachers criticized girls for engaging in "masculine" activities such as playing with blocks, and boys for engaging in "feminine" activities such as playing with dolls. Other studies also showed that nursery school teachers encouraged and discouraged different activities in boys and girls (Serbin et al., 1973).

There are several ways in which imitation may lead to

gender-stereotyped responses. The most obvious is that boys and girls may be exposed to different people and to different activities, collectively termed role models in social-learning terminology. Girls generally have greater access to women early in their lives, since their mothers or female caregivers will usually be present for much of the day. Fathers are usually only present intermittently, so that a boy will have to rely on older boys and on the media to provide role models of masculine behavior. Boys and girls may also watch different television programs and read different comics. Perhaps the most important influence of this type is that the two genders tend to play independently of one another (e.g., Lever, 1976) and are thus exposed to different models during play.

Another way in which gender-stereotyped responses might arise is if children only attend to what people of their own gender are doing. Mischel (1970) raised this possibility citing a study that found that children watching a film showed more eye movements toward the major characters of their own gender. A more recent study found that boys and girls attended to an equal extent to people of the same and opposite genders portrayed on slides, but the measure of attention used in this study was rather idiosyncratic (Bryan and Luria, 1978).

In seeking to account for gender-role development in terms of social-learning theory, Mischel (1966, 1970) made a clear distinction between learning and performance. He suggested that children learn behavior associated with their own and opposite gender, but that they only *perform* gender-appropriate activities. However, since lack of performance may impede learning right from the start for many activities, this distinction may not be so useful in practice. It also underestimates the importance of practice for learning skills, both intellectual and social: By performing gender-appropriate activities, boys and girls come to acquire skills necessary for competently performing these activities. Even so, some studies suggest that children possess knowledge of the other gender's responses but will not readily perform these responses. Hargreaves (1976, 1977) analyzed the content of children's drawings made according to the instruction to complete circles by drawing objects: Boys and girls showed different responses, boys showing more mechanical and scientific themes and girls showing more domestic themes. When the children were given a parallel form of the same test but asked to fill it out as the opposite gender would, boys' and girls' responses were reversed. This study not only demonstrated a gender difference in response styles but also suggested that at least some information about the activities of the opposite gender is learned but not performed.

Another question is whether boys and girls imitate activities simply because they are performed by a member of their own gender. Imitation is often thought to take place in this way, with boys and girls "identifying" with people of their own gender. However, Barkley et al. (1977) found that the important feature is whether or not the observed activity is considered gender-appropriate, rather than which gender is performing it. Thus girls imitated behavior they saw as feminine, regardless of the gender of the person displaying it. A large number of other studies, reviewed by Barkley et al. (1977), supported this conclusion.

There are, therefore, several ways in which boys and girls could acquire different forms of behavior, notably selective reward and punishment and imitation of people performing gender-appropriate activities. The social-learning view of gender, as elaborated by Mischel (1966, 1970) and others (e.g., Perry and Bussey, 1979), seeks to provide a comprehensive explanation of the processes by which socialization influences are transmitted to the next generation. Few, if any, psychologists doubt the existence of such processes, but many have raised the question of whether the social-learning view is adequate to account for the origins of all aspects of gender-related behavior.

Two major shortcomings of the social-learning approach have often been noted. First, doubts have been raised as to whether the different learning conditions acting on boys and

girls are sufficient to explain all the observed gender differences. Such doubts have led some psychologists to suggest
either a major or minor role for biological maturation (e.g.,
Hutt, 1972a, and Maccoby and Jacklin, 1980, respectively). Secondly, it is felt that the part played by the child is underesti-
mated by social-learning theorists. One critic has even labeled
the social-learning view the "hospital bed" theory of socialization: The child is seen as passive, like a patient lying in bed
who simply receives the hospital's treatment. Admittedly,
modern versions of social-learning theory have gone some way
toward rectifying this impression by considering how the child
views and selects material for imitation (Bandura, 1977; Barkley
et al., 1977). Long before such modifications to social-learning
theory were proposed, other psychologists had already sought
alternative ways of characterizing the developmental process –
ways that took greater account of the two-way interaction between the child and the environment.

The cognitive developmental approach:
an interactionist theory

Although nowadays most psychologists would say that they
favor some form of "interactionist" approach, since both the
nature and the nurture views on their own are too narrow, this
is seldom developed as a coherent theory. More often the interactionist position takes the form of trying to disentangle and
separate out the possible sources of influence, biological and
environmental, followed by an acknowledgment such as the
following: "Biological attributes and cultural concept could not
become analytically disentangled in a single cause-and-effect
relationship" (Tieger, 1980, p. 959). It is indeed difficult to understand the interaction of the organism and environment
without taking into account the dynamics of development, the
progression through time. This aspect has been considered in
cognitive developmental accounts, which provide the major alternative to the social-learning perspective.

The cognitive developmental view seeks to describe the progressive interaction between the child and the environment, and in particular how the child comes to understand the social world (Kohlberg, 1966). Kohlberg viewed the child as an active agent seeking to make sense of the world outside; the child's own attitudes and beliefs about gender roles were held to be of primary importance in guiding the child's interaction with the environment.

In some ways the difference between the social-learning and cognitive developmental approaches is one of different starting points and different emphasis: The former looks at the child from the viewpoint of an outside observer, whereas the latter views the child from within. If we take the example of a boy viewing a football match on television and immediately afterward going out to play football, the social-learning view would explain his behavior in terms of imitation and the (externally) available model, whereas the cognitive developmental view would emphasize the child's ability to understand that he is a boy and to select for viewing, and engaging in, "boys'" activities such as football rather than "girls'" activities such as sewing.

This difference of approach and emphasis means that cognitive developmental theory is stated in a language different from that of social-learning theory. The concept of gender identity – the child's ability to categorize him- or herself as a boy or a girl – which we introduced in connection with hormonal theories, is viewed as particularly important. According to Kohlberg (1966), who followed Money et al. (1957), gender identity appears between two and three years of age, but more recent evidence places it even earlier, between one and two years (Lewis, 1981).

Thus a two- or three-year-old child will have already learned that there are two categories of person and that she or he belongs to one of them. Kohlberg regarded this initial categorization as a necessary prerequisite for further learning about gender roles. A more recent study found that two- to three-year-old children were positive in their beliefs about their own gender and negative in their beliefs about the opposite one: This is consistent with Kohlberg's view that as children come to regard themselves as boys or girls, they will value gender-appropriate aspects of themselves positively and devalue aspects of the other gender (Kuhn et al., 1978). The two features of preference for and identification with one's gender were seen as guiding the processes of imitation and reinforcement, which assume such crucial importance in social-learning theory. The two theories differ in that cognitive developmental theory views imitation and reinforcement as being guided by the child's understanding of the meaning and significance of these events, whereas social-learning theory sees meaning and significance as arising from the imitation and reinforcement of gender-appropriate behavior.

Kohlberg (1966) claimed that, in the earliest years of life, a child knows relatively little about what distinguishes male and female and does not realize that sex remains constant throughout life. According to this view, a child three or four years of age may think that a girl can be changed into a boy by cutting her hair short or by being dressed as a boy. Only gradually do gender labels become applied more accurately, so that between the ages of five and six years the child will have come to realize that sex remains constant, irrespective of such changes as hair length or dress. These conclusions were based on studies in which the child was asked whether the gender of a pictured girl or boy could be transformed by various means. When children were asked direct questions about themselves – for example, what they would be when they grew up – the majority even of three-year-olds were in no doubt that their gender would remain constant (Shields and Duveen, 1982), despite claiming that a figure drawing *could* be changed by a change of clothes. When questioned, the children made clear distinctions between real and hypothetical – or "pretend" – transformations. Earlier studies employing pictorial transformations (Kohlberg, 1966; DeVries, 1969) are therefore called into question. The whole issue of "gender constancy" and how it relates to other aspects of gender development must now be viewed as problematic.

Children possess knowledge about gender-appropriate characteristics at an early age. Kuhn et al. (1978) presented two- to three-year-olds with two paper dolls, one called Michael and the other called Lisa. They were asked, in the form of a game, a number of questions about activities, characteristics, and adult roles. Kuhn et al. found that even at this age the children possessed quite an extensive knowledge about which activities were appropriate for boys and girls and about adult gender roles. At two years of age both boys and girls believed that girls would clean the house when they were grown up and that boys would be the boss and would mow the lawn.

There is also evidence that such early knowledge is related to the child's own behavior. Blakemore et al. (1979) found that knowledge of gender stereotypes was associated with preference for gender-appropriate toys in four- to six-year-olds. In a study of children aged three to four years, Eisenberg et al. (1982) found that although they chose toys along gender-appropriate lines and used considerable gender-role-oriented thinking to justify other children's likes and dislikes, they used more reasoning about the properties of the toys, such as what the toys would do, to justify their own preferences.

Another approach to gender that is broadly within the cognitive developmental framework derives from Bartlett's (1932) classic studies of memory, in which he demonstrated the importance of the subject's own organizing framework in the recall of verbal or graphical information. Such an organizing framework was conceptualized in terms of schemata, central cognitive structures that organize and direct our experience and at the same time are open to change. Following Bartlett and more recent discussions of the schema concept (notably Neisser, 1976), the term *gender schema* has been adopted to refer to cognitive structures concerned with processing information about gender (Liben and Signorella, 1980; Bem, 1981; Martin and Halverson, 1981). This has stimulated studies on whether gender is used as an organizing construct by children when they remember material in stories or pictures. Such studies show that children between the ages of five and eight years do indeed recall information on gender-stereotypical lines, and the extent to which they do so is a function of their own gender-stereotypical attitudes (Liben and Signorella, 1980; Carlsson and Jaderquist, 1983; Martin and Halverson, 1983). Whether this approach will provide a fruitful way of investigating the gender-related cognitive processes of younger children remains to be seen.

Another major aspect of Kohlberg's (1966) theory is that the *reasons* children give for males and females performing different activities undergo a series of developmental changes that coincide with changes in the child's general level of understanding about the physical and social world. Ullian (1976) investigated this aspect of the theory by interviewing six- to eighteen-year-olds about their beliefs concerning men and women. She asked a series of questions relating to nurturing, competence, activity level, and power. Examples of questions relating to power are "Who should be the boss in the family?" followed by "Why?" Ullian asserted that the answers to her questions indicated that there are six stages in the development of beliefs about masculinity and femininity: At the earliest age (six years), gender differences are viewed as being primarily the result of fixed biological attributes – that men work outside the home is seen as a consequence of their greater size and strength. By the third stage (ten years) gender differences are explained in terms of fixed social conventions, but this idea is soon replaced by more flexible notions of historical and social forces. At around fourteen to sixteen years, gender roles are viewed as a matter of inner feelings, and masculinity and femininity are seen as part of everyone's psychological makeup.

Essentially Ullian's evidence supported Kohlberg's stage theory, but it included very little information that would enable an independent judgment of the classifications she made. It is possible that her findings could be described in terms of a series of more gradual changes during development rather than as discrete stages. Ullian's two later stages occur after puberty, but she did not mention puberty as a possible source of change in gender-role concepts. Yet it is likely that reactions to physical maturation and adult gender-role requirements produce a marked change in the way a person thinks about masculinity and femininity.

We can conclude that cognitive developmental theory has been successful in stimulating research on the processes by which a child acquires and uses gender concepts to interact with the social world. But it has been less successful in addressing the question of changes with age: Kohlberg's and Ullian's theory of developmental stages in the understanding of gender is sketchy when compared with its application to other aspects of social development (e.g., moral development: Kohlberg, 1976). We address the question of changes with age more fully in a later section.

Nature, nurture, and models of development

In order to progress beyond the commonsense view of nature or nurture, it is helpful to consider "models" of development (Archer, 1980). In our discussion the term *model* refers to a precise but simplified representation that seeks to capture important principles underlying the original system. In constructing a general model of development, we ask where the controlling influence lies. Both the biological and the socialization views answer this question in relatively simple terms: Either the biological or environmental source of influence is regarded as being so much more important than the other that for practical purposes the lesser influence can be neglected (or regarded as having only a weak, modifying influence). This type of model is called the *main-effect model*. Mischel (1966), the social-learning theorist, would regard processes such as different types of reinforcement and modeling opportunities as overriding any biological differences between boys and girls. On the other hand, Gray (1971a) or Hutt (1972a, 1972b), biological theorists, would regard biological differences as being more important, so that environmental influences would only be capable of slightly amplifying or reducing the extent of such differences.

There are several ways of incorporating a control mechanism into a model of development. The most obvious of these is that there is some external or internal standard against which the performance of the individual is matched. This is easier to understand in the case of an external influence. For example, if it is decided that every child must learn a particular skill irrespective of his or her initial ability, performance will be monitored in relation to an "ideal" imposed from outside until it matches this. A similar but more continuous process could occur with gender-role learning, a boy's or girl's behavior being continually matched against standards shared by parents, teachers, and other children.

An internal controlling influence could operate through a similar matching process. The best examples of this are found in the control of physical processes, such as growth. The growth of a child is a regular and organized process; it is also self-stabilizing or target-seeking (Tanner, 1970), so that if the child's weight is depressed after illness or malnutrition, for example, weight gain will subsequently occur more rapidly until, in all but extreme cases, the child catches up to where he or she would have been. Various control mechanisms have been suggested for such catch-up effects (Tanner, 1970; Bateson, 1976). Essentially, they involve a negative feedback loop of the type found in many biological systems: Any variation due to the environment is compared to a reference value, in this case specifying the ideal outcome of growth, and discrepancies are corrected by appropriate action, such as by eating more or less. Similar catch-up effects have been observed in the case of intellectual development, again suggesting some form of internal reference value.

Most features of psychological development are more complex than these examples, and many psychologists view notions of overriding control by either the social environment or the biological organism as too simple to account for the complexities. Many developmental psychologists stress the notion of an *interaction* or continuous interplay between biology and the environment (e.g., Schaffer, 1974; Lewis, 1975; Tieger, 1980). In terms of models of development, one form of interactionist model sees the controlling influence as residing neither within the individual nor in the outside world (Bowers, 1973; Archer and Lloyd, 1975; Bateson, 1976), so that a far greater variety of possible outcomes can occur than with either type of main-effect model. When the interactionist model is applied to the development of psychological gender differences, a difficulty arises. Although there is a great deal of inconsistency in some of the research findings, many gender-related characteristics do show a measure of consistency in their outcome. Examples include aggression, spatial ability, mathematical, and verbal ability (Maccoby and Jacklin, 1974) and gender differences in major interests and occupational choice. It would seem, therefore, that a form of interactionist model that predicts variable outcomes could not account for these gender differences. Are they better explained by a main-effect model? Many gender differences can be viewed as a result of the socialization process, as we have indicated in this and other chapters. But we have also emphasized that development involves an interaction or continuous interplay between the child and the environment, and this aspect is absent from the social-learning main-effect model. How can we reconcile these two aspects? This can be done partly by realizing that the term *interactionist* is often used in two senses, one referring to any approach that recognizes the two-way interplay between the child and environment and the other – a more specialized meaning – referring to those cases where there is no overriding control on development from within the organism or from the environment. The interactionist model we have just described is of the second type. To account for consistencies in gender development, we require a model that involves both the notion of control and the principle of interaction used in the sense of interplay between organism and the environment. We now outline such a model, derived from Bateson (1976), and argue that it is the most appropriate one for describing the development of many gender differences.

The essential feature of Bateson's model is that the constant interplay of organism and environment leads to the establishment of an internal controlling influence on development. In effect, what happens is that the organism is born with the capacity to control its own development, as in the maturational main-effect model, but that it has no fixed control mechanism until it interacts with its environment, the exact nature of the control mechanism being determined by that environment. Bateson (1976) suggests that many behavioral systems, such as imprinting (Sluckin, 1972), are of this type. He does not refer to human gender-role learning, but the model would appear to fit this process – or rather, it would fit the cognitive developmental account of it.

Applying Bateson's model to gender development would produce the following. The individual comes into the world with no set notion of what male and female are, but develops a classification process at about two years of age. Subsequently this is elaborated and used as a way of making sense of the social world and of guiding action. Precisely what characteristics the child will use for distinguishing between appropriate and inappropriate action for his or her gender will depend on the social representations of his or her society. Hence the *content* of the internal reference value, the gender-role concept, depends on external influences; but the existence of the potential for classifying and acting on the basis of categories such as male or female is something that is part of the human biological makeup. In this way, human beings possess the intellectual equipment for incorporating aspects of their culture into a view of the world that emphasizes socially determined differences between categories. One might almost say that people are "programmed" to look at the social world in terms of differences and that social representations of gender provide one of the most readily available sets of material for this program to act upon. The construction of this internal system of gender rules occurs gradually throughout development without the child being consciously aware of it. Eventually, he or she will come to regard his or her own culturally induced variety of gender representations as equivalent to the natural order of things. In other words, nurture becomes second nature. (Similar views of gender development have been arrived at independently by Pleck, 1976, and Constantinople, 1979).

It is our opinion that social representations are very important for understanding gender differences (and we would place very much less emphasis on biological explanations). Nevertheless, the socialization process occurs in an interactive way, and gender concepts become incorporated into the mental fabric at an early age. It is scarcely surprising that they become very difficult to change later on.

Gender and developmental pathways

No account of development would be complete without considering changes with age. Major developmental theories, such as those of Freud, Erickson, and Piaget, together with Kohlberg's theory of moral development, have attempted to chart the pathway that children take on the way to young adulthood or beyond it throughout adult life (Lerner, 1976). However, most of these theories have little or nothing to say about the different pathways taken by males and females. Major theorists in the psychoanalytic tradition, such as Freud and Erickson, have been criticized for viewing the male as the standard model and the female as a deviant from this (see Chapter 4 and Gilligan, 1982). Similarly, Gilligan (1982) has remarked that Piaget's account of moral development is essentially an account of *male* moral development and that Kohlberg's later work, which was built on this, relied upon a study that used only male subjects. Gilligan interprets her more recent studies of *women's* moral development as having revealed fundamental differences from the male pattern, which by now has come to be described in all the well-known developmental texts as "moral development." She argues that whereas men tend to see morality in terms of rights and noninterference, women see it in interpersonal terms, principally helping and pleasing others. This argument was based mainly on illustrative examples, and it has been challenged convincingly by Colby and Damon (1983), who point out that studies of moral development that used Kohlberg's (and other) scoring systems do not reveal gender differences. Nevertheless, Gilligan's book ranges further than the specific issue of moral development. She calls attention to a different quality and pathway through life in female development and claims that this aspect has been ignored by most if not all major psychological theorists, whether they are dealing with adulthood or with developmental sequences. She goes on to suggest that "only when life-cycle theorists divide their attention and begin to live with women as they have lived with men will their vision encompass the experience of both sexes" (p. 23).

Gilligan's book can be viewed as part of a growing awareness that perhaps male and female development differ so fundamentally that they need to be considered as separate (though interrelated) developmental pathways. This view is also seen in some other contemporary accounts of gender development (Maltz and Borker, 1982; Block, 1983). Block argues that current socialization practices influence male and female cognitive development in different ways, boys being afforded more opportunities for independent problem solving and for engaging the wider world outside the home. This is seen as producing both a different view of and a different way of dealing with the social and physical world in boys and girls.

We consider Maltz and Borker's (1982) account of gender differences in communication patterns in more detail, to illustrate how male and female development can be viewed separately. Maltz and Borker begin by considering miscommunication in friendly conversations between women and men, which they characterize as follows. Men are more likely to interrupt, challenge or dispute their partner's utterances, to ignore the comments of the other speaker, to respond unenthusiastically, and to make more declarations of fact or opinion. Women, on the other hand, are more likely to ask questions and to maintain the flow of the conversation, to make more minimal positive responses, to use more personal pronouns, and to show silent forms of protest when interrupted. Maltz and Borker claim that these differences are not simply another expression of male power (cf. Henley's analysis of nonverbal communication in terms of power discussed in Chapter 5). Instead, they argue that, in a sense, men and women show cultural differences in their notions of what a friendly conversation entails and that these can be understood by viewing each gender group as a different subculture. In Chapter 5 we introduced Rogers's view that in some cultures women and men inhabit different conceptual worlds, but this idea was applied mainly to cultures where men and women spend most of their lives independently of one another. It may seem surprising – and even farfetched – to apply a similar view to our own culture, where men and women interact with one another much more freely. Maltz and Borker seek to counter this objection by claiming that the rules adults possess for operating in friendly interactions are learned from their peers between the ages of five and fifteen – a time when boys and girls interact mainly with their own gender.

Drawing on studies of children's play and social interactions (e.g., Lever, 1976), Maltz and Borker characterize girls' social play as follows. Girls tend to play in small groups with others of the same age, most often in pairs, and in relatively private settings. Play is cooperative and noncompetitive, and relationships tend to be exclusive, with the notions of the best friend crucial. Quarrels are not effectively dealt with, and usually lead to the breakup of the group. Girls use speech to create and maintain their friendship, to criticize in a subtle and acceptable way, and to interpret accurately what the other girls say. They learn, for example, to decipher the degree of closeness being offered, to recognize criticism, to learn when and in whom it is appropriate to confide, and generally to concentrate more on interpreting relationships and their contexts.

Maltz and Borker describe the world of boys' play groups as being very different. Boys play in larger, more hierarchically organized groups, where relative status is the main feature that is manipulated in the interactions. The social interactions of boys consist of posturing and counterposturing with speech used to assert status, to attract and keep an audience, and to assert oneself when others are speaking. A successful boy will be able to use these forms of speech appropriately – a boy who simply uses physical aggression will be unpopular and be viewed as a bully.

Maltz and Borker view the rules learned in these childhood groups as forming an essential basis for the way adult men and women use speech, women for negotiating and expressing relationships, and men for more culturally diverse ends but showing the common features of storytelling, arguing, and verbal posturing.

The socialization perspective we considered earlier concentrates on the transmission of specific gender-related messages. A major contribution of Maltz and Borker's approach is to provide an alternative view that considers gender development in terms of the separate social worlds of boys and girls. A similar change of emphasis can be found in other attempts to describe features specific to male or female development, which we present below.

David and Brannon (1976) have suggested that there are three phases in male-role development. The earliest of these involves the learning of negative rules associated with the avoidance of femininity. The second, which lasts until after the age of adolescence, is superimposed on the first and is characteristic of male peer groups; it consists of a series of positive guides, largely based on physical characteristics such as toughness, aggression, and sporting success. (But see above for the importance of language in boys' groups.) The third phase, which again operates in addition to what was learned before, consists of an adult-centered view of masculinity, based on intellectual and interpersonal competence and achievement. The second and third phases parallel a distinction made by Pleck (1976) between two forms of male role, "traditional" (physically based) and "modern," the second being historically superimposed on the first.

There are several interesting features raised by these views of male development. First, the sanctions against cross-gender behavior are greater for boys than for girls. They operate through the influence of parents, peers, and teachers and begin at an early age (Archer, 1984). Second, the children's notions of male-role requirements are, from an adult viewpoint, unrealistic. Boys tend to role-play unlikely occupations such as that of an astronaut (Greif, 1976); when asked about male role requirements, eight- to eleven-year-old boys replied that these involve, among other things, being able to fight off a bully, run fast, play many games, and climb (Hartley, 1957). The contradiction between boyhood and adult male roles produces inconsistencies and discontinuities in male development that are not found in female development (Archer, 1984).

In contrast to these features of male development, there are far fewer sanctions against girls' cross-gender behavior. This can be illustrated by contrasting the adult reactions to girl tomboys and to feminine boys. Tomboys are socially acceptable, whereas feminine boys are not; the latter may even be referred for treatment (Reckers and Yates, 1976). In addition, the role playing of girls involves components of the adult female role. Girls tend to play games such as mothers and fathers, nurses, and baby and bride (Greif, 1976).

Katz (1979) argued that tolerance of tomboyish behavior decreases drastically at adolescence, together with devaluation of girls' sporting achievement and academic excellence (cf. the quotation from the novel *Kinflicks* in Chapter 3). Interest becomes narrowly focused on activities related to dating, sexual attractiveness, and future marriage plans. Katz is suggesting a discontinuity in the development of girls at puberty: This contrasts with the form of discontinuity we have noted for male development, where the role content changed. For girls, there is less change in the content, although elements specifically associated with sexual and reproductive maturity are added. The major change is that the rules become more rigidly applied and acted upon. Katz also suggested that this narrow channeling of activities and interests is reflected in the declining academic performance found in adolescent girls. In Chapter 8, we discussed a similar explanation for the decline in adolescent girls' spatial ability (Siann, 1977), and in Chapter 3 we noted girls' decreased interest in sports at this time.

David and Brannon, as well as Katz, considered male and female development separately and in terms of chronological changes, but neither discussion considered development beyond young adulthood. A further perspective for viewing changes with age is to take account of differences throughout the whole life span, including adulthood.

Knox and Kupferer (1971) have suggested that although male socialization is heavily laden with the notions of achievement, power, independence, and avoidance of feminine activities in the younger years, when a man becomes a father he has to carry out many apparently feminine activities. Seemingly in contrast to this view, Gutmann (1975) has speculated that a couple's gender-role specialization becomes more marked upon the birth of the first child, but that flexibility increases as the children grow up, leading to a lack of specialization in old age. Feldman et al. (1981) compared Bem's self-attribution measures of sex typing (the Bem Sex Role Inventory – see Chapter 3) during nine stages of adult life. Gutmann's view was supported by his findings that young male parents scored higher on masculine items than did men at other stages in the life cycle and that there were more cross-gender attributions by grandparents.

Nash and Feldman (1981) made a comparison between young couples who were either living together, married without children, expecting their first child, or had recently had their first child. As families were established there was a shift toward more traditional gender roles, again supporting the view of Gutmann. A more detailed analysis revealed the following pattern. Gender-stereotyped behavior decreased and cross-gender behavior increased in the husband, thus representing a shift *away* from the masculine stereotype. A much larger increase in gender-stereotyped activities together with a smaller decrease in cross-gender behavior occurred in the wives. Thus, although there is an *overall* divergence in gender-role specialization, it arose mainly from the mothers showing a shift toward the traditionally feminine role; men did show a shift away from traditionally masculine activities, as Knox and Kupferer suggested, but it was small, so that the overall gap between the husbands' and wives' activities widened. These results show how important it is to view the separate paths of men and women as well as the differences between them.

Nash and Feldman (1981) also studied how responsiveness to babies differed at different times during the life span. Under nine years of age boys and girls were similar, but after adolescence girls were more responsive to a strange baby than boys were. Young men and women who were not parents showed similar reactions once again, and a follow-up study showed that increasingly in adolescence boys become more responsive to infants. Women who had borne children of their own were much more responsive to infants than fathers were, a gender difference that was still apparent in older people who had been parents. Grandfathers showed a higher level of responsiveness than fathers, but still not as high as grandmothers. This study again supports Gutmann's broad generalizations, this time using a behavioral rather than a self-report measure of role-related behavior.

In this chapter we have discussed a variety of ways of looking at the psychological development of gender that have been used in developmental psychology. We first discussed the commonsense view of the nature-nurture issue and then went beyond this to consider interactionist models of development. Next we looked at development in terms of descriptions of the different social worlds of boys and girls and considered progress along each developmental pathway. Most of the perspectives we have discussed – prenatal hormones and the brain, imitation of role models, "gender schemata" in childhood, the subcultures of boys and girls, and developmental pathways – are still being actively researched, and new findings are continually appearing. We have therefore sought to indicate the wide variety of approaches currently being used in the study of development.

10

Social change and the future

In the preceding chapters we have tried to maintain a clear distinction between sex and gender. We have used the term *sex* in biological contexts and have employed the word *gender* to denote a socially derived distinction between people. It is time to consider whether this precise usage produces better understanding or whether it is primarily a bit of academic pedantry.

Gender and social change

Practically, the distinction between sex and gender matters little. Most people class themselves and are categorized by others as the gender congruent with their biological sex. Nonetheless, we have seen that in certain cases, as a result of a genetic or developmental abnormality, perceived gender is not congruent with biological sex (Chapter 3). In Chapter 9, we discussed how individuals with some of these conditions have been studied in order to determine whether gender of upbringing can override biological attributes incongruent with it. We have also seen that in Omani society certain people who are biologically male choose to define themselves as *xanith*, a social category that one anthropologist has described as a third gender (Chapter 4). In our own society we have become aware, in recent years, of people who believe themselves to be living in physical bodies that contradict their psychological and socially determined gender-group membership. These transsexuals seek surgery to remove the stigmata of the wrong "sex" (the external genitals) and use hormones to modify secondary sexual characteristics to make their bodies congruent with the gender they have chosen.

Emphasizing the social construction of gender allows us to pursue possibilities for change in a number of directions. On the one hand, we can contemplate the gradual blurring of distinctions in the roles and activities of men and women and a movement toward a unisex or androgynous position that need only be tempered by the constraints of human reproduction. On the other hand, we can consider the possibility that comparison and differentiation are essential aspects of social organization and that biological sex provides a convenient emblem around which to construct social categories or gender groups.

Sandra Bem has contemplated the consequences of her goal of an androgynous society. She suggested that if a society were to give meaning to behavior in a manner that ignored the gender of the actor, the very notions of masculinity and femininity would cease to have significance (Bem, 1979). Insofar as we can specify the limits of masculinity and femininity we are presently able to measure androgyny (Chapter 2). Gender-stereotyped people describe their behavior in terms of stereotypes or commonsense beliefs, but androgynous individuals espouse aspects of both masculine and feminine behavior. These considerations led Bem to conclude that "when androgyny becomes a reality the *concept* of androgyny will have been transcended" (1979, p. 1053).

Pleck (1975) incorporated a similar vision of the androgynous society into a developmental theory of gender that he based partly on Bem's early research on the measurement of androgyny. Pleck suggested that there are three stages in gender-role development and that these are analogous to Kohlberg's levels of moral development (Kohlberg, 1976). Pleck only sketched out the stages, and the analogy with moral development was tenuous. The relevant point for our discussion is that Pleck's third stage, which he claims is not universally achieved, involves the transcendence of gender-role boundaries or androgyny. In using the concept of androgyny to describe the highest stage of development he implied that androgynous people are more mature. *Maturity* appears to be used in an ideological sense to denote that which he deems desirable and congruent with an androgyny view. We are as skeptical of his claim that ultimately gender-role development leads to an androgynous view of gender as we are of the probability of an androgynous society.

We believe that the androgynous society will not become a reality because some form of group differentiation seems essential to human social organization. Although it can be argued that the basis of social stratification need not be biological sex – it could, for example, be age – we believe that gender will continue to be an important basis for social comparison. There are many sources of support for this position, which we call the gender view. Social stratification based on age is possible and also occurs in some societies, but it is arbitrary and cumbersome. Age is a continuous dimension, and cutoff points must be selected and marked. To a limited degree rites of passage such as initiation at puberty perform such functions. On the other hand, sex is easily seen as a dichotomous variable, and in most cases identification as either male or female is made with no difficulty. These considerations provide a partial account of the virtually universal presence of gender as a principle of social organization.

Taking the argument a step further, it is difficult to imagine a completely androgynous society. In discussing infantile sexuality (Chapter 4) and gender identity (Chapter 9) we noted that awareness of one's gender develops very early and is essential to the construction of a sense of self. In turn, it is difficult to imagine an individual functioning adequately in society as we understand it without a firm sense of self. Thus early gender awareness aids the child in organizing the social world and reflects the child's understanding of it. Gender awareness arises not only from infants' experiences of their bodies but through interaction with adults in their society who are themselves molded by their membership in gender groups. As we proposed in the last chapter, nurture becomes second nature, and gender identity becomes an important schema in mental life (Constantinople, 1979; Liben and Signorella, 1980).

Additional support for the view that gender differences will persist comes from a thirty-nation study of gender stereotypes (Williams and Best, 1982). The authors concluded, "We also reject a unisex position in which one attempts to minimize or deny all differences between men and women maintaining that such behavioral differences are artefactual in nature and evil in consequence. There is too much biology, sociobiology and history involved to make the unisex position a comfortable one for the women and men of tomorrow" (Williams and Best, 1982, p. 308).

In adopting the gender view, we can look forward to changes in the *content* of gender roles and stereotypes, as indeed has occurred over the past fifty years, but we do not foresee the total abolition of gender categories. Pitcher and Schultz (1983) also make a distinction between attainable social change, which involves minimizing gender differences, and the total elimination of gender differentiation, which they believe to be unattainable. We find in their account endorsement for the realizable aims of the gender view.

If a society or a group within a society specifically set out to minimize gender differences, how would this best be achieved? Legislation in the field of employment discrimination and equal rights is one step some governments have taken to reduce structural barriers and to ensure a more equal distribution of resources. But how could the lessening of gender differences be achieved on a level closer to the individual? Insofar as we believe that early learning is particularly important, we may identify parents, teachers, peers, and the media as the main sources of influence in childhood and hence provide targets for intervention programs (Chapter 9).

Pitcher and Schultz offer the following recommendations for reducing stereotypical thinking in children: Increase fathers' involvement in child care, require boys to perform more domestic tasks and baby care, and remove or modify stereotypical features of preschool children's play such as "doll corners." They also consider the importance of same-gender peer groups in learning stereotypical views of gender. They use cross-cultural and historical evidence to suggest that same-age and same-gender peer groups are relatively recent phenomena and note encouragingly that some recent studies of American elementary schools have reported much more cross-gender interaction among children.

Early childhood is often regarded as the most effective time to intervene to produce social change. It is believed that later intervention must first overcome the effects of gender learning in the early years before change can take place. Yet Pitcher and Schultz, who regard the cognitive structures of preschool children as immature and subject to simple stereotyping, argue against intervention programs concentrating on the early years. They suggest that preschool children learn narrow gender concepts and tend to think in black and white terms (Ullian, 1976). They point out that research evidence has revealed little change in young children's gender concepts from 1964 to 1976 despite considerable change in adults' gender concepts.

Pitcher and Schultz argue that the greater cognitive maturity and sensitivity to social influences present in older children enables intervention programs to be more effective at these ages. At younger ages, they maintain, the *pattern* of gender differentiation – learning the distinction between the two gender categories – takes priority over understanding content, and this first step is important for later development. They view the content involved at this stage – which is usually primitive, stereotyped, and mutually exclusive – as relatively unimportant. Another way of describing the process they are considering is to say that preschool children are learning masculine and feminine prototypes around which concepts with fuzzy boundaries may later develop (Rosch, 1978). Thus direct teaching about gender roles is thought best undertaken in the middle school years.

The gender view: intergroup relations and social change

In adopting the gender view, we can think of genders as social groups and consider them in terms of social psychological theories of intergroup relations. Glynis Breakwell (1979) used this body of theory to analyze the women's movement. She viewed women as members of the social group "woman" and saw their identity as deriving from group membership and as reflecting the social value of the group. This value reflects the differentiation of the gender groups from one another. In the case of the group "woman," it stands in contrast to the group "man" and derives its value from that comparison. As we have noted many times, the category "woman" suffers in the comparison, and this leads us to consider whether it need always be so.

In the next three subsections we use the framework of intergroup relations theory to consider social change. First we look at the inequality of power between the gender groups and ask whether this necessarily leads to conflict. Next we examine what it means to belong to a gender group and the consequences of making the requirements for membership less obligatory. Finally, we consider the ways in which the gender constructs of women undervalue their achievements and restrict their potential.

Do men always have more power than women?

Breakwell's analysis of gender in terms of intergroup relations theory did not explicitly address the issue of the inevitability of inequality between men and women. Breakwell initially inferred inequality from attempts by women (as individuals or as organized groups) to bring about social change to alter their position relative to men. Later in her argument she explicitly rejected the idea that men and women are merely different but not unequal as an ideology that prevents women from changing their position and called it the "grand illusion."

In apparent contrast to Breakwell's view is that of Rogers (1978), which we considered in Chapter 5. She asserted that inequality is not an inevitable consequence of two gender groups. She argued that inequality will exist under circumstances where the two groups differ in their behavior but do not see one another as fundamentally different in aims and values (ideological differentiation). Where there is ideological differentiation as well as behavioral differentiation, Rogers suggested that the two gender groups can see each other as different and interdependent rather than as unequal and in conflict. Rogers argued that the position of women in traditional Islamic societies is of this nature. Her interpretation differs from that of many anthropologists; the material on Islamic societies is clearly open to different interpretations.

Rosenblatt and Cunningham (1976) have used cross-cultural evidence to develop an argument closer to Rogers's views than to Breakwell's. They noted that in most societies male activities have higher status and that men dominate the economic life of most communities, but they emphasized the importance of distinguishing public and private powers. Noting that private power is often held by women, they argued, as did Rogers, that in many societies the worlds of men and women are so different that the higher public status of men is irrelevant to the question of whether women see themselves as having less power. They also argued that a woman's status, feelings, and reputation are concerned with her relations with other women and not with how she is seen in relation to the world of men. Accordingly, the self-perceived status of women will not be less than that of men.

The Rosenblatt and Cunningham analysis highlights a crucial issue in deciding between the view of Rogers and Breakwell: How do we define *power?* Do we take the views of women themselves, or do we take an outside observer's analysis of the position of women in that society? The first option, the one adopted by Rogers (and to some extent by Rosenblatt and Cunningham), is open to the criticism that the views of certain women may be misleading. Women may believe that they are different and not unequal because men have encouraged them to do so in order to subjugate and keep them contented. The second option, that of Breakwell, is open to a different kind of criticism, that of an American or European ethnocentrism in the analysis of power. We have already noted in Chapter 5 that *power* is notoriously difficult to define, and any observer brings a particular cultural bias to the choice of status and power indicators. Thus both these criticisms raise fundamental issues and result in a dilemma that will continue to produce arguments.

Acknowledging that there are potential problems in transferring our own conceptions of power to other societies, we nevertheless argue here that a wholly subjective view of power is inadequate: Slaves cannot obtain power simply by being contented with their social position relative to other slaves. We agree, along with Breakwell, that inequality is independent of whether or not a disadvantaged group perceives that inequality. Here we can see the usefulness of Lukes's (1975) three-dimensional approach, with its emphasis on consciousness in the exercise of power.

Breakwell suggested that conflict is inevitable if members of the less powerful group experience dissatisfaction with their position and perceive that they are less powerful. The outcome of this dissatisfaction and conflict depends on the degree of social mobility that group membership permits. If there is little opportunity to move out of the lower-status group, then the members of that group will attempt collectively to change the social position of their group. If movement out of the group is readily available, there will be emphasis on individual change. If individual women feel that they can maintain their identities and at the same time relinquish traditional feminine characteristics by adopting masculine roles and behavior, they can in a sense change their group membership. It has been argued that throughout history individual women have achieved positively valued identities in this way (Williams and Giles, 1978). This is an option that is open only to a few women who are prepared to abandon those feminine characteristics that may be crucial to the identity of most women and are able to do so. For the majority who do not wish to relinquish their feminine traits, change of this sort would be unacceptable. (Indeed, Rossi [Chapter 7] argued that a feminine approach to childcare – which she believes is better suited to the needs of children – should not be lost in the pursuit of equality.) Instead, more collective action that would benefit the majority of women is urged by those of a feminist outlook.

What are the possible forms that social change can take? Breakwell has suggested three approaches. One is for women to seek membership in the more powerful masculine groups, that is, become tractor drivers and neurosurgeons. A second involves changing the values ascribed to the existing characteristics of lower-status group members with related changes in intergroup relations. A third entails fundamental changes in group structures. We consider these strategies in the next two subsections.

What are the requirements for belonging to a gender group?

In this section we consider Breakwell's first strategy for social change, attempting to gain membership in the male gender group. In the last section we stated that individual women, because of the rigidity of membership requirements, can only gain membership in male groups with some difficulty. This led us to ask what the requirements are and how rigidly they are enforced.

Male and female gender constructs provide prescriptions for gender-group membership. To be fully accepted as a man, one must look, act, and feel like a man. Although there is an overall consensus as to what this entails, there is also considerable variation within particular societies. In group relations theory, men and women are seen as distinct "conceptual groups" as opposed to "concrete groups." The latter are more formalized in terms of goals and entry requirements, whereas conceptual groups do not meet for an overt purpose nor do they have specified entry requirements.

Breakwell used the notion of a conceptual group in analyzing the position of women. The social group "woman" exists in many different forms both as a social entity and in terms of the criteria for group membership. Breakwell argued that various standards are imposed from outside (i.e., by men) in deciding what it means to be a woman, and these are often incompatible with individual women's conceptions of themselves. Some women will, therefore, see themselves as marginal to their gender group; that is, they are neither affiliated with it nor free of it. Breakwell went on to argue that marginal individuals will be dissatisfied with their position and wish to change it. Both types of analysis – that based on intergroup inequality and that based on marginality – predict pressure to change.

Breakwell outlined the various strategies for change open to someone who is in a marginal position. The first is to expand the criteria for group membership so as to include the marginal individual. This would entail lessening the obligatory nature of gender constructs. In this way a woman would still feel part of the social world of women even if she chose to pursue a career instead of having a family or if she lived in a homosexual relationship. Similarly, a man who was a househusband or in a homosexual relationship would still feel and be accepted as part of the social world of men. At present we would expect all these people to feel excluded from full acceptance by their gender group. Because of their marginal position they will also find it difficult to alter the criteria for group membership so as to enable them to become accepted. In such cases, social change has to come from another direction. One common strategy is to affiliate with like-minded individuals and to press for social change through collective action. The difficulty with this strategy is that the new group may remain marginal or only be accepted in restricted circles and will not be accepted by the majority of the gender group. In this respect, the more the women's movement is identified with marginal women, such as lesbians and Marxists, the less will be its influence on widening the criteria for group membership. Even the wider influence of broader-based feminism has largely affected only the habits of an educated elite and may not be transmitted to the cultural mainstream of society. Nevertheless, individual women will obtain a positive self-concept by belonging to a marginal group: It is more satisfactory to be a member of a marginal group than to be an isolated individual.

The gender view predicts that even if gender constructs were made much more flexible, so that marginal individuals were able to become affiliated to their gender group, the majority of people will still opt to belong to only one gender group. Most will opt for their sex-appropriate gender role, but a few individuals, convinced that they really belong to the opposite gender group, will want to adopt that life-style and appearance.

But do we mean that change will be restricted to making gender constructs more flexible? This is only one avenue of change that we can derive from the analysis of intergroup relations. There are two other possibilities that we consider in the next subsection.

Revaluation of gender relations and structural change

In this subsection we consider two more forms of social change that can be derived from intergroup-relations theory. If members of a group view their own characteristics as undervalued, they can try to alter the values ascribed to them and to their behavior. Similarly, if they view their potential as being underdeveloped, they can seek to change the existing social order. Both these methods of achieving change involve altered self-perception by members of the group, but they depend for their ultimate success on members of the dominant group acknowledging these changes.

We first consider how the value of women's achievements and characteristics may be increased. Until comparatively recently the activities of women and their artistic and scientific achievements were neglected. This imbalance has begun to be redressed by books on the place of women in history (e.g., Power, 1975) and on their artistic achievements (e.g., Moers, 1978; Peterson and Wilson, 1978; Perry, 1979). In the biological and social sciences, many topics of interest to women have been neglected or viewed only from a male standpoint. There is now more interest in these subjects. In psychology, pregnancy, childbirth, and the menopause have been discovered as legitimate areas of research (e.g., Bardwick, 1971; Sherman, 1971; Paige, 1973; Macfarlane, 1977). In sociology, too, there are studies of housework and childbirth that seek to increase the value of these activities (Oakley, 1974, 1979).

Penelope Leach (1979), in her book *Who Cares?*, argued that child care is greatly undervalued in our society; and she advocated a new approach to parenthood that would recognize and reward it as an important and high-status activity. Among the measures she suggested were paying mothers to stay at home and look after their young children. Alice Rossi (Chapter 7) advocated a more cooperative approach to counteract the social isolation felt by many mothers and their children.

Both Leach and Rossi have accepted that child care is a woman's role, and their solutions for social change are to aid women in performing their role and to accord value to its enactment. Their writings provide a sharp contrast to the prevailing spirit of the women's movement of the late 1970s in Britain and North America, which was aiming to enable women to escape from child care and to concentrate on activities outside the home.

Whether or not we agree that women should have primary responsibility for children, how easy would it be to change the status of the role of housewife? In Chapter 8 we considered research that suggested that a loss of status occurred when an occupation changed from being mainly male to mainly female. An increase occurs when men undertake the same activity, and this may even be reflected in language – for example, *cook* becomes *chef* when a man does it. In some occupations that used to be predominantly female and lower-paid, an influx of men occurred when pay was increased. In addition, men come to occupy the high-status positions within these occupations (e.g., primary school teaching and nursing). It is, therefore, possible that a sudden increase in the pay and status of child care might result in attracting men, particularly as the higher-paid organizers of women's activities. This would, of course, be quite the opposite of Leach's and Rossi's intentions.

There are, therefore, two dilemmas in adopting a strategy for social change based on increasing the status of the child-care role: first, whether concentration on this strategy will be to the detriment of widening women's economic choices; and second, whether it would simply attract more men – who would organize the women.

The second strategy for social change is to concentrate on the development of women's unrealized potential in order to alter the existing social structure. In Chapters 2 and 8 we noted that women on average leave full-time education before men and that their attainments in higher education are likely to be lower than those of men. In the United States this picture has changed dramatically in recent years. In 1979 women began to outnumber men at universities, and by 1981 there were 108 women in college for every 100 men (*New York Times*, March 21, 1983). The general picture, however, is that few women embark on occupational training and that women tend to take up unskilled, low-status, repetitive jobs. Although women make up half the full-time undergraduates under the age of thirty-five in the United States, 55 percent of today's graduate students are men.

It is probably too soon to tell whether the trends showing more women in education and training – for example, the increased proportion of women in universities – will be maintained (cf. Blackstone, 1978, on British universities) so that more women realize their educational potential. In employment, media publicity tends to concentrate on a few cases of women entering stereotypically male occupations and hence may be misleading in reflecting overall trends. Despite twenty years or so of equal-opportunity legislation in the United States and ten years of it in Great Britain, there are still powerful influences, such as the career structure and entry age, that discourage women from trying to succeed in the masculine world of work. Perhaps the current paucity of full-time job openings and the rise of part-time work will provide a specific opportunity for women to realize their potential in the future.

Sport provides a particularly clear example of the delay in achieving female potential. In Chapter 3 we noted that although, on average, the physical potential of women for various sports activities is lower than that of men, the gap between the performance, in athletic events, of men and women has narrowed in recent years. More and more professional sports are ceasing to be male preserves.

In Chapter 4 we considered the denial and underdevelopment of women's capacity for sexual enjoyment. Studies of female sexuality, such as the Hite report (1976), have sought to overcome female inhibitions and to encourage more women to seek sexual activity and to develop their capacity for fulfillment.

A final example of women engaging in activities beyond the bounds of the traditional feminine role and stereotype is in the area of aggression: Many would hesitate to refer to this as unrealized potential. Aggression can mean either assertiveness or fighting and violence (Chapter 5). Assertiveness is often regarded as being necessary to compete effectively with men in their social world. Although few would regard violence as a positive characteristic, some women are prepared to engage in traditionally masculine activities such as professional boxing and wrestling, political terrorism, and violent crime. Changes may occur in the structure of armed forces as more women carry arms.

These examples represent various ways in which women seek to develop their potential and redefine the limits of what has traditionally been seen as feminine. The extent of the future development of women's potential in these areas will depend on the future flexibility and definition of gender constructs. If women can engage in activities that were once exclusively masculine and still feel that they are feminine, the potential for change will be far more extensive than at present. This partly depends on the attitude of men toward women who engage in once traditional masculine activities. The more men come to accept women who seek to develop their potential beyond the boundaries of traditional gender constructs, the more women will see that such development need not conflict with a positive self-image.

Implications of the gender view for the future

We have used intergroup-relations theory to consider the implications for social change in gender constructs. This is one way to explore the possible course of future events. Another way is to predict the future by extrapolation from the present: It is assumed that current trends have an impetus that will carry them into the future. In this manner, it is predicted that more women will enter higher education and the work force, participate in professional sport, and commit violent crimes.

We are skeptical about the possibility of accurate predictions based solely on an analysis of the possibilities for social change derived from intergroup-relations theory or on projections from current changes in gender constructs. Both focus only on sources of change directly related to gender constructs, without adequate recognition that the futures of women and men are embedded in other issues in the wider society. Changes in the wider society are likely to have greater consequences for the futures of women and men than current changes in gender constructs alone.

It is difficult to predict the course of wider changes in society that will affect gender-role changes. Predictions about the numbers of women in the labor force must take account of the absolute number of jobs and their specific requirements. If the absolute number of jobs is decreasing, it will be less likely that more women will enter the labor force in the future; but if jobs are increasing in service sectors and many are part-time, women's participation may increase at the expense of men's. During the twentieth century in the United States and Britain, unemployment and changes in work requirements resulting from war have been associated with more widespread changes in occupational gender roles than have changes in social attitudes toward gender constructs.

Army recruitment in the United States provides an example of wider societal trends affecting the occupational roles of women. Owing to a shortage of available male recruits with the abolition of the draft, the Pentagon reconsidered in 1978 an earlier policy and decided to recruit more women and to allow them combat roles. The military planners intended almost to double the proportion of enlisted women from 1978 to 1983 (Davidson, 1978).

The Pentagon's plans covered only a five-year period. We now turn to a recent attempt to predict changes in child care and family life. Lois Hoffman (1977) identified several trends that she assumed would be maintained and would affect the future. The first was that motherhood would continue to occupy a smaller and smaller proportion of a woman's life, and the second was that the employment of women with young children would become increasingly common. The first of these was based on the expectation of a declining birth rate and longer life expectancy; and the second, on full employment. By the 1980s both of these assumptions were being called into question and had come to illustrate the difficulty of making accurate predictions. Although at the time Hoffman was writing the birth rate was declining both in Britain and the United States, there are signs that the decline has stopped. Similarly, rising unemployment calls into question the assumption that more women with children will work outside the home. Other developments – for example, in medical technology – may produce further complications that will make prediction even more difficult. We may have to consider the social consequences of parents' being able to choose the sex of their children.

Given these uncertainties in prediction based on extrapolation from the present, we finally turn to some more imaginative visions of the future. We have chosen two examples. The first is George Orwell's (1949) *Nineteen Eighty-four*, in which the author describes his vision of the structure of a society in the future; our interest lies in his description of an imaginary society of the future and in his fantasies about gender roles and the relationships of men and women. The second example is a fantasy offered by the social psychologist Marie Jahoda (1975) on the possible future relations of women and men, in this case without situating them in a society of the future.

Nineteen Eighty-four was written before the women's movement of the 1960s had stimulated analysis and consciousness of gender roles. It reflects many assumptions about gender roles presumably prevalent in British society in the 1940s. The leader (Big Brother) and most of the soldiers and heroes of the party are men. Boys and men are socialized to play an active, heroic role. The early childhood of a model citizen, Comrade Ogilvy, entailed the following: At the age of three he had refused all toys except a drum, a submachine gun, and a model helicopter, and at six he had joined the Spies – an organization designed to make children watch their parents for signs of unorthodoxy. The women were conditioned to reject their sexual feelings and remain chaste, since men's sexual instincts were held to be less controllable than those of women.

But many other aspects of the relationships between Orwell's women and men are different from those of Britain in the 1940s. In the world of "Newspeak" and "Thoughtcrime," gender roles are seen as incidental to the overall control of people's lives and habits by the party. Socialization is aimed at producing loyal party members and at preventing any loyalties the party could not control. Emotional attachments between children and their parents are discouraged. So, too, is eroticism, and the authorities try to remove pleasure from the sexual act: "Sexual intercourse was to be looked on as a slightly disgusting minor operation, like having an enema" (1949, p. 56).

In Orwell's version of the future sexuality is denigrated and gender constructs exaggerated in directions that would help the state achieve its ends. Jahoda's scheme is aimed at providing the individual with a more satisfactory erotic life. To achieve this end she makes some radical proposals.

Jahoda was frank in admitting that her fantasy was outrageous and not easily implemented. Having considered both the benefits and the limitations of the two-generation family (parents and their children), she proposed a new form of three-generational family. It would include three adults, either two men and one woman or two women and one man. A young girl would first marry a middle-aged man and through him learn about sexuality and perhaps bear children. In middle age she might take a second husband, a young man whom she would initiate into the sexual culture. In her old age, the by now middle-aged man could take a second, younger wife and produce children of his own. So the cycle would evolve, giving age and sexual experience new meaning. Jahoda's fantasy is exciting to contemplate, as it challenges such fundamental values as monogamous marriage and age in relation to sexual partners, and it almost touches the Oedipal taboo, that universal principle of human social organization (Chapter 4).

This fantasy permits us to see clearly the values it challenges, but less imaginative schemes often encourage us to forget an important consequence of social change. In choosing a new solution to an old problem – for example, caring for the young communally, as is done in the *kibbutzim* of Israel – we are also choosing not to do something, in this case not to encourage the development of family life. Change involves giving up old ways as well as adopting new ones.

Given the importance of gender in a person's self-concept and the difficulties in giving up old ways, it seems inevitable that social change will come about slowly, and perhaps the transition will be painful. Were a society able to provide meaningful freedom of choice in domains such as education, child care, and careers, individuals would still experience difficulty in exercising this freedom. The return to an emphasis on the nuclear family in *kibbutzim* is an indication of the difficulties to be encountered in bringing major change to gender constructs (Tiger and Shepher, 1975). We are not counseling the maintenance of the status quo but, rather, trying to approach the question of change with an awareness of the difficulties both in predicting the course of social history and in implementing proposals once they have been developed.

References

Ainsworth, M. D. S. 1965. Further research into the adverse effects of maternal deprivation. In J. Bowlby (ed.), *Child Care and the Growth of Love* (2nd ed.). Harmondsworth: Penguin.

Alcock, J. 1975. *Animal Behavior: An Evolutionary Approach*. Sunderland, Mass.: Sinauer.

Alther, L. 1977. *Kinflicks*. Harmondsworth: Penguin.

American Psychiatric Association. 1968. *Diagnostic and Statistical Manual of Mental Disorders* (2nd ed.). Washington, D.C.

American Psychiatric Association. 1980. *Diagnostic and Statistical Manual*. (3rd ed.). Washington, D.C.

Anastasi, A. 1958. *Differential Psychology* (3rd ed.). New York: Macmillan.

Annual Abstract of Statistics. 1983. Vol. 119. London: Her Majesty's Stationery Office.

Archer, J. 1971. Sex differences in emotional behavior: a reply to Gray and Buffery. *Acta Psychologica*, 35:415–29.

Archer, J. 1973. Test for emotionality in rats and mice: a review. *Animal Behavior*, 21:205–35.

Archer, J. 1975. Rodent sex differences in emotional and related behaviour. *Behavioural Biology*, 14:451–79.

Archer, J. 1976a. Biological explanations of psychological sex differences. In B. B. Lloyd and J. Archer (eds.), *Exploring Sex Differences*. New York: Academic Press.

Archer, J. 1976b. The organization of aggression and fear in vertebrates. In P. P. G. Bateson and P. Klopfer (eds.), *Perspectives in Ethology*, vol. 2. New York: Plenum.

Archer, J. 1979. *Animals Under Stress*. London: Edward Arnold.

Archer, J. 1980. Sex roles and models of development. Paper presented at British Psychological Society Annual Conference, Aberdeen, April 1980.

Archer, J. 1984. Gender roles as developmental pathways. *British Journal of Social Psychology*, 23:245–56.

Archer, J., and Lloyd, B. B. 1975. Sex differences: biological and social interactions. In R. Lewin (ed.), *Child Alive*. London: Temple Smith.

Archer, J., and Lloyd, B. B. 1980. Problems and issues in research on sex differences. In J. Sants (ed.), *Developmental Psychology and Society*. London: Macmillan.

Archer, J., and Westeman, K. 1981. Sex differences in the aggressive behaviour of school children. *British Journal of Social and Clinical Psychology*, 20:31–6.

Ardener, E. 1972. Belief and the problem of women. In J. LaFontaine (ed.), *The Interpretation of Ritual*. London: Tavistock.

Ardrey, R. 1967. *The Territorial Imperative*. London: Collins.

Baker, S. 1980. Biological influences on human sex and gender. *Signs*, 6:80–96.

Bandura, A. 1977. *Social Learning Theory*. Englewood Cliffs, N.J.: Prentice-Hall.

Bandura, A., Ross, D., and Ross, S. A. 1961. Transmission of aggression through imitation of aggressive models. *Journal of Abnormal and Social Psychology*, 63:575–82.

Barash, D. P. 1977. *Sociobiology and Behavior*. New York: Elsevier.

Bardwick, J. M. 1971. *Psychology of Women: A Study of Bio-cultural Conflicts*. New York: Harper & Row.

Barkley, R. A., Ullman, D. G., Otto, L., and Brecht, J. M. 1977. The effects of sex-typing and sex appropriateness of modelled behavior on children's imitation. *Child Development*, 48:721–5.

Baron, R. A. 1977. *Human Aggression*. New York: Plenum.

Barry, W. A. 1970. Marriage research and conflict: an integrative review. *Psychological Bulletin*, 73:41–54.

Bart, P. B. 1971. Depression in middle-aged women. In V. Cornick and B. K. Moran (eds.), *Women in Sexist Society*. New York: Basic Books.

Bartlett, F. C. 1932. *Remembering*. Cambridge: Cambridge University Press.

Bateson, P. P. G. 1976. Rules and reciprocity in development. In P. P. G. Bateson and R. A. Hinde (eds.), *Growing Points in Ethology*. Cambridge: Cambridge University Press.

Bayley, N., and Oden, M. 1955. The maintenance of intellectual ability in gifted adults. *Journal of Gerontology*, 10:91–101.

Bayley, N., and Schaefer, E. S. 1964. Correlations of maternal and child behaviors with the development of mental abilities: data from the Berkeley Growth Study. *Monographs of the Society for Research in Child Development*, vol. 29, serial no. 97.

Beach, F. A. 1966. Review of *Human Sexual Response* by W. H. Masters and V. E. Johnson. *Scientific American*, 215(2):107–10.

Beail, N., and McQuire, J. (eds.). 1982. *Fathers: Psychological Perspectives*. London: Junction Books.

Beck, A. T., and Greenberg, R. L. 1974. Cognitive therapy with depressed women. In V. Franks and B. Vasanti (eds.), *Women in Therapy*. New York: Brunner–Mazel.

Beer, W. R. 1983. *Househusband: Men and Housework in American Families*. New York: Praeger/Bergin.

Bem, S. L. 1974. The measurement of psychological androgyny. *Journal of Consulting and Clinical Psychology*, 42:155–62.

Bem, S. L. 1979. Theory and measurement of androgyny: a reply to the Pedhazur–Tetenbaum and Locksley–Colten critiques. *Journal of Personality and Social Psychology*, 37:1047–54.

Bem, S. L. 1981. Gender schema theory: a cognitive account of sex typing. *Psychological Review*, 88:354–64.

Best, D. L., Williams, J. E., Cloud, J. M., Davis, S. W., Robertson, L. S., Edwards, J. R., Giles, H., and Fowles, J. 1977. Development of sex-trait stereotypes among young children in the United States, England, and Ireland. *Child Development*, 48:1375–84.

Bibring, E. 1953. The mechanism of depression. In P. Greenacre (ed.), *Affective Disorders*. New York: International Universities Press.

Biller, H. B. 1976. Paternal deprivation and sex role development. In M. E. Lamb (ed.), *The Role of the Father in Child Development*. New York: Wiley.

Birke, L. I. A. 1982. From sin to sickness: hormonal theories of lesbianism. In R. Hubbard, M. S. Henifin, and B. Fried (eds.), *Biological Woman: The Convenient Myth*. Cambridge, Mass.: Schenkman.

Birke, L. I. A., and Best, S. 1980. The tyrannical womb: menstruation, menopause, and science. In Brighton Women and Science Collective (ed.), *Alice through the Microscope: The Power of Science over Women's Lives*. London: Virago.

Birke, L. I. A., and Best, S. 1982. Changing minds: women, biology, and the menstrual cycle. In R. Hubbard, M. S. Henifin, and B. Fried (eds.), *Biological Woman: The Convenient Myth*. Cambridge, Mass.: Schenkman.

Birns, B. 1976. The emergence and socialization of sex differences in the earliest years. *Merrill-Palmer Quarterly*, 22:229–54.

Blackstone, T. 1978. Success or failure? *Times Higher Educational Supplement*, 8 September: 11.

Blakemore, J. E. O., LaRue, A., and Olejnik, A. B. 1979. Sex-appropriate toy preference and the ability to conceptualize toys as sex-role related. *Developmental Psychology*, 15:339–40.

Blizard, D. A. 1983. Sex differences in running-wheel behaviour in the rat: the inductive and activational effects of gonadal hormones. *Animal Behaviour*, 31:378–84.

Block, J. H. 1976a. Debatable conclusions about sex differences. *Contemporary Psychology*, 21:517–22.

Block, J. H. 1976b. Issues, problems, and pitfalls in assessing sex differences: a critical review of *The Psychology of Sex Differences*. *Merrill–Palmer Quarterly*, 22:283–308.

Block, J. H. 1978. Another look at sex differentiation in the socialization behaviors of mothers and daughters. In J. Sherman and F. Denmark (eds.), *Psychology of Women: Future Directions of Research*. New York: Psychological Dimensions.

Block, J. H. 1983. Differential premises arising from differential socialization of the sexes: some conjectures. *Child Development*, 54:1335–54.

Blum, J. E., Fosshage, J. L., and Jarvik, L. F. 1972. Intellectual changes and sex differences in octogenarians: a twenty-year longitudinal study of ageing. *Developmental Psychology*, 7:178–87.

Blurton-Jones, N. G. 1972. Categories of child-child interaction. In N. Blurton-Jones (ed.), *Ethological Studies of Child Behaviour*. Cambridge: Cambridge University Press.

Blurton-Jones, N. G., and Konner, M. J. 1973. Sex differences in the behaviour of London and Bushman children. In R. P. Michael and J. H. Crook (eds.), *Comparative Ecology and Behavior of Primates*. New York: Academic Press.

Boles, D. B. 1980. X-linkage of spatial ability: a critical review. *Child Development*, 51:625–35.

Bowers, K. S. 1973. Situationism in psychology: an analysis and critique. *Psychological Review*, 80:307–36.

Bowlby, J. 1951. *Maternal Care and Mental Health*. Geneva: World Health Organisation.

Bowlby, J. 1965. *Child Care and the Growth of Love* (2nd ed.). Harmondsworth: Penguin.

Bowlby, J. 1969. *Attachment and Loss*. Vol. 1: *Attachment*. London: Hogarth Press.

Brackbill, Y., and Schroder, K. 1980. Circumcision, gender differences, and neonatal behavior: an update. *Developmental Psychobiology*, 13:607–14.

Brain, M. 1978. Transsexualism in Oman (correspondence). *Man*, 13:322–3.

Breakwell, G. 1979. Women: group and identity? *Women's Studies International Quarterly*, 2:9–17.

Breen, D. 1975. *The Birth of a First Child: Towards an Understanding of Femininity*. London: Tavistock.

Brimer, M. A. 1969. Sex differences in listening comprehension. *Journal of Research and Development in Education*, 3:72–9.

Broverman, D. M., Klaiber, E. L., Kobayashi, Y., and Vogel, W. 1968. Roles of activation and inhibition in sex differences in cognitive abilities. *Psychological Review*, 75:23–50.

Broverman, I. K., Broverman, D. M., Clarkson, F. E., Rosenkrantz, P. S., and Vogel, S. R. 1970. Sex role stereotypes and clinical judgements of mental health. *Journal of Consulting and Clinical Psychology*, 34:1–7.

Brown, G. W., and Harris, T. O. 1978. *Social Origins of Depression: A Study of Psychiatric Disorder in Women*. London: Tavistock.

Brown, G. W., Harris, T. O., and Bifulco, A. In press. Long term effects of early loss of parent. In M. Rutter, C. Izard, and P. Read (eds.), *Depression in Childhood: Developmental Perspectives*. New York: Guilford Press.

Bryan, J. W., and Luria, Z. 1978. Sex-role learning: a test of the selective attention hypothesis. *Child Development*, 49:13–23.

Buffery, A. W. H., and Gray, J. A. 1972. Sex differences in the development of spatial and linguistic skills. In C. Ounsted and D. C. Taylor (eds.), *Gender Differences: Their Ontogeny and Significance*. London: Churchill.

Burns, R. B. 1977. Male and female perceptions of their own and the other sex. *British Journal of Social and Clinical Psychology*, 16:213–20.

Burnstyn, J. N. 1971. Brain and intellect: science applied to a social issue, 1860–1875. *XIIe Congrès International d'Histoire des Sciences*, 9:13–16.

Byrne, D. G. 1981. Sex differences in the reporting of symptoms of depression in the general population. *British Journal of Clinical Psychology*, 20:83–92.

Campbell, A. 1982. Female aggression. In P. Marsh and A. Campbell (eds.), *Aggression and Violence*. Oxford: Basil Blackwell.

Carlsson, M., and Jaderquist, P. 1983. Note on sex-role opinions as conceptual schemata. *British Journal of Social Psychology*. 22:65–68.

Cerullo, M., Stacy, J., and Breines, W. 1977–8. Alice Rossi's sociobiology and anti-feminist backlash. *Berkeley Journal of Sociology*, 22:67–77.

Chang, J. 1977. *The Tao of Love and Sex: The Ancient Chinese Way to Ecstasy*. London: Wildwood House.

Chesler, P. 1972. *Women and Madness.* New York: Doubleday.

Chodorow, N. 1978. *The Reproduction of Mothering.* Berkeley: University of California Press.

Clancy, K., and Gove, W. 1974. Sex differences in mental illness: an analysis of response bias in self-reports. *American Journal of Sociology,* 80:205–16.

Clare, A. 1979. The treatment of premenstrual symptoms. *British Journal of Psychiatry,* 135:576–9.

Clare, A. W. 1983. Psychiatric and social aspects of premenstrual complaint. *Psychological Medicine Monograph Supplement* 4.

Clarke, A. E., and Ruble, D. N. 1978. Young adolescents' beliefs concerning menstruation. *Child Development,* 49:231–4.

Clarke, A. M., and Clarke, A. D. B. (eds.). 1976. *Early Experience: Myth and Evidence,* London: Open Books.

Clarke-Stewart, K. A. 1977. The father's impact on mother and child. Society for Research in Child Development meeting, New Orleans, March.

Coates, S. 1974. Sex differences in field independence among preschool children. In R. C. Friedman, R. M. Richart, and R. L. Vande Wiele (eds.), *Sex Differences in Behavior.* New York: Wiley.

Colby, A., and Damon, W. 1983. Listening to a different voice: a review of Gilligan's "In a different voice." *Merrill–Palmer Quarterly,* 29:473–81.

Condry, J., and Condry, S. 1976. Sex differences: a study of the eye of the beholder. *Child Development,* 47:812–19.

Constantinople, A. 1973. Masculinity–femininity: an exception to a famous dictum? *Psychological Bulletin,* 80:389–407.

Constantinople, A. 1979. Sex role acquisition: in search of the elephant. *Sex Roles,* 5:121–33.

Cowley, J. E., Levitui, T. E., and Quinn, R. P. 1973. Seven deadly half-truths about women. *Psychology Today,* 6:94–6.

Crook, J. H. 1972. Sexual selection, dimorphism, and social organization in the primates. In B. Campbell (ed.), *Sexual Selection and the Descent of Man.* Chicago: Aldine.

Culp, R. E., Crook, A. S., and Housley, P. C. 1983. A comparison of observed and reported adult-infant interactions: effects of perceived sex. *Sex Roles,* 9:475–9.

Dalton, K. 1969. *The Menstrual Cycle.* Harmondsworth: Penguin.

Dalton, K. 1971. Prospective study into puerperal depression. *British Journal of Psychiatry,* 118:689–92.

Dalton, K. 1979. *Once a Month.* London: Fontana.

Daly, M. 1978. Cost of mating. *American Naturalist,* 112:771–4.

Danziger, K. 1971. *Socialization*. Harmondsworth: Penguin.

Darwin, C. 1871. *The Descent of Man, and Selection in Relation to Sex* (1901 ed.). London: John Murray.

David, D. S., and Brannon, R. 1976. The male sex role: our culture's blueprint of manhood, and what it's done for us lately. In D. S. David and R. Brannon (eds.), *The Forty-Nine Percent Majority: The Male Sex-Role*. Reading, Mass.: Addison–Wesley.

Davidson, C. 1978. US armed forces to use woman power. *Times* (London), 21 July: 8.

Davidson, T. 1977. Wifebeating: a recurring phenomenon throughout history. In M. Roy (ed.), *Battered Women: A Psychological Study of Domestic Violence*. New York: Van Nostrand.

Dawkins, R., and Carlisle, T. R. 1976. Parental investment, mate selection, and a fallacy. *Nature*, 262:131–3.

Dawson, J. L. M. 1972. Effects of sex hormones on cognitive style in rats and men. *Behavior Genetics*, 2:21–42.

Deaux, K. 1976a. Sex: a perspective on the attribution process. In J. H. Harvey, W. J. Ickes, and R. F. Kidd (eds.), *New Directions in Attribution Research*, vol 1. New York: Wiley.

Deaux, K. 1976b. *The Behavior of Women and Men*. Monterey, Calif.: Brooks–Cole.

Deaux, K. 1977. Sex differences. In T. Blass (ed.), *Personality Variables in Social Behavior*. New York: Halsted Press.

Decarie, T. G., Goulet, J., Brossard, M. D., Rafman, S., and Shaffran, R. 1974. *The Infant's Reaction to Strangers*. Trans. J. Diamanti. New York: International Universities Press.

DeFries, J. C., Johnson, R. C., Kuse, A. R., McClearn, G. E., Polovina, J., Vandenburg, S. G., and Wilson, J. R. 1979. Familial resemblance for specific cognitive abilities. *Behavior Genetics*, 9:23–43.

Deleuze, G., and Guattari, F. 1977. *Anti-Oedipus: Capitalism and Schizophrenia*. Trans. R. Hunley et al. New York: Viking.

Department of Health and Social Services. 1982. *Health and Personal Social Statistics for England*. London: Her Majesty's Stationery Office.

Depp, F. C. 1976. Violent behavior patterns on psychiatric wards. *Aggressive Behavior*, 2:295–306.

Deutsch, H. 1945. *The Psychology of Women*. New York: Grune & Stratton.

DeVries, R. 1969. Constancy of generic identity in the years three to six. *Monographs of Society for Research in Child Development*, vol. 34, no. 127, (3).

Doering, C. H., Brodie, H. K. H., Kraemer, H., Becker, H., and Hamburg, D. A. 1974. Plasma testosterone levels and psychologic measures in men over a 2 month period. In R. C. Friedman, R. M. Richart, and R. L. Vande Wiele (eds.), *Sex Differences in Behavior*. New York: Wiley.

Doise, W. 1978. *Groups and Individuals: Explanations in Social Psychology*. Cambridge: Cambridge University Press.

Dörner, G. 1976. *Hormones and Brain Differentiation*. Amsterdam: Elsevier.

Douglas, J. D. 1967. *The Social Meanings of Suicide*. Princeton, N.J.: Princeton University Press.

Durrett, M. E. 1959. The relationship of early infant regulation and later behavior in play interviews. *Child Development*, 30:211–16.

Dyer, K. 1977. Female athletes are catching up. *New Scientist*, 75:722–3.

Eagly, A. H. 1983. Gender and social influence: a social psychological analysis. *American Psychologist*, 38:971–81.

Ebert, P. D., and Hyde, J. S. 1976. Selection for agonistic behavior in wild female *Mus musculus*. *Behavior Genetics*, 6:291–304.

Effects of sexual activity on beard growth in man. 1970. *Nature*, 30:869–70.

Ehlers, C. L., Rickler, K. C., and Hovey, J. E. 1980. A possible relationship between plasma testosterone and aggressive behavior in a female outpatient population. In M. Giris and L. G. Kiloh (eds.), *Limbic Epilepsy and the Dyscontrol Syndrome*. New York: Elsevier.

Ehrenkranz, J., Bliss, E., and Sheard, M. H. 1974. Plasma testosterone correlation with aggressive behavior and social dominance in men. *Psychosomatic Medicine*, 36:469–75.

Ehrhardt, A. A., and Baker, S. W. 1974. Fetal androgens, human central nervous system differentiation, and behavior sex differences. In R. C. Friedman, R. M. Richart, and R. L. Vande Wiele (eds.), *Sex Differences in Behavior*. New York: Wiley.

Ehrhardt, A. A., Ince, S. E., and Meyer-Bahlberg, H. F. L. 1981. Career aspirations and gender role development in young girls. *Archives of Sexual Behavior*, 10:281–99.

Eisenberg, N., Murray, E., and Hite, T. 1982. Children's reasoning regarding sex-typed toy choices. *Child Development*, 53:81–6.

El-Badry, M. A. 1969. Higher female than male mortality in some countries of South Asia: a digest. *American Statistical Association Journal*, 64:1234–44.

Ellis, H. 1903. Variation in man and woman. *Popular Science Monthly*, 62:237–53.

Ellis, L. 1982. Developmental androgen fluctuations and the dimensions of mammalian sex (with emphasis upon the behavioral dimension and the human species). *Ethology and Sociobiology*, 3:171–9.

Ellis, L. J., and Bentler, P. M. 1973. Traditional sex-determined role standards and sex stereotypes. *Journal of Personality and Social Psychology*, 25:28–34.

Ellman, M. 1968. *Thinking about Women*. New York: Harcourt, Brace & World.

Eme, R. F. 1979. Sex differences in childhood psychopathology: a review. *Psychological Bulletin*, 86:574–95.

Englander-Golden, R., Whitmore, M. R., and Dienstbier, R. A. 1978. Menstrual cycle as a focus of study and self-reports of moods and behaviors. *Motivation and Emotion*, 2:75–86.

Evans, B. 1979. *Life Change*. London: Pan Books.

Fagot, B. 1974. Sex differences in toddlers' behavior and parental reaction. *Developmental Psychology*, 4:554–8.

Fagot, B. I. 1977. Consequences of moderate cross-gender behavior in pre-school children. *Child Development*, 48:902–7.

Fairweather, H. 1976. Sex differences in cognition. *Cognition*, 4:31–80.

Feldman, L. B. 1982. Sex roles and family dynamics. In F. Walsh (ed.), *Normal Family Processes*. New York: Guilford.

Feldman, S. S., Biringen, Z. C., and Nash, S. C. 1981. Fluctuations of sex-related self-attributions as a function of stage of family life-cycle. *Developmental Psychology*, 17:24–35.

Ferri, E. 1976. *Growing up in a One-Parent Family*. Windsor: National Foundation for Educational Research.

Feshbach, S. 1970. Aggression. In P. H. Mussen (ed.), *Carmichael's Manual of Child Psychology*. New York: Wiley.

Fling, S., and Manosevitz, M. 1972. Sex-typing in nursery-school children's play interests. *Developmental Psychology*, 7:146–52.

Flor-Henry, P. 1974. Psychosis, neurosis, and epilepsy. *British Journal of Psychiatry*, 124:114–50.

Foucault, M. 1979. *The History of Sexuality*. London: Allen Lane.

Fox, C. A., Ismail, A. A., Love, D. N., Kirkham, K. E., and Loraine, J. A. 1972. Studies on the relationship between plasma testosterone levels and human sexual activity. *Journal of Endocrinology*, 52:51–8.

Fox, N. 1977. Attachment of kibbutz infants to mother and metapelet. *Child Development*, 48:1228–39.

Frank, F. 1957. The causality of microtine cycles in Germany. *Journal of Wildlife Management*, 21:113–21.

Frazier, S. H., and Carr, A. C. 1967. Phobic Reactions. In A. M. Freedman and H. I. Kaplan (eds.), *Comprehensive Textbook of Psychiatry*. Baltimore: Williams & Wilkins.

Fredga, K., Gropp, A., Winking, H., and Frank, F. 1976. Fertile XX-
and XY-type females in the wood lemming *Myopus schisticolor*.
Nature, 261:225–7.

Freedman, D. G. 1964. A biological view of man's social behavior. In
W. Etkin (ed.), *Social Behavior from Fish to Man*. Chicago: University of Chicago Press.

French, M. 1978. *The Women's Room*. London: Deutsch.

Freud, S. 1905. *Three Essays on the Theory of Sexuality*, vol. 7, std. ed.
London: Hogarth Press, 1953.

Freud, S. 1917. (1915). *Mourning and Melancholia*, vol. 14, std. ed.
London: Hogarth Press, 1957.

Freud, S. 1920. *Beyond the Pleasure Principle*, vol. 18, std. ed. London:
Hogarth Press, 1955.

Freud, S. 1923. *The Ego and the Id*, vol. 19, std. ed. London: Hogarth
Press, 1961.

Freud, S. 1924. *The Dissolution of the Oedipus Complex*, vol. 19, std. ed.
London: Hogarth Press, 1961.

Freud, S. 1925. *Some Psychical Consequences of the Anatomical Distinction
between the Sexes*, vol. 19, std. ed. London: Hogarth Press, 1961.

Freud, S. 1931. *Female Sexuality*, vol. 21, std. ed. London: Hogarth
Press, 1961.

Freud, S. 1940. *An Outline of Psychoanalysis*, vol. 23, std. ed. London:
Hogarth Press, 1964.

Fried, B. 1982. Boys will be boys: the language of sex and gender. In
R. Hubbard, M. S. Henfin, and B. Fried (eds.), *Biological Woman:
The Convenient Myth*. Cambridge, Mass.: Schenkman.

Frieze, I. 1978. Achievement and nonachievement in women. In I. H.
Frieze, J. E. Parsons, P. S. Johnson, D. N. Ruble, and G. L.
Zellman (eds.), *Women and Sex Roles: A Social Psychological Perspec-
tive*. New York: Norton.

Frieze, I. H., Whitley Jr., B. E., Hanusa, B. H., and McHugh, M. C.
1982. Assessing the theoretical models for sex differences in causal attributions for success and failure. *Sex Roles*, 8:333–43.

Frisch, H. L. 1977. Sex stereotypes in adult–infant play. *Child Development*, 48:1671–5.

Frodi, A., Macaulay, J., and Thome, P. R. 1977. Are women always
less aggressive than men? A review of the experimental literature.
Psychological Bulletin, 84:634–60.

Gagnon, J. H., and Simon, W. 1973. *Sexual Conduct: The Social Sources
of Human Sexuality*. Chicago: Aldine.

Galenson, E., and Roiphe, H. 1977. Some suggested revisions concerning early female development. In H. P. Blum (ed.), *Female*

Psychology: Contemporary Psychoanalytic Views. New York: International Universities Press.

Garai, J. E. 1970. Sex differences in mental health. *Genetic Psychology Monographs*, 81:123–42.

Garai, J. E., and Scheinfeld, A. 1968. Sex differences in mental and behavioural traits. *Genetic Psychology Monographs*, 77:169–299.

Garvey, C. 1977. *Play*. Cambridge: Harvard University Press.

Gavron, H. 1966. *The Captive Housewife: Conflict of Housebound Mothers*. London: Routledge & Kegan Paul.

Gelles, R. J. 1972. *The Violent Home*. Beverly Hills, Calif.: Sage.

General Household Survey. *1979*. (1981). Office of Population Censuses and Social Surveys, Survey Division. London: Her Majesty's Stationery Office.

Ghiselin, M. T. 1974. *The Economy of Nature and the Evolution of Sex*. Berkeley: University of California Press.

Gilligan, C. 1982. *In a Different Voice*. Cambridge, Mass.: Harvard University Press.

Glucksmann, A. 1974. Sexual dimorphism in mammals. *Biological Review*, 49:423–75.

Goldberg, P. A. 1968. Are women prejudiced against women? *Transaction*, 5:28–30.

Goldberg, S. 1973. *The Inevitability of Patriarchy*. New York: Morrow.

Gough, H. G., and Heilbrun, A. B. 1965. *Adjective Checklist Manual*. Palo Alto, Calif.: Consulting Psychologists' Press.

Gould, S. J. 1978. Women's brains. *New Scientist*, 80:364–6.

Gould, S. J. 1980. *Ever Since Darwin: Reflections in Natural History*. Harmondsworth: Penguin.

Gove, W. R. 1972. Sex, marital status, and suicide. *Journal of Health and Social Behavior*, 13:204–13.

Gove, W. R., and Tudor, J. F. 1973. Adult sex roles and mental illness. *American Journal of Sociology*, 78:812–35.

Goy, R. W. 1968. Organizing effects of androgen on the behaviour of rhesus monkeys. In R. P. Michael (ed.), *Endocrinology and Human Behaviour*. Oxford: Oxford University Press.

Goy, R. W., and McEwan, B. S. 1980. *Sexual Differentiation in the Brain*. Cambridge, Mass.: MIT Press.

Graber, B. (ed.). 1982. *Circumvaginal Musculature and Sexual Function*. Basel: Karger.

Gray, J. A. 1971a. Sex differences in emotional behaviour in mammals including man: endocrine bases. *Acta Psychologica*, 35:29–46.

Gray, J. A. 1971b. *The Psychology of Fear and Stress*. London: Weidenfeld & Nicolson.

Gray, J. A. 1979. Emotionality in male and female rodents: a reply to Archer. *British Journal of Psychology*, 70:425–40.

Gray, J. A., and Buffery, A. W. H. 1971. Sex differences in emotional and cognitive behaviour in mammals including man: adaptive and neural bases. *Acta Psychologica*, 35:89–111.

Gray, J. A., and Drewett, R. F. 1977. The genetics and development of sex differences. In R. B. Cattell and R. M. Dreger (ed.), *Handbook of Modern Personality Theory*. New York: Halsted Press.

Green, J. 1982. Recent trends in the treatment of premenstrual syndrome: a critical review. In R. C. Friedman (ed.), *Behavior and the Menstrual Cycle*. New York: Dekker.

Greene, J. G. 1981. Types of life-events in relation to symptoms at the climacterium. *Bulletin of the British Psychological Society*, 34:187 (abstr.).

Greer, G. 1970. *The Female Eunuch*. London: MacGibbon and Kee.

Greif, E. B. 1976. Sex-role playing in preschool children. In J. S. Bruner, A. Jolly, and K. Sylva (eds.), *Play*. Harmondsworth: Penguin.

Grossman, M., and Bart, R. B. 1982. Taking the men out of the menopause. In R. Hubbard, M. S. Henifin, and B. Fried (eds.), *Biological Woman: the Convenient Myth*. Cambridge, Mass.: Schenkman.

Gutmann, D. 1975. Parenthood: a key to the comparative study of the life cycle. In N. Datan and L. Ginsberg (eds.), *Life Span Developmental Psychology*. New York: Academic Press.

Guttentag, M., and Secord, P. F. 1983. *Too Many Women?: The Sex Ratio Question*. Beverly Hills, Calif.: Sage.

Hamburg, D. A., and Lunde, D. T. 1967. Sex hormones in the development of sex differences in human behaviour. In E. E. Maccoby (ed.), *The Development of Sex Differences*. London: Tavistock.

Hargreaves, D. 1976. What are little boys and girls made of? *New Society*, 37:542–4.

Hargreaves, D. 1977. Sex roles in divergent thinking. *British Journal of Educational Psychology*, 47:25–32.

Harlow, H. 1958. The nature of love. *American Psychologist*, 13:673–85.

Harris, L. J. 1978. Sex differences in spatial ability: possible environmental, genetic, and neurological factors. In M. Kinsbourne (ed.), *Asymmetrical Function of the Brain*. Cambridge: Cambridge University Press.

Hartley, R. E. 1957. Sex-role pressures and the socialization of the male child. *Psychological Reports*, 5:457–68.

Hartnett, O. 1978. Sex-role stereotyping at work. In J. Chetwynd and O. Hartnett (eds.), *The Sex-Role System*. London: Routledge & Kegan Paul.

Heilbrun, A. B. 1965. An empirical test of the modelling theory of sex-role learning. *Child Development*, 36:789–99.

Heim, A. 1970. *Intelligence and Personality*. Harmondsworth: Penguin.

Heiman, J. R. 1975. The physiology of erotica: women's sexual arousal. *Psychology Today*, April: 90–4.

Henley, N. M. 1977. *Body Politics, Power, Sex, and Non Verbal Communication*. Englewood Cliffs, N.J.: Prentice-Hall.

Herbert, J. 1976. Hormonal basis of sex differences in rats, monkeys, and humans. *New Scientist*, 70:284–6.

Hersov, L. 1977. Adoption. In M. Rutter and L. Hersov (eds.), *Child Psychiatry*. Oxford: Blackwell Scientific.

Hetherington, E. M. 1965. A development study of the effects of sex of the dominant parent on sex-role preference, identification, and imitation in children. *Journal of Personality and Social Psychology*, 2:188–94.

Hill, J. 1978. The psychological impact of unemployment. *New Society*, 43:118–20.

Hite, S. 1976. *The Hite Report*. New York: Macmillan.

Hite, S. 1981. *The Hite Report on Male Sexuality*. New York: Knopf.

Hocquenghem, G. 1978. *Homosexual Desire*. Trans. D. Dangoor. London: Allison and Busby.

Hoffman, L. W. 1977. Changes in family roles, socialization, and sex differences. *American Psychologist*, 32:644–57.

Horner, M. S. 1972. Toward an understanding of achievement-related conflicts in women. *Journal of Social Issues*, 28:157–75.

Horney, K. 1924. On the genesis of the castration complex in women. *International Journal of Psychoanalysis*, 5:50–65.

Hrdy, S. B. 1981. *The Woman That Never Evolved*. Cambridge, Mass.: Harvard University Press.

Hutt, C. 1972a. *Males and Females*. Harmondsworth: Penguin.

Hutt, C. 1972b. Sexual dimorphism: its significance in human development. In F. J. Monks, W. W. Hartup, and J. De Wit (eds.), *Determinants of Behavioral Development*. New York: Academic Press.

Hyde, J. 1979. *Understanding Human Sexuality*. New York: McGraw-Hill.

Hyde, J. S. 1981. How large are cognitive gender differences? A meta-analysis using W2 and D. *American Psychologist*, 36:892–901.

Hyde, J. S., Rosenberg, B. G., and Behrman, J. A. 1977. Tomboyism. *Psychology of Women Quarterly*, 2:73–5.

Imperato-McGinley, J., Guemero, L., Gautier, T., and Peterson, R. E. 1974. Steroid 5α-reductase deficiency in man: an inherited form of male pseudohermaphroditism. *Science*, 186:1213–15.

Imperato-McGinley, J., Peterson, R. E., and Gautier, T. 1976. Gender identity and hermaphroditism. *Science*, 191:872.

Ingham, J. G., and Miller, P. McC. 1976. The concept of prevalence applied to psychiatric disorders and symptoms. *Psychological Medicine*, 6:217–25.

Irigaray, L. 1977. Women's exile. *Ideology and Consciousness* 1:62–76.

Jacklin, C. N. 1979. Epilogue. In M. A. Wittig and A. C. Peterson (eds.), *Sex Related Differences in Cognitive Functioning: Developmental Issues*. New York: Academic Press.

Jacobson, M. B., and Effertz, J. 1974. Sex roles and leadership: perceptions of the leaders and the led. *Organizational Behavior and Human Performance*, 12:383–96.

Jahoda, M. 1975. Technicalities and fantasy about men and women. *Futures: The Journal of Forecasting and Planning*, 7:414–19.

Janiger, O., Riffenburgh, R., and Kersh, R. 1972. Cross-cultural study of pre-menstrual symptoms. *Psychosomatics*, 13:226–35.

Jenni, D. A. 1974. Evolution of polyandry in birds. *American Zoologist*, 14:129–44.

Johanson, D. C., and Edey, M. A. 1981. *Lucy: The Beginnings of Humankind*. New York: Granada.

Johnson, R. N. 1972. *Aggression in Man and Animals*. Philadelphia: Saunders.

Johnston, J. 1973. *Lesbian Nation: The Feminist Solution*. New York: Simon & Schuster.

Jost, A. 1972. A new look at the mechanisms controlling sex differentiations in mammals. *John Hopkins Medical Journal*, 130:38–53.

Jourard, S. M. 1964. *The Transparent Self: Self-Disclosure and Well-Being*. Princeton: Van Nostrand.

Kagan, J. 1978. Sex differences in the human infant. In T. E. McGill, D. A. Dewsbury, and B. D. Sachs (eds.), *Sex and Behavior: Status and Prospects*. New York: Plenum.

Kagan, J., and Moss, H. A. 1962. *Birth to Maturity*. New York: Wiley.

Kahne, H. 1975. Economic perspectives on the roles of women in the American economy. *Journal of Economic Literature*, 13:1249–92.

Kamin, L. J. 1978. Sex differences in susceptibility of IQ to environmental influence. *Child Development*, 49:517–18.

Kangas, J., and Bradway, K. 1971. Intelligence at middle age: thirty-eight year follow-up. *Developmental Psychology*, 5:333–7.

Kaplan, M. 1983. A woman's view of the DSM-III. *American Psychologist*, 38:786–92.

Kaplan, M. 1983. The issue of sex bias in DSM-III: Comments on the articles by Spitzer, Williams, and Kass. *American Psychologist,* 38:802–3.

Kass, F., Spitzer, R. L., and Williams, J. B. W. 1983. An empirical study of the issue of sex bias in the diagnostic criteria of DSM-III axis II personality disorders. *American Psychologist,* 38:799–801.

Katchadourian, H. A., and Lunde, D. T. 1980. *Fundamentals of Human Sexuality* (3rd ed.). New York: Holt, Rinehart & Winston.

Katongole, C., Naftolin, F., and Short, R. V. 1971. Relationship between blood levels of luteinizing hormone and testosterone in bulls, and the effects of sexual stimulation. *Journal of Endocrinology,* 50:457–60.

Katz, D., and Braly, K. W. 1933. Racial prejudice and racial stereotypes. *Journal of Abnormal and Social Psychology,* 30:175–93.

Katz, P. A. 1979. Development of female identity. In C. B. Kopp (ed.), *Becoming Female.* New York: Plenum.

Keating, F. 1978. Ladies didn't run until 1928: now they face the sex test hurdle. *Guardian,* 3 August.

Kennedy, I. 1980. "Great caution must be exercised in visiting the status of mentally ill on anyone": The Reith Lectures, "Unmasking Medicine." *Listener,* 4 December: 745–8.

Kessler, S. J., and McKenna, W. 1978. *Gender: An Ethnomethodological Approach.* New York: Wiley.

Kiesler, S., Sproull, L., and Eccles, J. S. 1983. Second-class citizens? *Psychology Today,* March: 41–8.

Kinsey, A. C., Pomeroy, W. B., and Martin, C. E. 1948. *Sexual Behavior in the Human Male.* Philadelphia: Saunders.

Kinsey, A. C., Pomeroy, W. B., Martin, C. E., and Gebhard, P. H. 1953. *Sexual Behavior in the Human Female.* Philadelphia: Saunders.

Kipnis, D. M. 1976. Intelligence, occupational status, and achievement orientation. In B. B. Lloyd and J. Archer (eds.), *Exploring Sex Differences.* New York: Academic Press.

Klaus, M. H., and Kennell, J. H. 1976. *Maternal–Infant Bonding.* Saint Louis: Mosby.

Klorman, R., Hastings, J. E., Weerts, T. C., Melamed, B. G., and Lang, P. J. 1974. Psychometric description of some specific fear questionnaires. *Behavior Therapy,* 5:401–9.

Knorr, D., Bidlingmaier, F., Butenandt, O., Fendel, H., and Ehrt-Wehle, R. 1974. Plasma testosterone in male puberty. I. Physiology of plasma testosterone. *Acta Endocrinologica,* 75:181–94.

Knox, W. E., and Kupferer, H. J. 1971. A discontinuity in the socialization of males in the United States. *Merrill–Palmer Quarterly,* 17:251–61.

Kohlberg, L. 1966. A cognitive developmental analysis of children's sex role concepts and attitudes. In E. E. Maccoby (ed.), *The Development of Sex Differences*. Stanford, Calif.: Stanford University Press.

Kohlberg, L. 1976. Moral stages and moralization: The cognitive-developmental approach. In T. Lickona (ed.), *Moral Development and Behavior: Theory, Research, and Social Issues*. New York: Holt, Rinehart & Winston.

Kolakowski, D., and Malina, R. M. 1974. Spatial ability, throwing accuracy, and man's hunting heritage. *Nature*, 251:410–12.

Komarovsky, M. 1950. Functional analysis of sex roles. *American Sociological Review*, 15:508–16.

Kotelchuck, M. 1976. The infant's relationship to the father: experimental evidence. In M. Lamb (ed.), *The Role of the Father in Child Development*. New York: Wiley.

Kreuz, L. E., and Rose, R. M. 1972. Assessment of aggressive behavior and plasma testosterone in a young criminal population. *Psychosomatic Medicine*, 34:321–32.

Kuhn, D., Nash, S. C., and Bruchan, L. 1978. Sex role concepts of two- and three-year olds. *Child Development*, 49:445–51.

Lacan, J. 1966. The significance of the phallus. In *Ecrits*. Paris: Editions de Seuil. (Reprinted *Ecrits: A selection*. Trans. A. Sheridan. London: Tavistock 1977.)

Laing, R. D. 1967. *The Politics of Experience*. Harmondsworth: Penguin.

Lamb, M. E. 1976. *The Role of the Father in Child Development*. New York: Wiley.

Lamb, M. E. 1977a. Father–infant and mother–infant interaction in the first year of life. *Child Development*, 48:167–81.

Lamb, M. E. 1977b. The development of mother–infant and father–infant attachments in the second year of life. *Developmental Psychology*, 13:637–48.

Lambert, H. H. 1978. Biology and equality: a perspective on sex differences. *Signs: Journal of Women in Culture and Society*, 4:97–117.

Lambert, L., and Hart, S. 1976. Who needs a father? *New Society*, 37:80.

Lawick-Goodall, J. Van. 1971. *In the Shadow of Man*. London: Collins.

Leach, P. 1979. *Who Cares?* Harmondsworth: Penguin.

Leakey, L., and Lewin, R. 1979. *People of the Lake*. London: Collins.

Le Boeuf, B. J. 1974. Male–male competition and reproductive success in elephant seals. *American Zoologist*, 14:163–76.

Leete, R. 1976. Marriage and divorce. In *Population Trends*. London: Her Majesty's Stationery Office.

Lehrke, R. G. 1978. Sex linkage: a biological basis for greater male variability in intelligence. In R. T. Osborne, C. E. Noble, and N. Weyl (eds.), *Human Variation: The Biopsychology of Age, Race, and Sex.* New York: Academic Press.

Lerner, R. M. 1976. *Concepts and Theories of Human Development.* Reading, Mass.: Addison-Wesley.

Lever, J. 1976. Sex differences in the games children play. *Social Problems,* 23:55–62.

Levine, A., and Crumrine, J. 1975. Women and the fear of success: a problem in replication. *American Journal of Sociology,* 80:964–74.

Levy, J. 1969. Possible basis for the evolution of lateral specialization of the human brain. *Nature,* 224:614–15.

Levy, P. 1967. Substantive significance of significant differences between two groups. *Psychological Bulletin,* 67:37–40.

Lewis, M. 1975. Early sex differences in the human: studies of socioemotional development. *Archives of Sexual Behavior,* 4:329–35.

Lewis, M. 1981. Self-knowledge: A social cognitive perspective on gender identity and sex-role development. In M. E. Lamb and L. R. Sherrod (eds.), *Infant Social Cognition.* Hillsdale, N.J.: Erlbaum.

Liben, L. S., and Signorella, M. L. 1980. Gender-related schemata and constructive memory in children. *Child Development,* 51:11–18.

Lips, H. M. 1981. *Women, Men, and The Psychology of Power.* Englewood Cliffs, N.J.: Prentice-Hall.

Lipshitz, S. 1978. Women and psychiatry. In J. Chetwynd and O. Hartnett (eds.), *The Sex-role System.* London: Routledge & Kegan Paul.

Litman, G. K. 1978. Clinical aspects of sex-role stereotyping. In J. Chetwynd and O. Hartnett (eds.), *The Sex-role System.* London: Routledge & Kegan Paul.

Lloyd, B. B. 1976. Social responsibility and research on sex differences. In B. B. Lloyd and J. Archer (eds.), *Exploring Sex Differences.* New York: Academic Press.

Lloyd, B. B., and Archer, J. 1981. Problems and issues in research on gender differences. *Current Psychological Reviews,* 1:287–304.

Locke, B. Z., and Gardner, E. A. 1969. Psychiatric disorders among the patients of general practitioners and internists. *Public Health Report,* 84:167–73.

Locksley, A., and Colten, M. E. 1979. Psychological androgyny: a case of mistaken identity? *Journal of Personality and Social Psychology,* 37:1017–31.

Lorenz, K. 1966. *On Aggression*. New York: Harcourt, Brace & World.

Lovejoy, O. 1981. The origin of man. *Science*, 211:341–50.

Lowe, M. 1982. Social bodies: the interaction of culture and women's biology. In R. Hubbard, M. S. Henifin, and B. Fried (eds.), *Biological Woman: The Convenient Myth*. Cambridge, Mass.: Schenkman.

Lukes, S. 1975. *Power: A Radical View*. London: Macmillan.

Maccoby, E. E., Doering, C. H., Jacklin, C. N., and Kraemer, H. 1979. Concentrations of sex hormones in umbilical-cord blood: their relation to sex and birth order of infants. *Child Development*, 50:632–42.

Maccoby, E. E., and Jacklin, C. N. 1974. *The Psychology of Sex Differences*. Stanford, Calif.: Stanford University Press.

Maccoby, E. E., and Jacklin, C. N. 1980. Sex differences in aggression: a rejoinder and reprise. *Child Development*, 51:964–80.

Macfarlane, A. 1977. *The Psychology of Childbirth*. Cambridge, Mass.: Harvard University Press.

McGee, M. G. 1979. Human spatial abilities: psychometric studies and environmental, genetic, hormonal, and neurological influences. *Psychological Bulletin*, 86:889–918.

McGlone, J. 1980. Sex differences in human brain asymmetry: a critical survey. *Behavioral and Brain Sciences*, 3:215–27.

McGlone, J., and Davidson, W. 1973. The relation between cerebral speech laterality and spatial ability with special reference to sex and hand preference. *Neuropsychologia*, 11:105–13.

McGuinness, D. 1976. Sex differences in the organization of perception and cognition. In B. Lloyd and J. Archer (eds.), *Exploring Sex Differences*. New York: Academic Press.

Mack, J. 1976. Children half-alone. *New Society*, 38:6–8.

Mackie, L., and Pattullo, P. 1977. *Women at Work*. London: Tavistock.

Madigan, F. C. 1957. Are sex mortality differentials biologically caused? *Millbank Memorial Fund Quarterly*, 35:202–23.

Maltz, D. N., and Borker, R. A. 1982. A cultural approach to male–female miscommunication. In J. Gumperz (ed.), *Language and Social Identity*. Cambridge: Cambridge University Press.

Manual of International Statistical Classification of Diseases, Injuries, and Causes of Death. 1967. Geneva: World Health Organization.

Martin, C. L., and Halverson Jr., C. F. 1981. A schematic processing model of sex-typing and stereotyping in children. *Child Development*, 52:1119–34.

Martin, C. L., and Halverson Jr., C. F. 1983. The effects of sex-typing schemas on young children's memory. *Child Development*, 54:563–74.

Martin, M. K., and Voorhies, B. 1975. *The Female of the Species*. New York: Macmillan.

Mason, J. W., Tolson, W. W., Robinson, J. A., Brady, J. V., Tolliver, G. A., and Johnson, T. A. 1969. Urinary androsterone, etiocholanolone, and dehydroepiandrosterone responses to 72-hour avoidance sessions in the monkey. *Psychosomatic Medicine*, 30:710–20.

Masters, W. H., and Johnson, V. E. 1966. *Human Sexual Response*. Boston: Little, Brown.

Masters, W. H., and Johnson, V. E. 1970. *Human Sexual Inadequacy*. Boston: Little, Brown.

Masters, W. H., and Johnson, V. E. 1979. *Homosexuality in Perspective*. Boston: Little, Brown.

Maynard Smith, J. 1971. What use is sex? *Journal of Theoretical Biology*, 30:319–35.

Mayo, P. 1976. Sex differences in psychopathology. In B. Lloyd and J. Archer (eds.), *Exploring Sex Differences*. London: Academic Press.

Mazur, A., and Lamb, T. A. 1980. Testosterone, status, and mood in human males. *Hormones and Behavior*, 14:236–46.

Mead, M. 1935. *Sex and Temperament in Three Primitive Societies*. London: Routledge & Kegan Paul.

Mead, M. 1950. *Male and Female*. Harmondsworth: Penguin.

Megargee, G. 1969. Influence of sex roles on the manifestation of leadership. *Journal of Applied Psychology*, 53:377–82.

Melzack, R., and Wall, P. 1982. *The Challenge of Pain*. Harmondsworth: Penguin.

Meyer-Bahlberg, H. F. L., Boon, D. A., Shama, M., and Edwards, J. A. 1974. Aggressiveness and testosterone measures in man. *Psychosomatic Medicine*, 36:269–74.

Mischel, W. 1966. A social learning view of sex differences. In E. E. Maccoby (ed.), *The Development of Sex Differences*. Stanford, Calif.: Stanford University Press.

Mischel, W. 1970. Sex-typing and socialization. In P. H. Mussen (ed.), *Carmichael's Manual of Child Psychology*, vol. 2 (3rd ed.). New York: Wiley.

Mitchell, J. 1974. *Psychoanalysis and Feminism*. London: Allen Lane.

Mitchell, J., and Oakley, A. 1976. *The Rights and Wrongs of Women*. Harmondsworth: Penguin.

Mittwoch, U. 1973. *Genetics of Sex Differentiation*. New York: Academic Press.

Moers, E. 1978. *Literary Women*. London: Women's Press.

Money, J. 1976. Gender identity and hermaphroditism. *Science*, 191:872.

Money, J., and Ehrhardt, A. A. 1972. *Man and Woman, Boy and Girl.* Baltimore: Johns Hopkins University Press.

Money, J., Hampson, J. G., and Hampson, J. L. 1957. Imprinting and the establishment of gender role. *Archives of Neurology and Psychiatry.* 77:333–6.

Moos, R. H., Kopell, B. S., Melges, F. T., Yalom, I. D., Lunde, D. T., Clayton, R. B., and Hamberg, D. 1969. Fluctuations in symptoms and moods during the menstrual cycle. *Journal of Psychosomatic Research,* 13:37–44.

Morgan, E. 1972. *The Descent of Woman.* London: Souvenir Press.

Morgan, G. A., and Ricciuti, H. N. 1969. Infant's response to strangers during the first year. In B. M. Foss (ed.), *Determinants of Infant Behaviour,* vol. 4. London: Methuen.

Morgan, P. 1975. *Child Care: Sense and Fable.* London: Temple-Smith.

Morris, D. 1967. *The Naked Ape.* London: Jonathan Cape.

Morris, J. 1974. *Conundrum.* London: Faber & Faber.

Napier, J. 1971. *The Roots of Mankind.* London: Allen & Unwin.

Nash, S. C., and Feldman, S. S. 1981. Sex-role and sex-related attributions: constancy and change across the family life cycle. In M. E. Lamb and A. L. Brown (eds.), *Advances in Developmental Psychology,* vol. 1. Hillsdale, N.J.: Erlbaum.

National Commission on Marihuana and Drug Abuse. 1973. *Drug Use in America.* Washington, D.C.: U.S. Government Printing Office.

Neisser, U. 1976. *Cognition and Reality.* San Francisco: Freeman.

Nemeth, C. 1973. A critical analysis of research utilizing the prisoners' dilemma paradigm for the study of bargaining. In L. Berkowitz (ed.), *Advances in Experimental Social Psychology,* vol. 6. New York: Academic Press.

Oakes, M. 1978. Statistical Evaluation of Psychological Evidence. Doctoral dissertation, Hull University, England.

Oakley, A. 1974. *Housewife.* London: Allen Lane.

Oakley, A. 1979. *Becoming a Mother.* Oxford: Martin Robertson.

Oetzel, R. M. 1966. Annotated bibliography. In E. E. Maccoby (ed.), *The Development of Sex Differences.* Stanford, Calif.: Stanford University Press.

Ohno, S. 1976. The development of sexual reproduction. In C. R. Austin and R. V. Short (eds.), *Reproduction in Mammals.* vol. 6: *The Evolution of Reproduction.* Cambridge: Cambridge University Press.

O'Leary, V. E. 1974. Some attitudinal barriers to occupational aspirations in women. *Psychological Bulletin,* 81:809–26.

Olioff, M., and Stewart, J. 1978. Sex differences in the play behavior of prepubescent rats. *Physiology and Behavior,* 20:113–15.

Olweus, D., Mattsson, A., Schallin, D., and Low, H. 1980. Testosterone, aggression, physical and personality dimensions in normal adolescent males. *Psychosomatic Medicine*, 42:253–69.

Orwell, G. 1949. *Nineteen Eighty-four*. London: Secker & Warburg.

Osofsky, H. J., and Seidenberg, R. 1970. Is female menopausal depression inevitable? *American Journal of Obstetrics and Gynecology*, 36:611–15.

Ounsted, C., and Taylor, D. C. 1972. The Y chromosome message: a point of view. In C. Ounsted and D. C. Taylor (eds.), *Gender Differences: Their Ontogeny and Significance*. London: Churchill.

Paige, K. E. 1973. Women learn to sing the menstrual blues. *Psychology Today*, 7:41–6.

Parke, R. D. 1979. Perspectives on father–infant interaction. In J. D. Osofsky (ed.), *Handbook of Infancy*. New York: Wiley.

Parke, R. D., and Sawin, D. B. 1977. The family in early infancy: social interactional and attitudinal analysis. Paper presented at Society for Research in Child Development meeting, New Orleans. Reported in Parke (1979).

Parker, G. A., Baker, R. R., and Smith, V. G. F. 1972. The origin and evolution of gamete dimorphism and the male–female phenomenon. *Journal of Theoretical Biology*, 36:529–53.

Parkes, C. M. 1975. *Bereavement: Studies of Grief in Adult Life*. Harmondsworth: Penguin.

Parlee, M. B. 1973. The premenstrual syndrome. *Psychological Bulletin*, 80:454–65.

Parlee, M. B. 1975. Psychology: review essay. *Signs: Journal of Women in Culture and Society*, 1:119–38.

Parlee, M. B. 1982. The psychology of the menstrual cycle: biological and physiological perspectives. In R. Friedman (ed.), *Behavior and the Menstrual Cycle*. New York: Dekker.

Parsons, T., and Bales, R. F. 1955. *Family, Socialization, and Interaction Process*. Glencoe, Ill.: Free Press.

Payne, A. P., and Swanson, H. H. 1970. Agonistic behaviour between pairs of hamsters of the same and opposite sex in a neutral observation area. *Behaviour*, 36:259–69.

Pedhazur, E. J., and Tetenbaum, T. J. 1979. Bem Sex Role Inventory: a theoretical and methodological critique. *Journal of Personality and Social Psychology*, 37:996–1016.

Perry, D. G., and Bussey, L. 1979. The social learning theory of sex differences: imitation is alive and well. *Journal of Personality and Social Psychology*, 37:1699–712.

Perry, G. 1979. *Paula Modersohn–Becker*. London: Women's Press.

Perry, J. D., and Whipple, B. 1982. Multiple components of the female orgasm. In B. Graber (ed.), *Circumvaginal Musculature and Sexual Function*. Basle: Karger.

Persky, H., Smith, K. D., and Basu, G. K. 1971. Relation of psychologic measures of aggression and hostility to testosterone production in man. *Psychosomatic Medicine*, 33:265–77.

Petersen, K., and Wilson, J. J. 1978. *Women Artists*. London: Women's Press.

Phillips, D., and Segal, B. 1969. Sexual status and psychiatric symptoms. *American Sociological Review*, 34:58–72.

Phoenix, C. H. 1974. Prenatal testosterone in the nonhuman primate and its consequences for behavior. In R. C. Friedman, R. M. Richart, and R. L. Vande Wiele (eds.), *Sex Differences in Behavior*. New York: Wiley.

Pitcher, E. G., and Schultz, L. H. 1983. *Boys and Girls at Play: the Development of Sex Roles*. New York: Praeger.

Pleck, J. H. 1975. Masculinity–femininity: current and alternative paradigms. *Sex Roles*, 1:161–78.

Pleck, J. H. 1976. The male sex role: definitions, problems, and sources of change. *Journal of Social Issues*, 32:155–64.

Polatnick, M. 1973. Why men don't rear children: a power analysis. *Berkeley Journal of Sociology*, 45–85.

Power, E. 1975. *Medieval Women*. Cambridge: Cambridge University Press.

Purvis, K., and Haynes, N. B. 1974. Short-term effects of copulation, human chorionic gonadotrophin injection, and non-tactile association with a female on testosterone levels in the male rat. *Journal of Endocrinology*, 60:429–39.

Quadagno, D. M., Briscoe, R., and Quadagno, J. S. 1977. Effect of perinatal gonadal hormones on selected nonsexual behavior patterns: a critical assessment of the human and nonhuman literature. *Psychological Bulletin*, 84:62–80.

Rachman, S. 1978. *Courage and Fearfulness*. San Francisco: Freeman.

Rada, R. T., Kellner, R., and Winslow, W. W. 1976. Plasma testosterone and aggressive behavior. *Psychosomatics*, 17:138–42.

Radloff, L. 1975. Sex differences in depression: the effects of occupation and marital status. *Sex Roles*, 1:249–69.

Ralls, K. 1976. Mammals in which females are larger than males. *Quarterly Review of Biology*, 51:245–76.

Ralls, K. 1978. When bigger is best. *New Scientist*, 77:360–3.

Raymond, J. G. 1979. Transsexualism: an issue of sex-role stereotyping. In R. Hubbard and M. Lowe (eds.), *Genes and Gender*, vol. 2. New York: Gordian Press.

Rebelsky, F., and Hanks, C. 1971. Fathers' verbal interaction with infants in the first three months of life. *Child Development*, 42:63–8.

Reckers, G. A., and Yates, C. E. 1976. Sex-typed play in feminoid boys versus normal boys and girls. *Journal of Abnormal Child Psychology*, 4:1–8.

Reeves, A. C. 1971. Children with surrogate parents: cases seen in analytic therapy and an aetiological hypothesis. *British Journal of Medical Psychology*, 44:155–71.

Reinisch, J. M. 1976. Effects of prenatal hormone exposure on physical and psychological development in humans and animals: with a note on the state of the field. In E. J. Sachar (ed.), *Hormones, Behavior, and Psychopathology*. New York: Raven Press.

Reinisch, J. M. 1981. Prenatal exposure to synthetic progestins increases potential for aggression in humans. *Science*, 211:1171–3.

Rendina, I., and Dickerscheid, J. D. 1976. Father involvement with first-born infants. *Family Coordinator*, 25:373–9.

Resko, J. A. 1975. Fetal hormones and their effect on the differentiation of the CNS in primates. *Federation Proceedings*, 34:1650–5.

Rheingold, H., and Cook, K. 1975. The contents of boys' and girls' rooms as an index of parents' behavior. *Child Development*, 46:459–63.

Richards, M. P. M. 1982. How should we approach the study of fathers? In L. McKee and M. O'Brien (eds.), *The Father Figure*. London: Tavistock.

Richards, M. P. M., Bernal, J. F., and Brackbill, Y. 1976. Early behavioral differences: gender or circumcision? *Developmental Psychobiology*, 9:89–95.

Richardson, D. C., Bernstein, S., and Taylor, S. P. 1979. The effect of situational contingencies on female retaliative behavior. *Journal of Personality and Social Psychology*, 37:2044–8.

Robinson, J. R., and Converse, P. E. 1966. Summary of the US Time Use Survey, May 30, 1966. Quoted in I. H. Frieze, J. E. Parsons, P. B. Johnson, D. N. Ruble, and G. L. Zellman, *Women and Sex Roles*. New York: Norton, 1978.

Rogers, S. C. 1978. Woman's place: a critical review of anthropological theory. *Comparative Studies in Society and History*, 20:123–62.

Rosaldo, M. Z., and Lamphere, L. (eds.). 1974. *Woman, Culture, and Society*. Stanford, Calif.: Stanford University Press.

Rosch, E. 1978. Principles of categorization. In E. Rosch and B. B.

Lloyd (eds.), *Cognition and Categorization*. Hillsdale, N.J.: Erlbaum.

Rose, R. M., Gordon, T. P., and Bernstein, I. S. 1972. Plasma testosterone levels in male rhesus: influences of sexual and social stimuli. *Science*, 178:643–5.

Rose, S. P. R., and Rose, H. 1974. "Do not adjust your mind, there is a fault in reality": ideology in neurobiology. *Cognition*, 2:479–502.

Rosenblatt, P. C., and Cunningham, M. R. 1976. Sex differences in cross-cultural perspective. In B. B. Lloyd and J. Archer (eds.), *Exploring Sex Differences*. New York: Academic Press.

Rosenblatt, P. C., Walsh, R. P., and Jackson, D. A. 1976. *Grief and Mourning in Cross-Cultural Perspective*. New Haven: Human Relations Area File Press.

Rosenkrantz, P. S., Vogel, S. R., Bee, H., Broverman, I. K., and Broverman, D. M., 1968. Sex role stereotypes and self-concepts in college students. *Journal of Consulting and Clinical Psychology*, 32:287–95.

Rossi, A. S. 1964. Equality between the sexes: an immodest proposal. *Daedalus*, 93:607–52.

Rossi, A. [S.] 1973. Maternalism, sexuality and the new feminism. In J. Zubin and J. Money (eds.), *Contemporary Sexual Behavior: Critical Issues for the 1970s*. Baltimore: Johns Hopkins University Press.

Rossi, A. S. 1977. A biosocial perspective on parenting. *Daedalus*, 106:1–31.

Roy, M. 1977. A survey of 150 cases. In M. Roy (ed.), *Battered Women: A Psychosociological Study of Domestic Violence*. New York: Van Nostrand.

Rubin, J. Z., Provenzano, F. J., and Luria, Z. 1974. The eye of the beholder: parents' views on the sex of new borns. *American Journal of Orthopsychiatry*, 44:512–19.

Rubin, R. T., Reinisch, J. M., and Haskett, R. F. 1981. Postnatal gonadal steroid effects on human behavior. *Science*, 211:1318–24.

Ruble, D. N. 1977. Premenstrual symptoms: a reinterpretation. *Science*, 197:291–2.

Ruble, D. N., and Brooks-Gunn, J. 1979. Menstrual symptoms: a social cognition analysis. *Journal of Behavioral Medicine*. 2:171–94.

Rushton, J. P., Brainerd, C. J., and Pressley, M. 1983. Behavioral development and construct validity: the principle of aggregation. *Psychological Bulletin*, 94:18–38.

Rutter, M. 1972. *Maternal Deprivation Reassessed*. Harmondsworth: Penguin.

Rutter, M. 1979. Maternal deprivation 1972–1978: New findings, new concepts, new approaches. *Child Development*, 50:283–305.

Rutter, M. 1981. *Maternal Deprivation Reassessed* (2nd ed.). Harmondsworth: Penguin.

Sahlins, M. 1977. *The Use and Abuse of Biology.* London: Tavistock.

Sayers, J. 1982. *Biological Politics: Feminist and Anti-Feminist Perspectives.* London: Tavistock.

Schaar, K. 1974. Suicide rate among women psychologists. *APA Monitor,* 5(1):10.

Schafer, R. 1977. Problems in Freud's psychology of women. In H. P. Blum (ed.), *Female Psychology: Contemporary Psychoanalytic Views.* New York: International Universities Press.

Schaffer, H. R. 1974. Early social behavior and the study of reciprocity. *Bulletin of the British Psychological Society,* 27:209–16.

Schaffer, H. R., and Emerson, P. 1964. *The Development of Attachments in Infancy.* Monographs of the Society for Research in Child Development, 29.

Schonberg, W. B., Costango, D. J., and Carpenter, R. S. 1976. Menstrual cycle: phases and reaction to frustration. *Psychological Record,* 26:321–5.

Secord, P. F., and Backman, C. W. 1964. *Social Psychology.* New York: McGraw-Hill.

Selander, R. K. 1972. Sexual selection and dimorphism in birds. In B. Campbell (ed.), *Sexual Selection and the Descent of Man.* Chicago: Aldine.

Seligman, M. E. P. 1975. *Helplessness: On Depression, Development, and Death.* San Francisco: Freeman.

Serbin, L. A., O'Leary, K. D., Kent, R. N., and Tonick, I. J. 1973. A comparison of teacher response to the preacademic problems and problem behavior of boys and girls. *Child Development,* 44:796–804.

Shapiro, B. H., Goldman, A. S., Bongiovanni, A. M., and Marino, J. M. 1976. Neonatal progesterone and feminine sexual development. *Nature,* 264:795–6.

Shapiro, D. Y. 1979. Social behaviour, group structure, and the control of sex reversal in hermaphroditic fish. In J. S. Rosenblatt, R. A. Hinde, C. Beer, and M. C. Busnel (eds.), *Advances in the Study of Behavior,* vol. 10. New York: Academic Press.

Sharman, G. B. 1976. Evolution of viviparity in mammals. In C. R. Austin and R. V. Short (eds.), *Reproduction in Mammals,* vol. 6: *The Evolution of Reproduction.* Cambridge: Cambridge University Press.

Shepherd, G. 1978. The Omani Xanith, (correspondence). *Man,* 13:663–5.

Shepherd, M., Cooper, B., Brown, A. C., and Kalton, G. W. 1966.

Psychiatric Illness in General Practice. London: Oxford University Press.

Sherfey, M. J. 1973. *The Nature and Evolution of Female Sexuality.* New York: Vintage.

Sherman, J. A. 1967. Problems of sex differences in space perception and aspects of intellectual functioning. *Psychological Review,* 74:290–99.

Sherman, J. A. 1971. *On the Psychology of Women.* Springfield, Ill.: Thomas.

Sherman, J. A. 1978. *Sex-related Cognitive Differences: An Essay on Theory and Evidence.* Springfield, Ill.: Thomas.

Shields, M., and Duveen, G. 1982. Animism and gender concepts in young children's representations of persons. Paper presented at British Psychological Society London conference, December 1982.

Shields, S. A. 1975. Functionalism, Darwinism, and the psychology of women: a study in social myth. *American Psychologist,* 30:739–54.

Short, R. V. 1980. The origins of sexuality. In C. R. Austin and R. V. Short (eds.), *Reproduction in Mammals,* vol. 8: *Human Sexuality.* Cambridge: Cambridge University Press.

Siann, G. 1977. Sex differences in spatial ability in children: its bearing on theories accounting for sex differences in spatial abilities in adults. Doctoral dissertation, University of Edinburgh.

Simpson, J. L. 1976. *Disorders of Sexual Differentiation.* New York: Academic Press.

Slocum, S. 1975. Woman the gatherer: male bias in anthropology. In R. Reiter (ed.), *Toward an Anthropology of Women.* New York: Monthly Review Press.

Sluckin, W. 1972. *Imprinting and Early Learning* (2nd ed.). London: Methuen.

Sluckin, W. (ed.). 1979. *Fear in Animals and Man.* Wokingham: Van Nostrand Reinhold.

Sluckin, W., Herbert, M., and Sluckin, A. 1983. *Maternal Bonding.* Oxford: Basil Blackwell.

Smith, C., and Lloyd, B. B. 1978. Maternal behavior and perceived sex of infant. *Child Development,* 49:1263–5.

Smith, P. K. 1980. Shared care of young children: alternative models to monotropism. *Merrill–Palmer Quarterly,* 26:371–90.

Smith, P. K., and Connolly, K. 1972. Patterns of play and social interaction in preschool children. In N. G. Blurton-Jones (ed.), *Ethological Studies of Child Behaviour.* Cambridge: Cambridge University Press.

Smith, P. K., and Green M. 1975. Aggressive behavior in English nurseries and play groups: sex differences and response of adults. *Child Development,* 46:211–14.

Snow, M. E., Jacklin, C. N., and Maccoby, E. E. 1983. Sex-of-child differences in father–child interaction at one year of age. *Child Development,* 54:227–32.

Social Trends. 1977, 1979, 1984. Central Statistics Office, London: Her Majesty's Stationery Office, nos. 8, 9, and 14.

Sommer, B. 1973. The effect of menstruation on cognitive and perceptual–motor behavior: a review. *Psychosomatic Medicine.* 35:515–34.

Sommer, B. 1982. Cognitive behavior and the menstrual cycle. In R. C. Friedman (ed.), *Behavior and the Menstrual Cycle.* New York: Dekker.

Speltz, M. L., and Bernstein, D. A. 1976. Sex differences in fearfulness: verbal report, overt avoidance, and demand characteristics. *Journal of Behavior Therapy and Experimental Psychiatry,* 7:177–22.

Spence, J. T., Helmreich, R., and Stapp, J. 1975. Ratings of self and peers on sex role attributes and their relation to self-esteem and conceptions of masculinity and femininity. *Journal of Personality and Social Psychology,* 32:29–39.

Spender, D. 1980. *Man Made Language.* London: Routledge & Kegan Paul.

Srole, L., and Fischer, A. K. 1980. The Midtown Manhattan longitudinal study vs. "the mental Paradise Lost" doctrine. *Archives of General Psychiatry,* 37:209–21.

Stafford, R. E. 1961. Sex differences in spatial visualization as evidence of sex-linked inheritance. *Perceptual and Motor Skills,* 13:428.

Stassinopoulos, A. 1972. *The Female Woman.* London: Davis–Poynter.

Statistical Abstracts of the USA. 1978. Washington, D.C.: U.S. Government Printing Office.

Statistical Abstracts of the USA. 1982–83. Washington, D. C.: U.S. Government Printing Office.

Steinman, D. L., Wincze, J. P., Sakheim, K., Barlow, D. H., and Mavissakalian, M. 1981. A comparison of male and female patterns of sexual arousal. *Archives of Sexual Behavior,* 10:529–47.

Steinmetz, S. K. 1977. Wifebeating, husbandbeating: a comparison of the use of physical violence between spouses to resolve marital fights. In M. Roy (ed.), *Battered Women: A Psychological Study of Domestic Violence.* New York: Van Nostrand.

Stengel, E. 1964. *Suicide and Attempted Suicide.* London: Penguin. (Rev. ed., 1970.)

Sternglanz, S. H., and Serbin, L. A. 1974. Sex-role stereotyping in children's television programs. *Developmental Psychology,* 10:710–15.

Stockard, J., and Johnson, M. M. 1979. The social origins of male dominance. *Sex Roles*, 5:199–218.

Stoll, C. S. 1978. *Female and Male: Socialization, Social Roles, and Social Structure*. Dubuque, Iowa: William C. Brown.

Strauss, B., Schultheiss, M., and Cohen, R. 1983. Autonomic reactivity in the menstrual phase. *British Journal of Clinical Psychology*, 22:1–9.

Stroebe, M. S., and Stroebe, W. 1983. Who suffers more? Sex differences in health risks of the widowed. *Psychological Bulletin*, 93:279–301.

Swanson, H. H. 1973. Sex differences in the agonistic behaviour of the Mongolian gerbil. *Journal of Endocrinology*, 57:38–9.

Symonds, A. 1971. Phobias after marriage: women's declaration of independence. *American Journal of Psychoanalysis*, 31:144–52.

Symons, D. 1979. *The Evolution of Human Sexuality*. Oxford: Oxford University Press.

Szasz, T. S. 1970. *The Manufacture of Madness*. New York: Harper & Row.

Tanner, J. M. 1970. Physical Growth. In P. H. Mussen (ed.), *Carmichael's Manual of Child Psychology*, vol 1. New York: Wiley.

Tanner, J. M. 1978. *Foetus into Man*. Cambridge, Mass.: Harvard University Press.

Tavris, C., and Offir, C. 1977. *The Longest War: Sex Differences in Perspective*. New York: Harcourt Brace Jovanovich.

Tennes, K. M., and Lampl, E. E. 1964. Stranger and separation anxiety. *Journal of Mental and Nervous Diseases*, 139:247–54.

Terman, L. M. 1925. *Mental and Physical Traits of a Thousand Gifted Children*. Genetic Studies of Genius, vol. I. Stanford, Calif.: Stanford University Press.

Thomas, H. 1983. Familial correlational analyses, sex differences, and the X-linked gene hypothesis. *Psychological Bulletin*, 93:427–40.

Thompson, R. J., Jr., and Lozes, J. 1976. Female gang delinquency. *Corrective and Social Psychiatry*, 22:1–5.

Tiefer, L. 1978. The context and consequences of contemporary sex research: a feminist perspective. In T. E. McGill, D. A. Dewsbury, and B. D. Sachs (eds.), *Sex and Behavior: Status and Prospects*. New York: Plenum.

Tieger, T. 1980. On the biological basis of sex differences in aggression. *Child Development*, 51:943–63.

Tiger, L. 1970. The possible biological origins of sexual discrimination. *Impact of Science on Society*, 20:29–45.

Tiger, L., and Shepher, J. 1975. *Women in the Kibbutz*. New York: Harcourt Brace Jovanovich.

Tizard, B., and Hodges, J. 1978. The effect of early institutional rearing on the development of eight-year-old children. *Journal of Child Psychology and Psychiatry*, 19:99–118.

Touhey, J. C. 1974. Effects of additional women professionals on ratings of occupational prestige and desirability. *Journal of Personality and Social Psychology*, 29:86–9.

Tresemer, D. W. 1975. Measuring "sex differences." *Sociological Inquiry*, 45:29–32.

Tresemer, D. W. 1977. *Fear of Success*. New York: Plenum.

Trivers, R. L. 1972. Parental investment and sexual selection. In B. Campbell (ed.), *Sexual Selection and the Descent of Man*. Chicago: Aldine.

Ullian, D. Z. 1976. The development of conceptions of masculinity and femininity. In B. B. Lloyd and J. Archer (eds.), *Exploring Sex Differences*. New York: Academic Press.

Unger, R. K. 1979. Toward a redefinition of sex and gender. *American Psychologist*, 34:1085–94.

Vandenberg, S. G., and Kuse, A. R. 1979. Spatial ability: a critical review of the sex-linked major gene hypothesis. In M. A. Wittig and A. C. Peterson (eds.), *Sex-Related Differences in Cognitive Functioning*. New York: Academic Press.

Vernon, P. E. 1955. The assessment of children. *Studies in Education*, 1:189–215.

Vernon, P. E. 1969. *Intelligence and Cultural Environment*. London: Methuen.

Vila, J., and Beech, H. R. 1978. Vulnerability and defensive reactions in relation to the human menstrual cycle. *British Journal of Social and Clinical Psychology*, 17:93–100.

Vila, J., and Beech, H. R. 1980. Premenstrual symptomatology: an interaction hypothesis. *British Journal of Social and Clinical Psychology*, 19:73–80.

Waddington, C. H. 1977. *Tools for Thought*. London: Jonathan Cape.

Waldron, I. 1976. Why do women live longer than men? (part 1). *Journal of Human Stress*, 2:2–13.

Walum, L. R. 1977. *The Dynamics of Sex and Gender: A Sociological Perspective*. Chicago: Rand McNally.

Washburn, S. L., and Lancaster, C. S. 1968. The evolution of hunting. In R. B. Lee and I. DeVore (eds.), *Man the Hunter*. Chicago: Aldine.

Weeks, J. 1978. Movements of affirmation: sexual meanings and homosexual identities. Paper presented at British Sociological Association Conference, University of Sussex.

Weissman, M. M. 1979. The myth of involutional melancholia. *Journal of the American Medical Association,* 242:742–4.

Weissman, M. M., and Klerman, G. L. 1977. Sex differences and the epidemiology of depression. *Archives of General Psychiatry,* 34:98–111. Reprinted in E. Howell and M. Bayes (eds.), *Women and Mental Health.* New York: Basic Books, 1981.

Weldburn, V. 1980. *Postnatal Depression,* Glasgow: Fontana.

White, D., and Wollett, A. 1981. The family at birth. Paper presented at British Psychological Society London Conference, December 1981.

White, J. W. 1983. Sex and gender issues in aggression research. In R. G. Geen and E. I. Donnerstein (eds.), *Aggression: Theoretical and Empirical Reviews,* vol. 2: *Issues in Research.* New York: Academic Press.

Whiting, B., and Edwards, C. P. 1973. Cross-cultural analysis of sex differences in the behavior of children aged 3 through 11. *Journal of Social Psychology,* 91:171–88.

Whitlock, F. A. 1973. Suicide in England and Wales, part 1: the county boroughs. *Psychological Medicine,* 3:350–65.

Wikan, U. 1977. Man becomes woman: transsexualism in Oman as a key to gender roles. *Man,* 12:304–19.

Wikan, U. 1978. The Omani *Xanith* (correspondence). *Man,* 13:667–71.

Williams, G. C. 1975. *Sex and Evolution.* Princeton, N.J.: Princeton University Press.

Williams, J., and Giles, H. 1978. The changing status of women in society: an intergroup perspective. In H. Taijfal (ed.), *Differentiation between Social Groups.* New York: Academic Press.

Williams, J. B. W., and Spitzer, R. L. 1983. The issue of sex bias in DSM-III: A critique of "A woman's view of DSM-III" by Marcie Kaplan. *American Psychologist,* 38:793–8.

Williams, J. E., and Bennett, S. M. 1975. The definition of sex stereotypes via the adjective check list. *Sex Roles,* 1:327–37.

Williams, J. E., and Best, D. L. 1982. *Measuring Sex Stereotypes: A Thirty Nation Study.* Beverly Hills, Calif.: Sage.

Williams, J. H. 1977. *Psychology of Women.* New York: Norton.

Wilson, J. R., and Vandenberg, S. G. 1978. Sex differences in cognition: evidence from the Hawai family study. In T. E. McGill, D. A. Dewsbury, and B. D. Sachs (eds.), *Sex and Behavior: Status and Prospects.* New York: Plenum.

Witelson, S. F. 1976. Sex and the single hemisphere: specialization of the right hemisphere for spacial processing. *Science,* 193:425–7.

Witkin, H. A. 1967. A cognitive-style approach to cross-cultural research. *International Journal of Psychology,* 2:233–50.

Witkin, H. A., Dyk, R. B., Paterson, H. F., Goodenough, D. R., and Karp, S. A. 1962. *Psychological Differentiation.* New York: Wiley.

Wittig, M. A., and Petersen, A. C. (eds.). 1979. *Sex Related Differences in Cognitive Functioning.* New York: Academic Press.

Wolkind, S., and Rutter, M. 1973. Children who have been "in care": an epidemiological study. *Journal of Child Psychology and Psychiatry,* 14:97–105.

Woman's Own, February 4, 1978.

Worobey, J., Laub, K. W., and Schilmoeller, G. L. 1983. Maternal and paternal responses to infant distress. *Merrill–Palmer Quarterly,* 29:33–45.

Wyer, R. S., and Malinowski, C. 1972. Effects of sex and achievement level upon individualism and competitiveness in social interaction. *Journal of Experimental Social Psychology,* 8:303–14.

Zerssen, D. von. 1976. Physique and personality. In A. R. Kaplan (ed.), *Human Behavior Genetics.* Springfield, Ill.: Thomas.

Author index

General index